SIMPSONS™ COMICS CLUBHOUSE

MATT GROENING

SIMPSONS COMICS CLUBHOUSE

Materials previously published in
Simpsons Comics #109-111, and The Simpsons Summer Shindig #4-5

Published in the UK by Titan Books, a division of Titan Publishing Group Ltd., 144 Southwark St., London SE1 0UP, under licence from Bongo Entertainment, Inc.

FIRST EDITION: JANUARY 2015

ISBN 9781783296576

2 4 6 8 10 9 7 5 3 1

Publisher: Matt Groening
Creative Director: Nathan Kane
Managing Editor: Terry Delegeane
Director of Operations: Robert Zaugh
Art Director: Jason Ho
Art Director Special Projects: Serban Cristescu
Assistant Art Director: Mike Rote
Production Manager: Christopher Ungar
Assistant Editor: Karen Bates
Production: Art Villanueva
Administration: Ruth Waytz, Pete Benson
Legal Guardian: Susan A. Grode

Printed by TC Trans … 4/2014

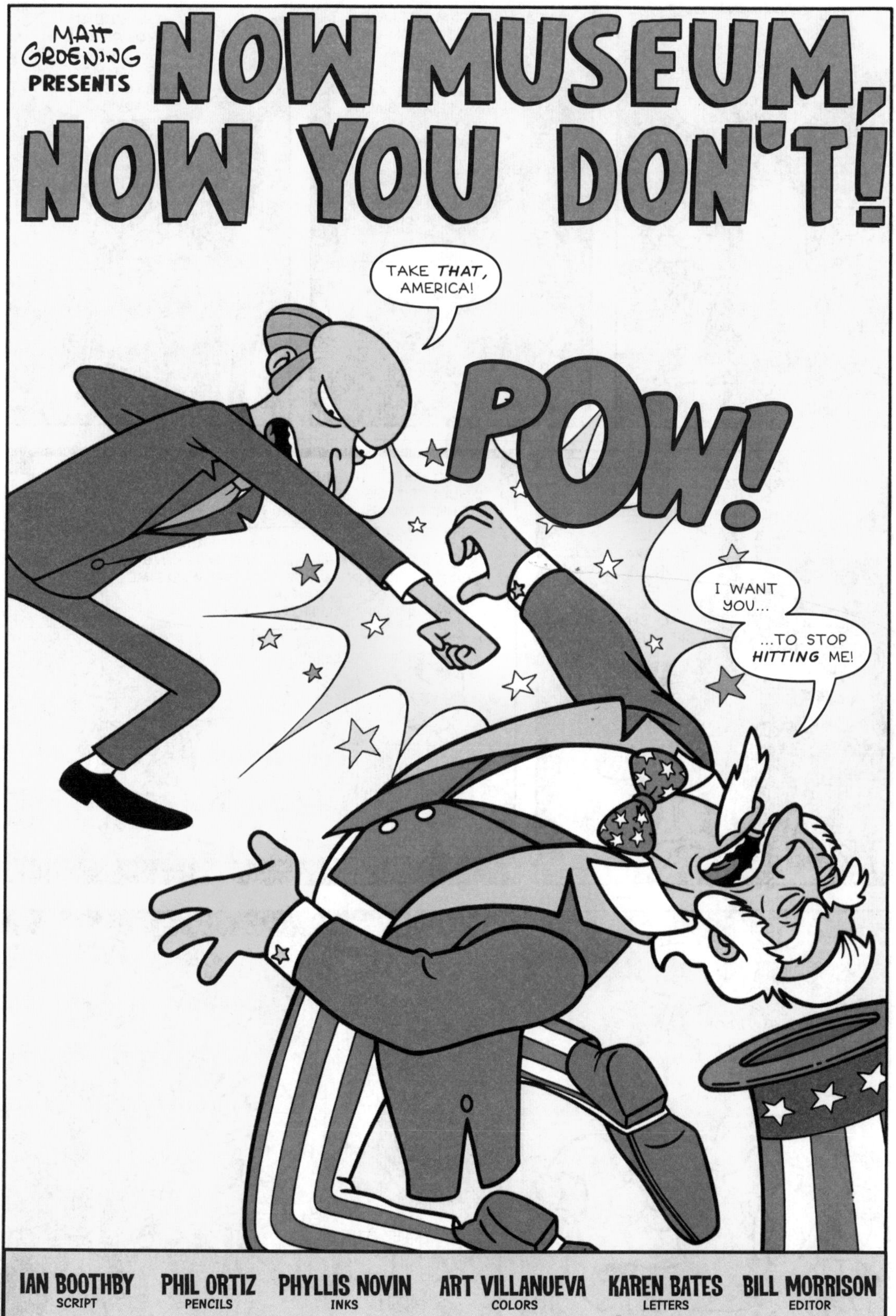
MATT GROENING PRESENTS
NOW MUSEUM, NOW YOU DON'T!
TAKE THAT, AMERICA!
POW!
I WANT YOU...
...TO STOP HITTING ME!
IAN BOOTHBY SCRIPT
PHIL ORTIZ PENCILS
PHYLLIS NOVIN INKS
ART VILLANUEVA COLORS
KAREN BATES LETTERS
BILL MORRISON EDITOR

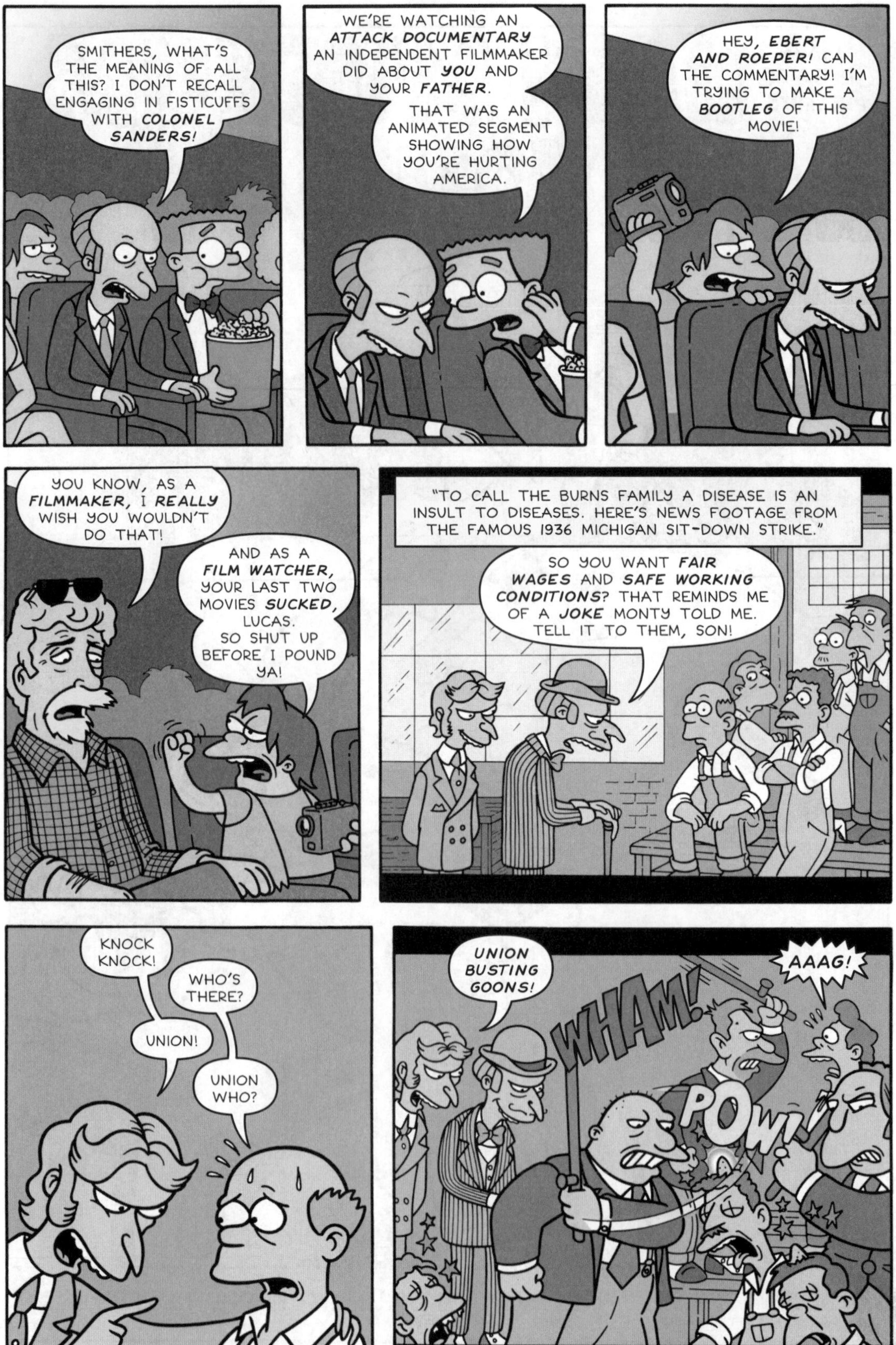
SMITHERS, WHAT'S THE MEANING OF ALL THIS? I DON'T RECALL ENGAGING IN FISTICUFFS WITH COLONEL SANDERS!
WE'RE WATCHING AN ATTACK DOCUMENTARY AN INDEPENDENT FILMMAKER DID ABOUT YOU AND YOUR FATHER.
THAT WAS AN ANIMATED SEGMENT SHOWING HOW YOU'RE HURTING AMERICA.
HEY, EBERT AND ROEPER! CAN THE COMMENTARY! I'M TRYING TO MAKE A BOOTLEG OF THIS MOVIE!
YOU KNOW, AS A FILMMAKER, I REALLY WISH YOU WOULDN'T DO THAT!
AND AS A FILM WATCHER, YOUR LAST TWO MOVIES SUCKED, LUCAS. SO SHUT UP BEFORE I POUND YA!
"TO CALL THE BURNS FAMILY A DISEASE IS AN INSULT TO DISEASES. HERE'S NEWS FOOTAGE FROM THE FAMOUS 1936 MICHIGAN SIT-DOWN STRIKE."
SO YOU WANT FAIR WAGES AND SAFE WORKING CONDITIONS? THAT REMINDS ME OF A JOKE MONTY TOLD ME. TELL IT TO THEM, SON!
KNOCK KNOCK!
WHO'S THERE?
UNION!
UNION WHO?
UNION BUSTING GOONS!
AAAG!
WHAM!
POW!

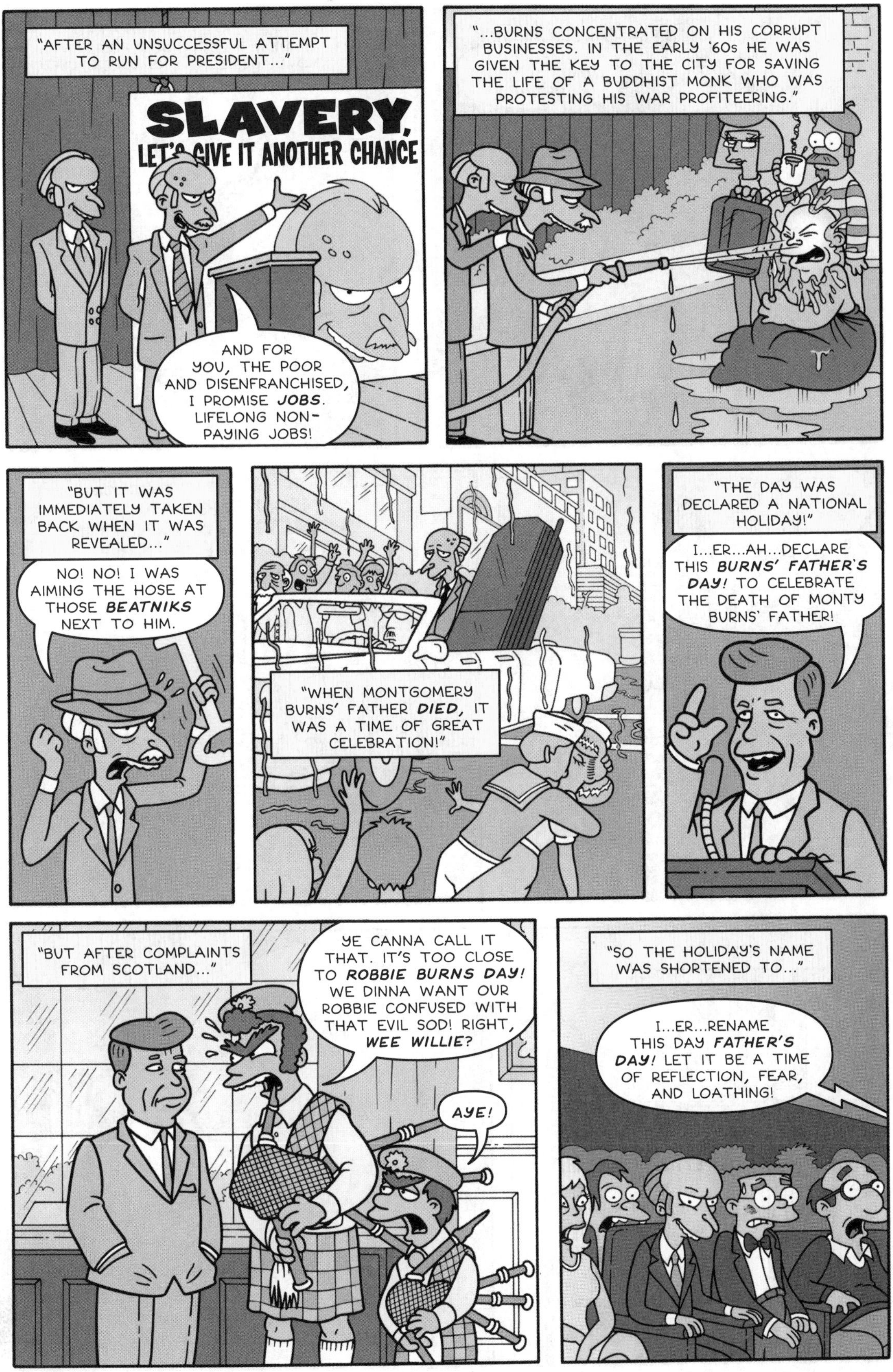

"AFTER AN UNSUCCESSFUL ATTEMPT TO RUN FOR PRESIDENT..."
SLAVERY, LET'S GIVE IT ANOTHER CHANCE
AND FOR YOU, THE POOR AND DISENFRANCHISED, I PROMISE JOBS. LIFELONG NON-PAYING JOBS!
"...BURNS CONCENTRATED ON HIS CORRUPT BUSINESSES. IN THE EARLY '60s HE WAS GIVEN THE KEY TO THE CITY FOR SAVING THE LIFE OF A BUDDHIST MONK WHO WAS PROTESTING HIS WAR PROFITEERING."
"BUT IT WAS IMMEDIATELY TAKEN BACK WHEN IT WAS REVEALED..."
NO! NO! I WAS AIMING THE HOSE AT THOSE BEATNIKS NEXT TO HIM.
"WHEN MONTGOMERY BURNS' FATHER DIED, IT WAS A TIME OF GREAT CELEBRATION!"
"THE DAY WAS DECLARED A NATIONAL HOLIDAY!"
I...ER...AH...DECLARE THIS BURNS' FATHER'S DAY! TO CELEBRATE THE DEATH OF MONTY BURNS' FATHER!
"BUT AFTER COMPLAINTS FROM SCOTLAND..."
YE CANNA CALL IT THAT. IT'S TOO CLOSE TO ROBBIE BURNS DAY! WE DINNA WANT OUR ROBBIE CONFUSED WITH THAT EVIL SOD! RIGHT, WEE WILLIE?
AYE!
"SO THE HOLIDAY'S NAME WAS SHORTENED TO..."
I...ER...RENAME THIS DAY FATHER'S DAY! LET IT BE A TIME OF REFLECTION, FEAR, AND LOATHING!

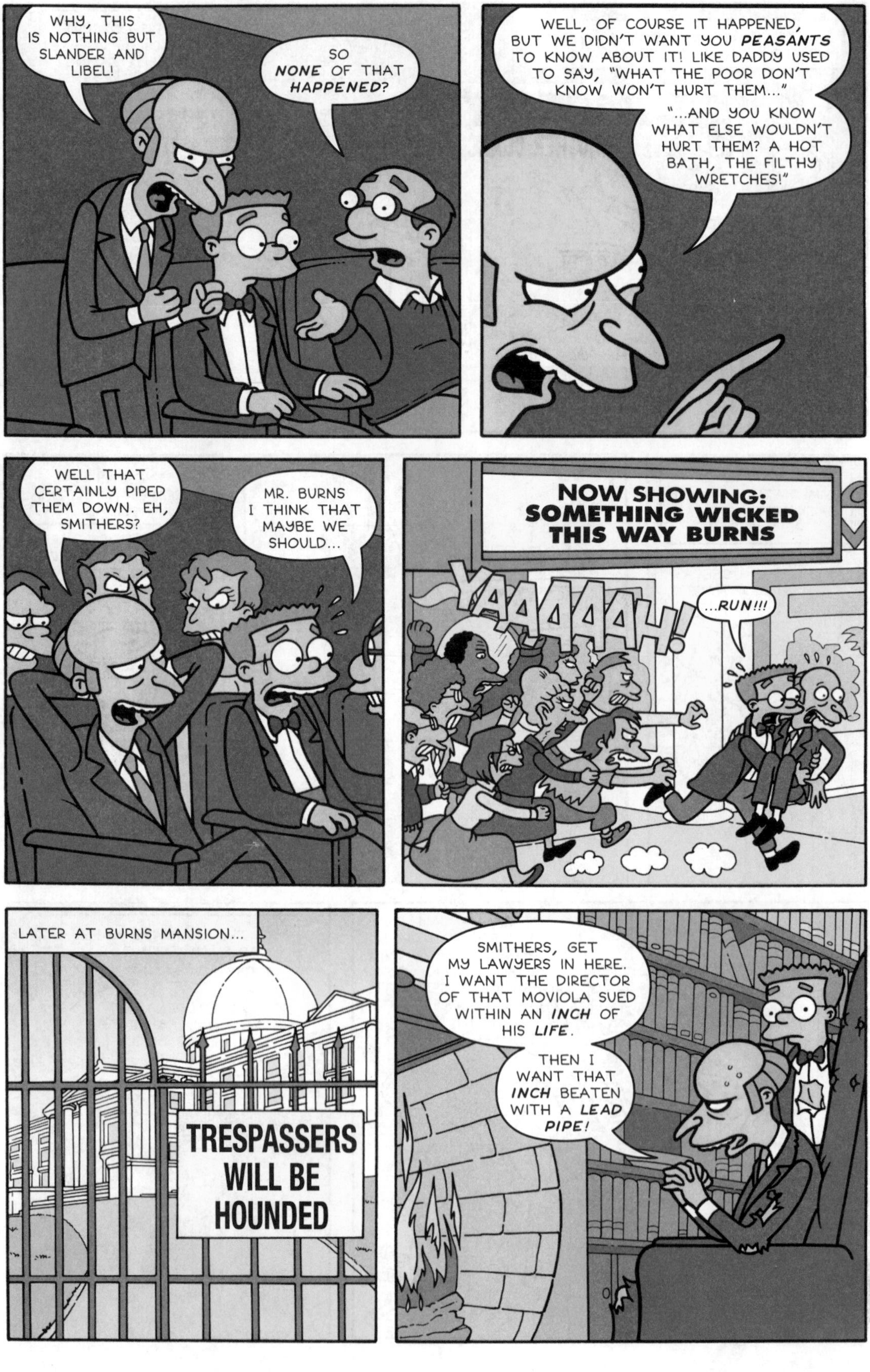
WHY, THIS IS NOTHING BUT SLANDER AND LIBEL!
SO NONE OF THAT HAPPENED?
WELL, OF COURSE IT HAPPENED, BUT WE DIDN'T WANT YOU PEASANTS TO KNOW ABOUT IT! LIKE DADDY USED TO SAY, "WHAT THE POOR DON'T KNOW WON'T HURT THEM..."
"...AND YOU KNOW WHAT ELSE WOULDN'T HURT THEM? A HOT BATH, THE FILTHY WRETCHES!"
WELL THAT CERTAINLY PIPED THEM DOWN. EH, SMITHERS?
MR. BURNS I THINK THAT MAYBE WE SHOULD...
NOW SHOWING:
SOMETHING WICKED THIS WAY BURNS
YAAAAAH!
...RUN!!!
LATER AT BURNS MANSION...
TRESPASSERS WILL BE HOUNDED
SMITHERS, GET MY LAWYERS IN HERE. I WANT THE DIRECTOR OF THAT MOVIOLA SUED WITHIN AN INCH OF HIS LIFE.
THEN I WANT THAT INCH BEATEN WITH A LEAD PIPE!

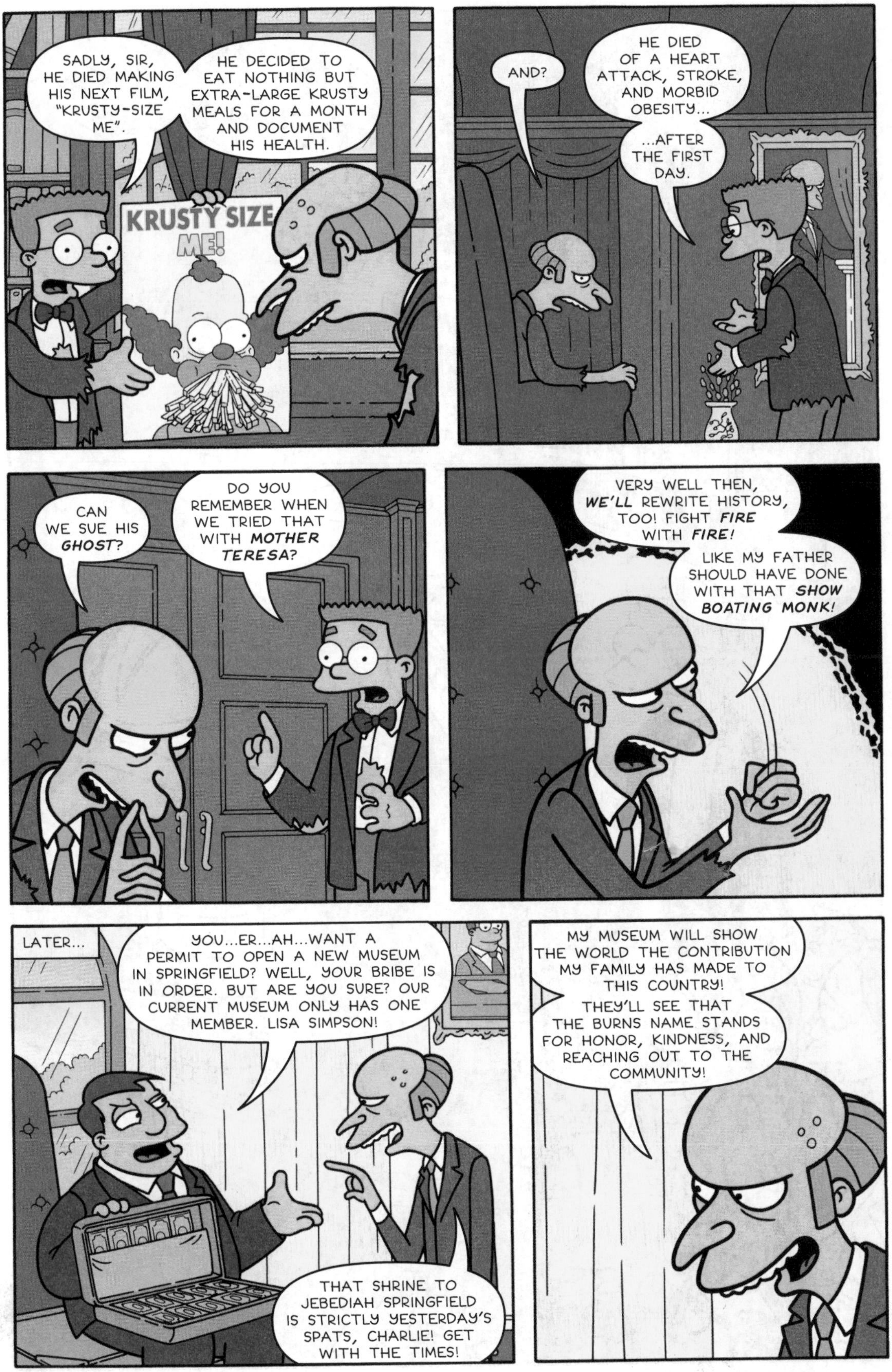
SADLY, SIR, HE DIED MAKING HIS NEXT FILM, "KRUSTY-SIZE ME".
HE DECIDED TO EAT NOTHING BUT EXTRA-LARGE KRUSTY MEALS FOR A MONTH AND DOCUMENT HIS HEALTH.
KRUSTY SIZE ME!
AND?
HE DIED OF A HEART ATTACK, STROKE, AND MORBID OBESITY...
...AFTER THE FIRST DAY.
CAN WE SUE HIS GHOST?
DO YOU REMEMBER WHEN WE TRIED THAT WITH MOTHER TERESA?
VERY WELL THEN, WE'LL REWRITE HISTORY, TOO! FIGHT FIRE WITH FIRE!
LIKE MY FATHER SHOULD HAVE DONE WITH THAT SHOW BOATING MONK!
LATER...
YOU...ER...AH...WANT A PERMIT TO OPEN A NEW MUSEUM IN SPRINGFIELD? WELL, YOUR BRIBE IS IN ORDER. BUT ARE YOU SURE? OUR CURRENT MUSEUM ONLY HAS ONE MEMBER. LISA SIMPSON!
THAT SHRINE TO JEBEDIAH SPRINGFIELD IS STRICTLY YESTERDAY'S SPATS, CHARLIE! GET WITH THE TIMES!
MY MUSEUM WILL SHOW THE WORLD THE CONTRIBUTION MY FAMILY HAS MADE TO THIS COUNTRY!
THEY'LL SEE THAT THE BURNS NAME STANDS FOR HONOR, KINDNESS, AND REACHING OUT TO THE COMMUNITY!

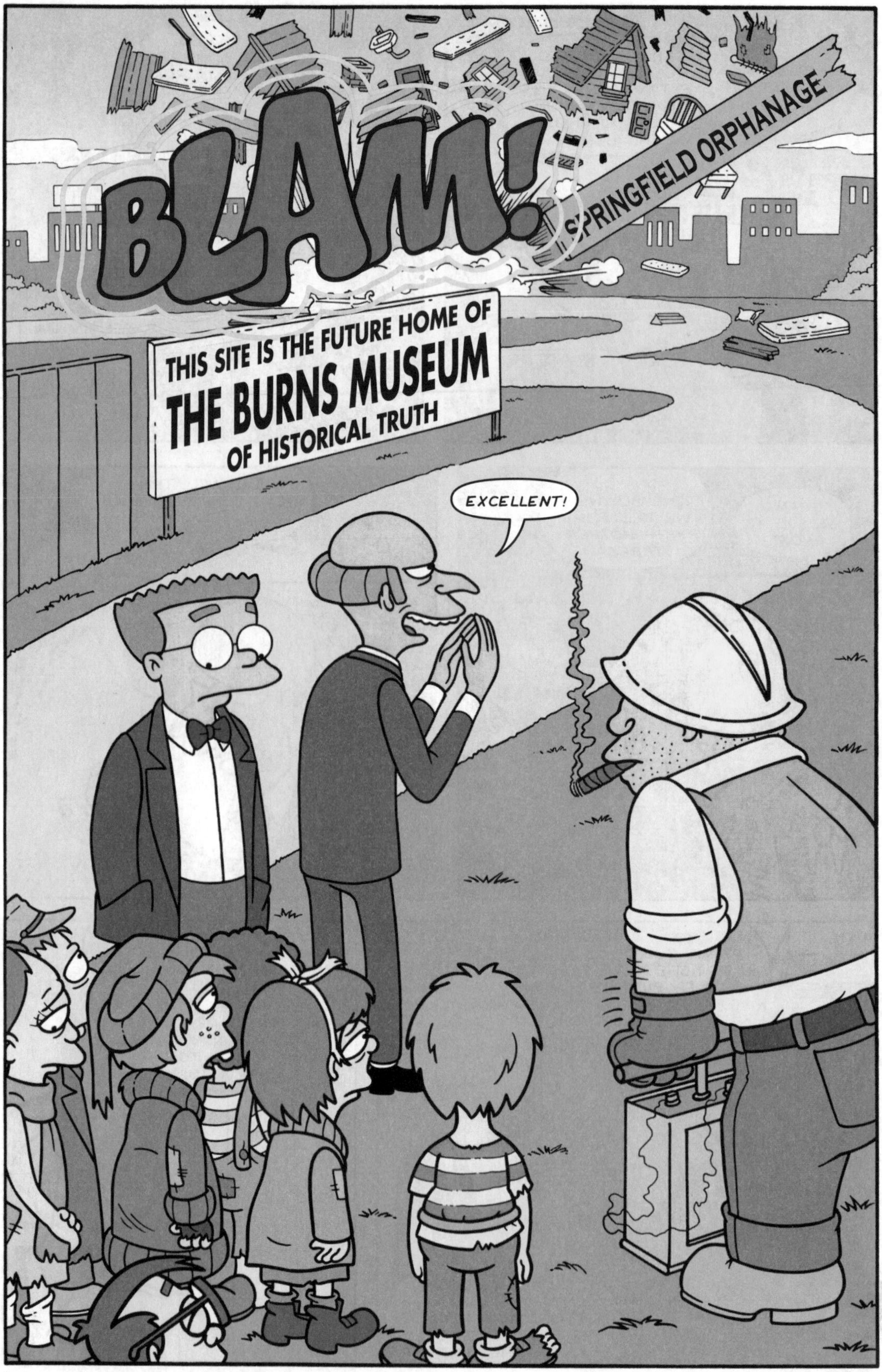
BLAM!
SPRINGFIELD ORPHANAGE
THIS SITE IS THE FUTURE HOME OF
THE BURNS MUSEUM
OF HISTORICAL TRUTH
EXCELLENT!

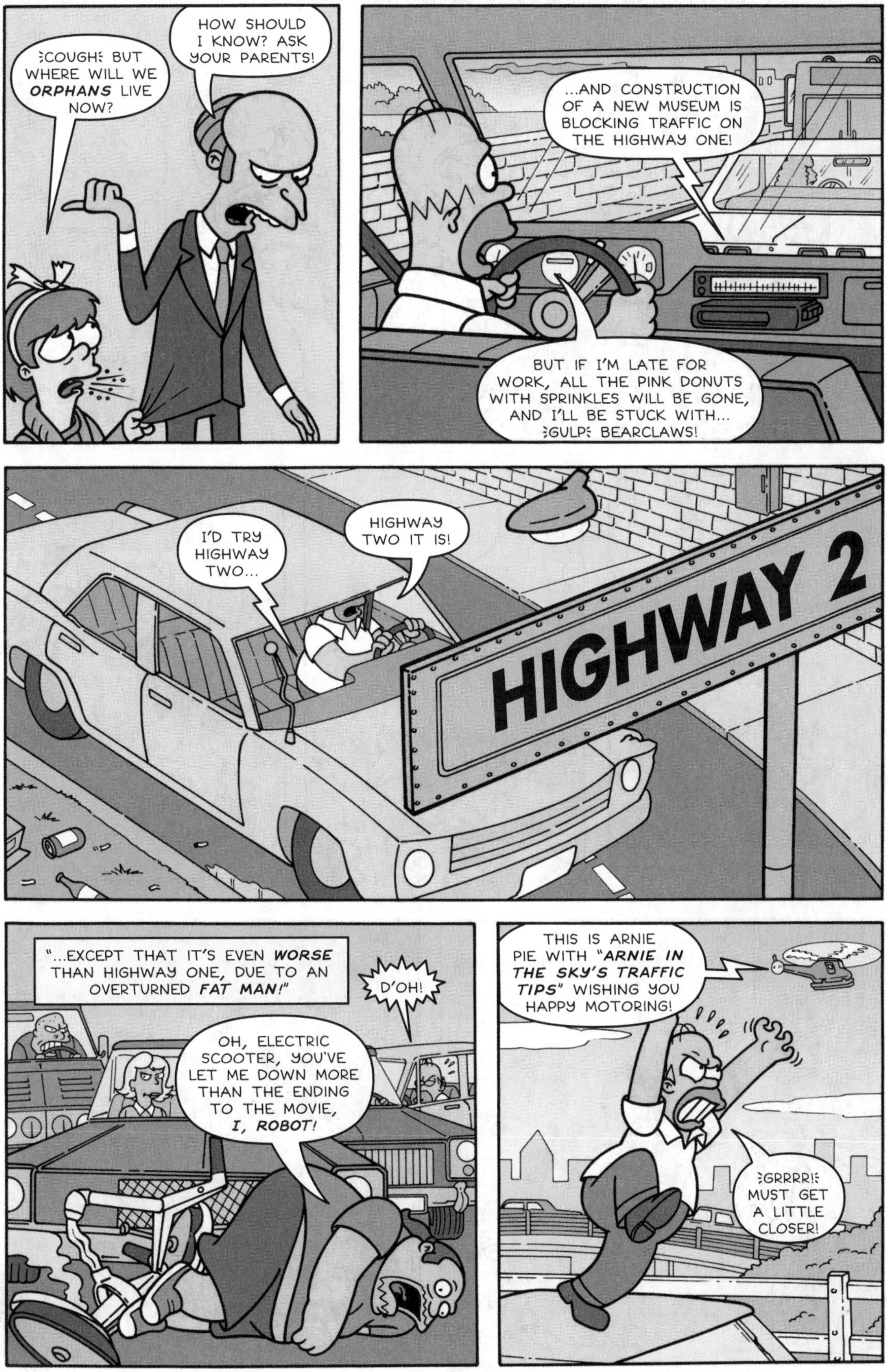

⁝COUGH⁝ BUT WHERE WILL WE ORPHANS LIVE NOW?
HOW SHOULD I KNOW? ASK YOUR PARENTS!
...AND CONSTRUCTION OF A NEW MUSEUM IS BLOCKING TRAFFIC ON THE HIGHWAY ONE!
BUT IF I'M LATE FOR WORK, ALL THE PINK DONUTS WITH SPRINKLES WILL BE GONE, AND I'LL BE STUCK WITH... ⁝GULP⁝ BEARCLAWS!
I'D TRY HIGHWAY TWO...
HIGHWAY TWO IT IS!
HIGHWAY 2
"...EXCEPT THAT IT'S EVEN WORSE THAN HIGHWAY ONE, DUE TO AN OVERTURNED FAT MAN!"
D'OH!
OH, ELECTRIC SCOOTER, YOU'VE LET ME DOWN MORE THAN THE ENDING TO THE MOVIE, I, ROBOT!
THIS IS ARNIE PIE WITH "ARNIE IN THE SKY'S TRAFFIC TIPS" WISHING YOU HAPPY MOTORING!
⁝GRRRR!⁝ MUST GET A LITTLE CLOSER!

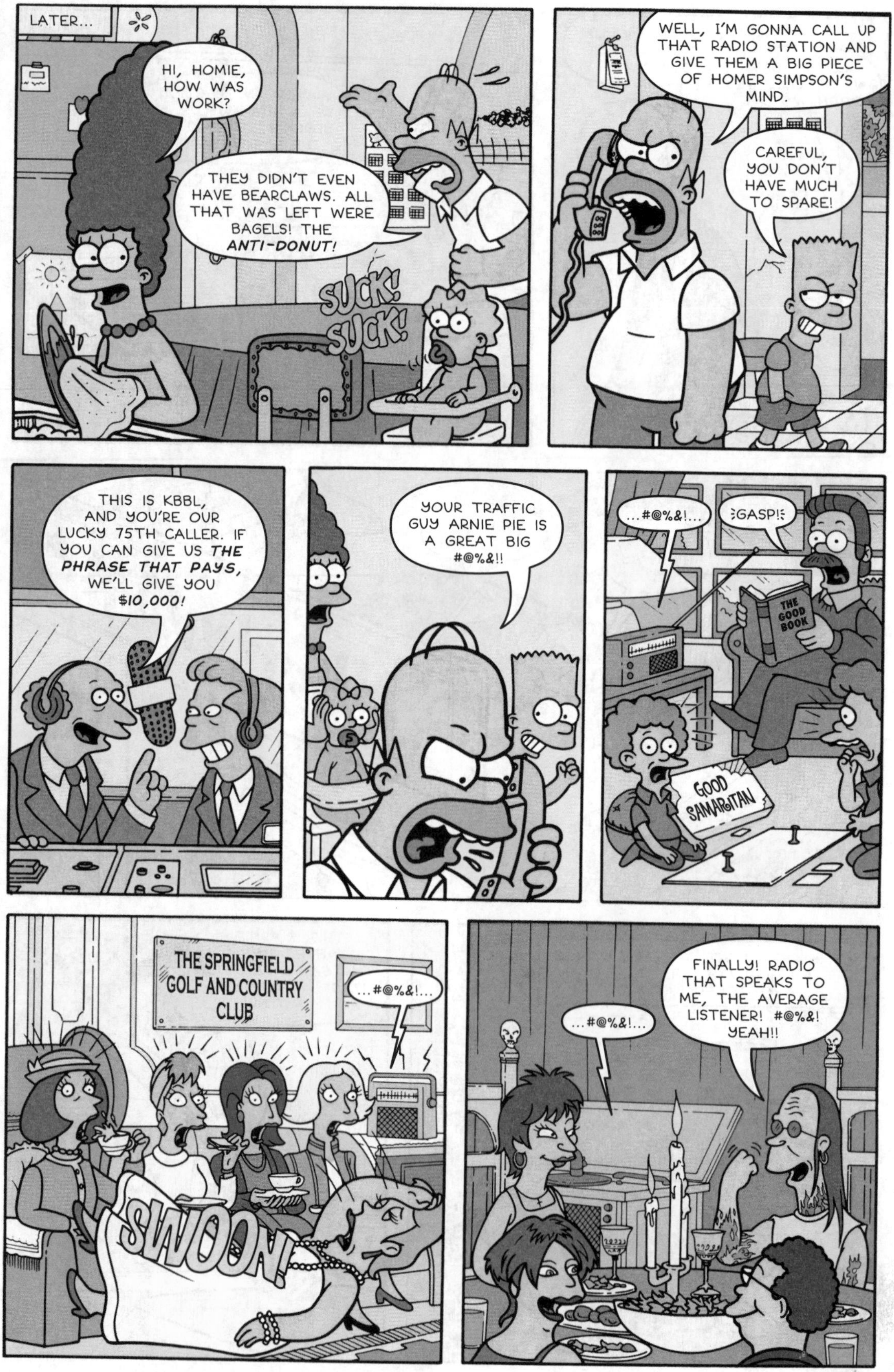
LATER...
HI, HOMIE, HOW WAS WORK?
THEY DIDN'T EVEN HAVE BEARCLAWS. ALL THAT WAS LEFT WERE BAGELS! THE *ANTI-DONUT*!
SUCK! SUCK!
WELL, I'M GONNA CALL UP THAT RADIO STATION AND GIVE THEM A BIG PIECE OF HOMER SIMPSON'S MIND.
CAREFUL, YOU DON'T HAVE MUCH TO SPARE!
THIS IS KBBL, AND YOU'RE OUR LUCKY 75TH CALLER. IF YOU CAN GIVE US ***THE PHRASE THAT PAYS,*** WE'LL GIVE YOU ***$10,000!***
YOUR TRAFFIC GUY ARNIE PIE IS A GREAT BIG #@%&!!
...#@%&!...
GASP!
THE GOOD BOOK
GOOD SAMARITAN
THE SPRINGFIELD GOLF AND COUNTRY CLUB
...#@%&!...
SWOON!
...#@%&!...
FINALLY! RADIO THAT SPEAKS TO ME, THE AVERAGE LISTENER! #@%&! YEAH!!

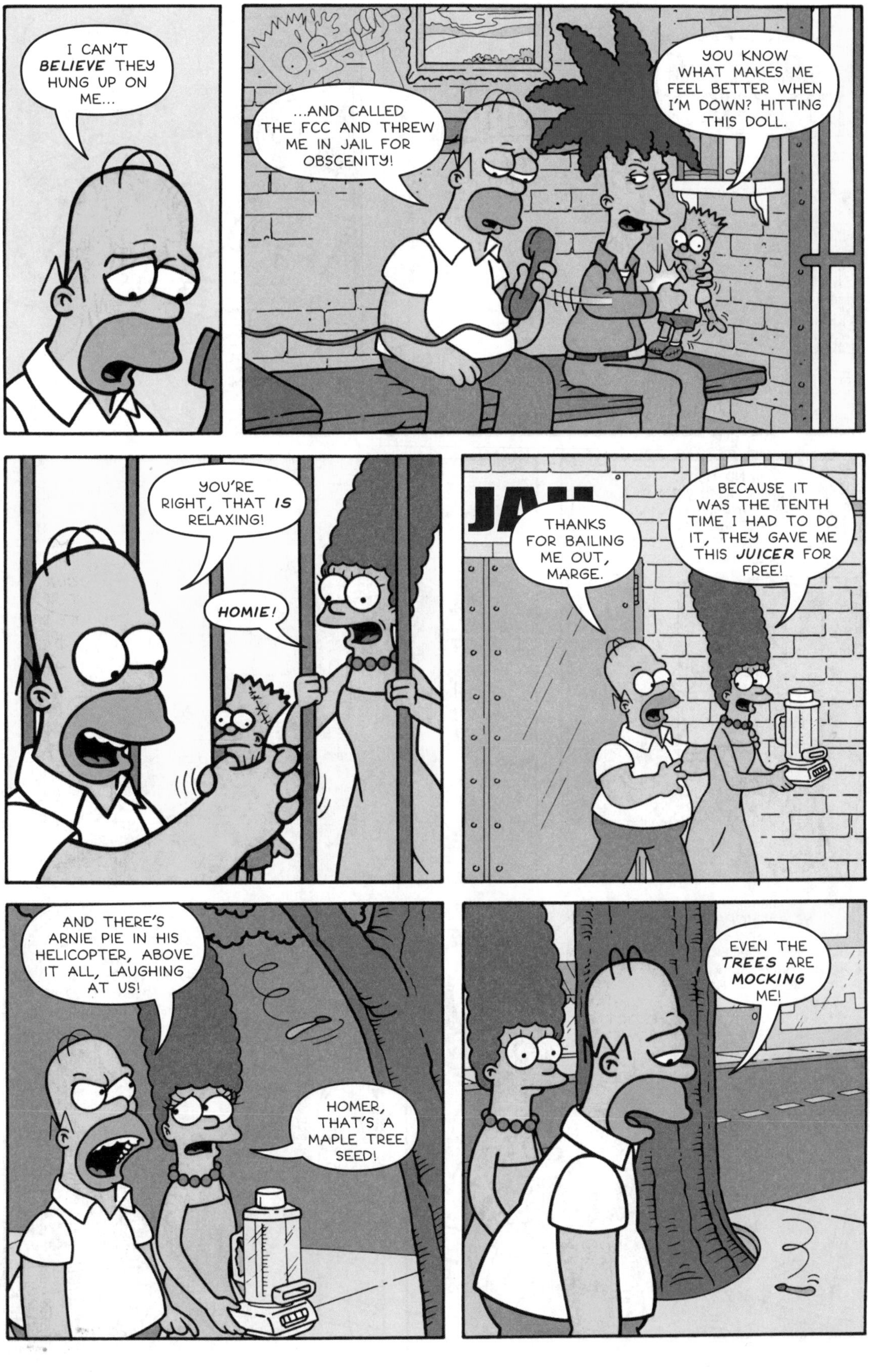

I CAN'T BELIEVE THEY HUNG UP ON ME...
...AND CALLED THE FCC AND THREW ME IN JAIL FOR OBSCENITY!
YOU KNOW WHAT MAKES ME FEEL BETTER WHEN I'M DOWN? HITTING THIS DOLL.
YOU'RE RIGHT, THAT IS RELAXING!
HOMIE!
JAIL
THANKS FOR BAILING ME OUT, MARGE.
BECAUSE IT WAS THE TENTH TIME I HAD TO DO IT, THEY GAVE ME THIS JUICER FOR FREE!
AND THERE'S ARNIE PIE IN HIS HELICOPTER, ABOVE IT ALL, LAUGHING AT US!
HOMER, THAT'S A MAPLE TREE SEED!
EVEN THE TREES ARE MOCKING ME!

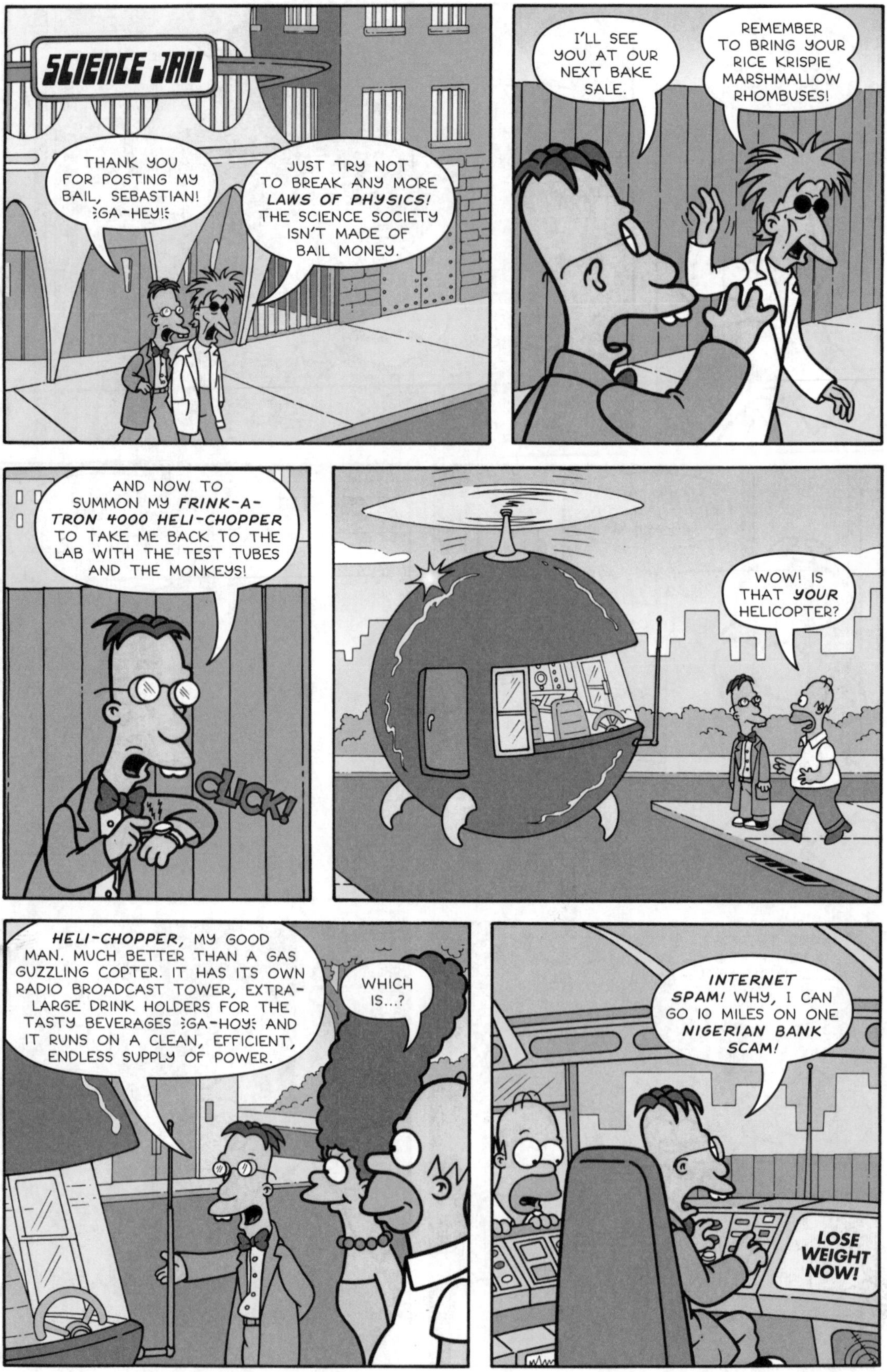
SCIENCE JAIL
THANK YOU FOR POSTING MY BAIL, SEBASTIAN! ~GA-HEY!~
JUST TRY NOT TO BREAK ANY MORE *LAWS OF PHYSICS!* THE SCIENCE SOCIETY ISN'T MADE OF BAIL MONEY.
I'LL SEE YOU AT OUR NEXT BAKE SALE.
REMEMBER TO BRING YOUR RICE KRISPIE MARSHMALLOW RHOMBUSES!
AND NOW TO SUMMON MY *FRINK-A-TRON 4000 HELI-CHOPPER* TO TAKE ME BACK TO THE LAB WITH THE TEST TUBES AND THE MONKEYS!
CLICK!
WOW! IS THAT *YOUR* HELICOPTER?
HELI-CHOPPER, MY GOOD MAN. MUCH BETTER THAN A GAS GUZZLING COPTER. IT HAS ITS OWN RADIO BROADCAST TOWER, EXTRA-LARGE DRINK HOLDERS FOR THE TASTY BEVERAGES ~GA-HOY~ AND IT RUNS ON A CLEAN, EFFICIENT, ENDLESS SUPPLY OF POWER.
WHICH IS...?
INTERNET SPAM! WHY, I CAN GO 10 MILES ON ONE *NIGERIAN BANK SCAM!*
LOSE WEIGHT NOW!

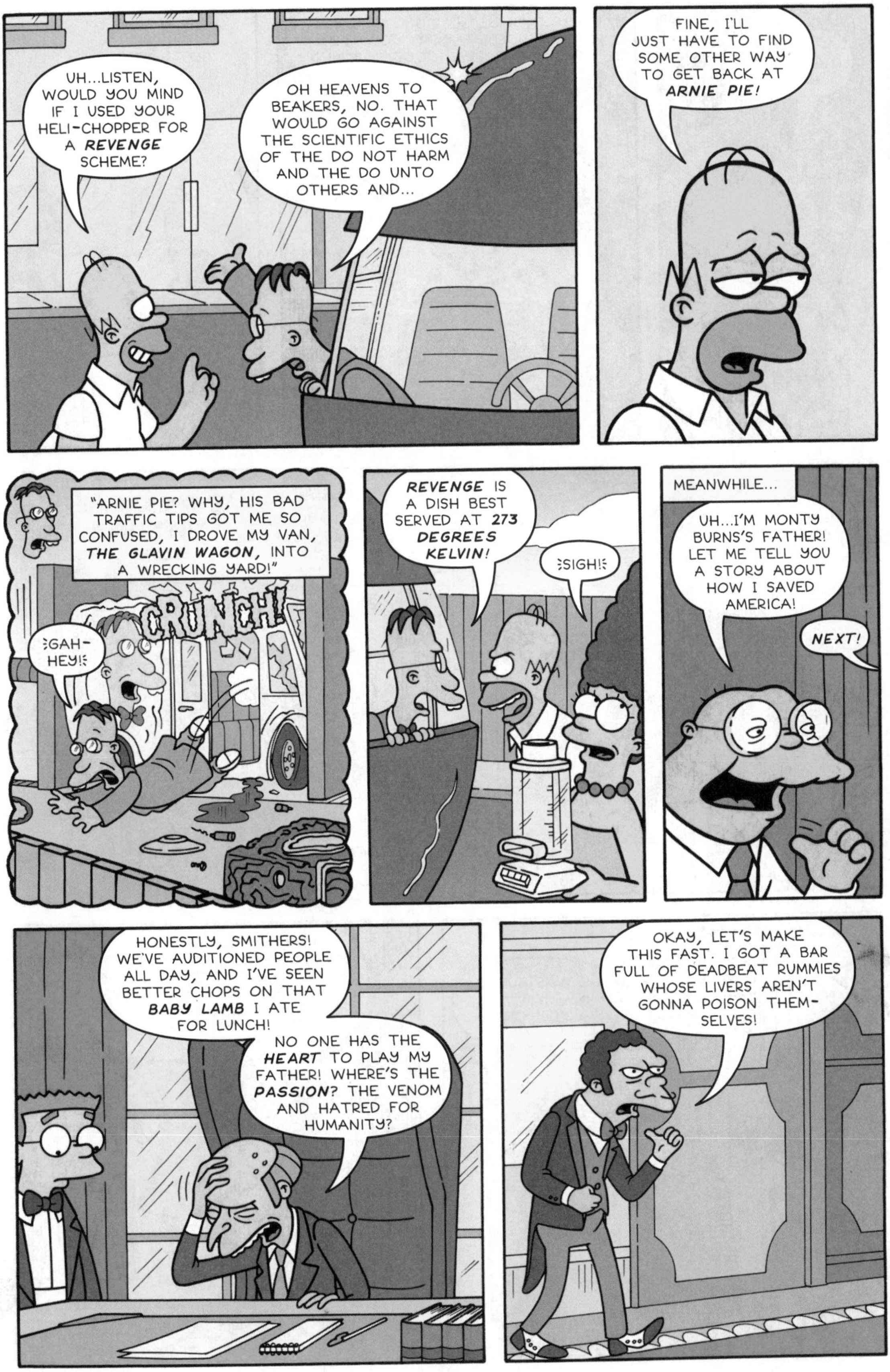
UH...LISTEN, WOULD YOU MIND IF I USED YOUR HELI-CHOPPER FOR A REVENGE SCHEME?
OH HEAVENS TO BEAKERS, NO. THAT WOULD GO AGAINST THE SCIENTIFIC ETHICS OF THE DO NOT HARM AND THE DO UNTO OTHERS AND...
FINE, I'LL JUST HAVE TO FIND SOME OTHER WAY TO GET BACK AT ARNIE PIE!
"ARNIE PIE? WHY, HIS BAD TRAFFIC TIPS GOT ME SO CONFUSED, I DROVE MY VAN, THE GLAVIN WAGON, INTO A WRECKING YARD!"
CRUNCH!
GAH-HEY!
REVENGE IS A DISH BEST SERVED AT 273 DEGREES KELVIN!
SIGH!
MEANWHILE...
UH...I'M MONTY BURNS'S FATHER! LET ME TELL YOU A STORY ABOUT HOW I SAVED AMERICA!
NEXT!
HONESTLY, SMITHERS! WE'VE AUDITIONED PEOPLE ALL DAY, AND I'VE SEEN BETTER CHOPS ON THAT BABY LAMB I ATE FOR LUNCH!
NO ONE HAS THE HEART TO PLAY MY FATHER! WHERE'S THE PASSION? THE VENOM AND HATRED FOR HUMANITY?
OKAY, LET'S MAKE THIS FAST. I GOT A BAR FULL OF DEADBEAT RUMMIES WHOSE LIVERS AREN'T GONNA POISON THEM-SELVES!

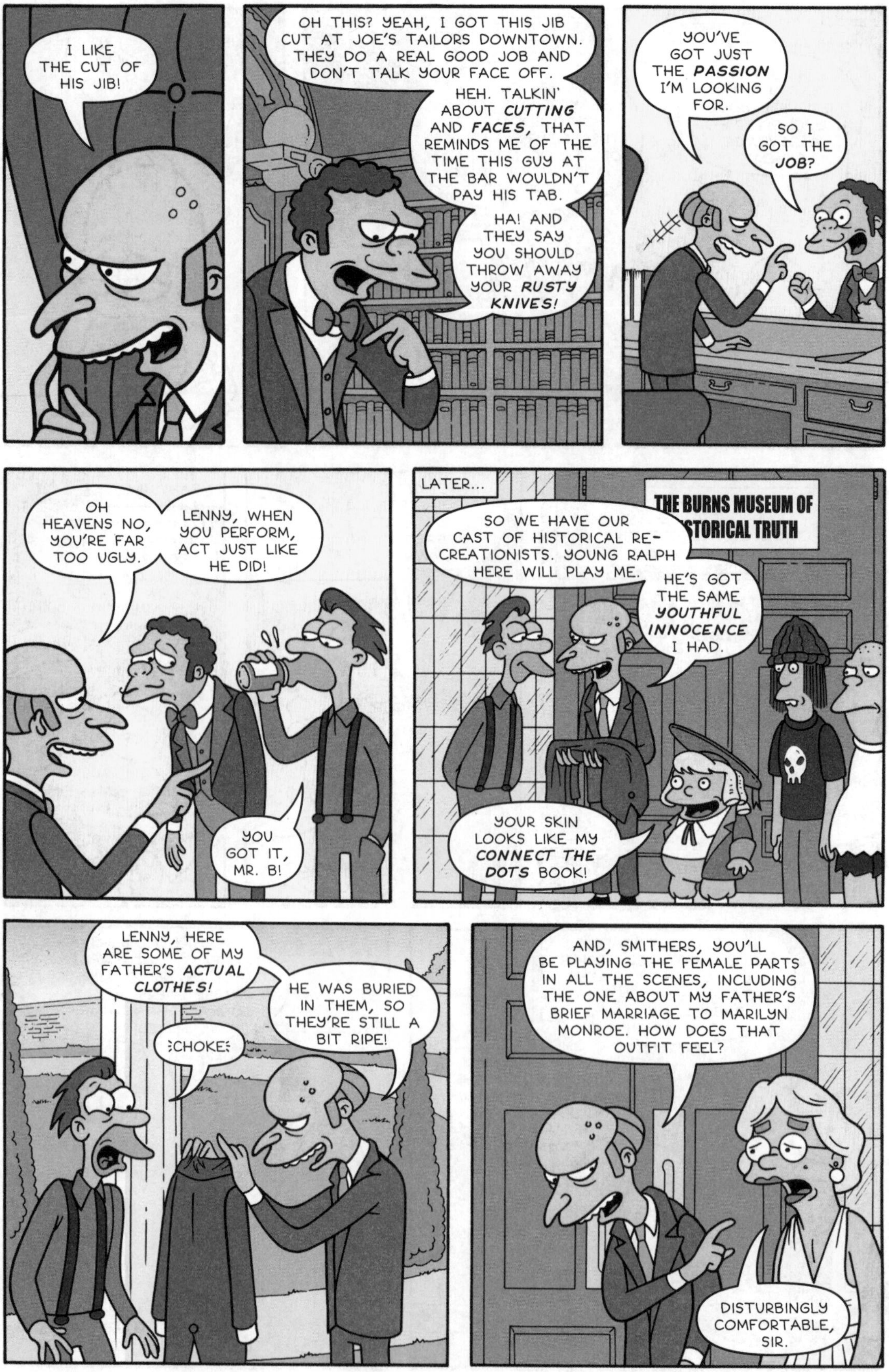

I LIKE THE CUT OF HIS JIB!
OH THIS? YEAH, I GOT THIS JIB CUT AT JOE'S TAILORS DOWNTOWN. THEY DO A REAL GOOD JOB AND DON'T TALK YOUR FACE OFF.
HEH. TALKIN' ABOUT CUTTING AND FACES, THAT REMINDS ME OF THE TIME THIS GUY AT THE BAR WOULDN'T PAY HIS TAB.
HA! AND THEY SAY YOU SHOULD THROW AWAY YOUR RUSTY KNIVES!
YOU'VE GOT JUST THE PASSION I'M LOOKING FOR.
SO I GOT THE JOB?
OH HEAVENS NO, YOU'RE FAR TOO UGLY.
LENNY, WHEN YOU PERFORM, ACT JUST LIKE HE DID!
YOU GOT IT, MR. B!
LATER...
THE BURNS MUSEUM OF HISTORICAL TRUTH
SO WE HAVE OUR CAST OF HISTORICAL RE-CREATIONISTS. YOUNG RALPH HERE WILL PLAY ME.
HE'S GOT THE SAME YOUTHFUL INNOCENCE I HAD.
YOUR SKIN LOOKS LIKE MY CONNECT THE DOTS BOOK!
LENNY, HERE ARE SOME OF MY FATHER'S ACTUAL CLOTHES!
HE WAS BURIED IN THEM, SO THEY'RE STILL A BIT RIPE!
CHOKE
AND, SMITHERS, YOU'LL BE PLAYING THE FEMALE PARTS IN ALL THE SCENES, INCLUDING THE ONE ABOUT MY FATHER'S BRIEF MARRIAGE TO MARILYN MONROE. HOW DOES THAT OUTFIT FEEL?
DISTURBINGLY COMFORTABLE, SIR.

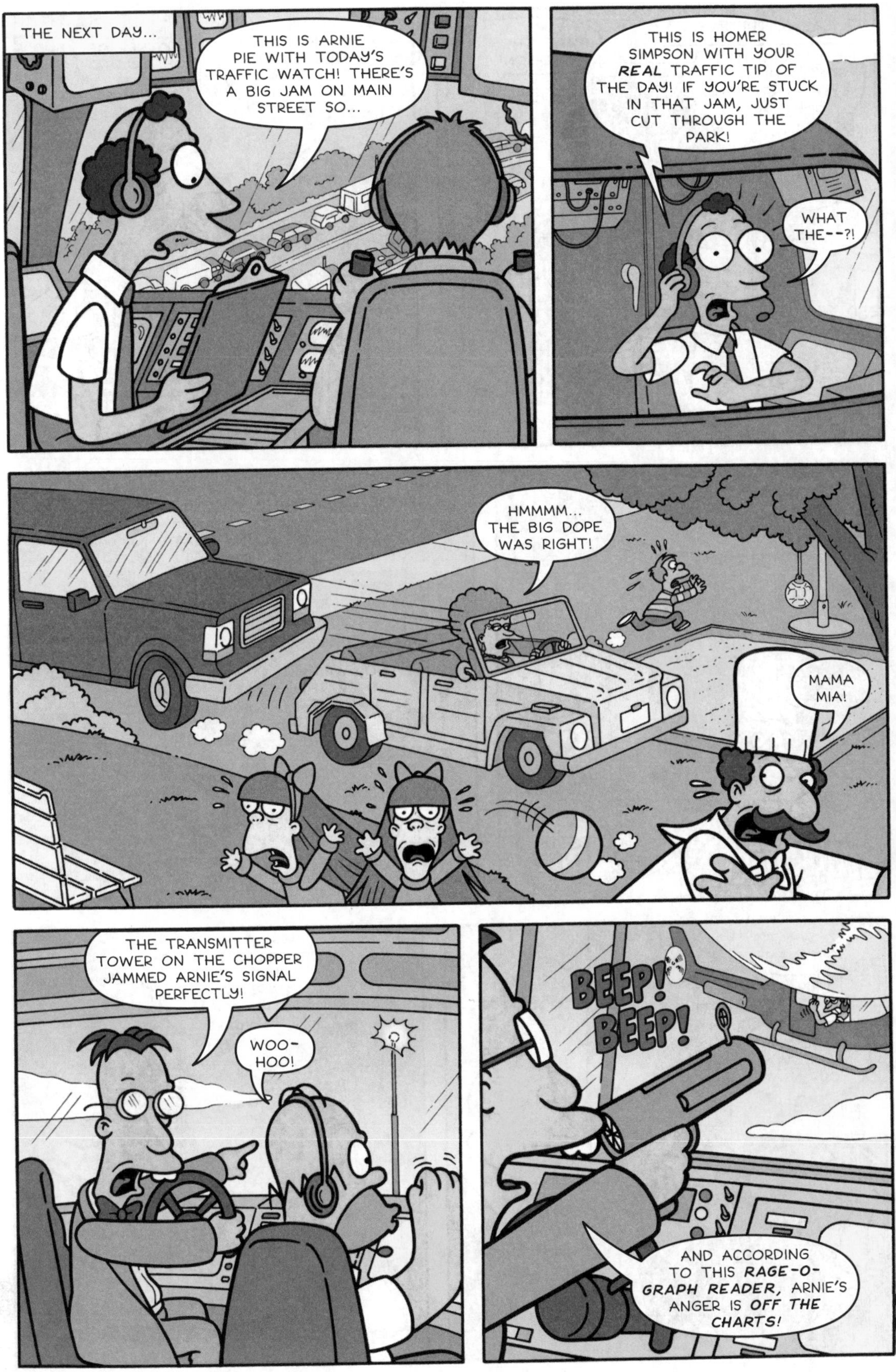
THE NEXT DAY...
THIS IS ARNIE PIE WITH TODAY'S TRAFFIC WATCH! THERE'S A BIG JAM ON MAIN STREET SO...
THIS IS HOMER SIMPSON WITH YOUR REAL TRAFFIC TIP OF THE DAY! IF YOU'RE STUCK IN THAT JAM, JUST CUT THROUGH THE PARK!
WHAT THE--?!
HMMMM... THE BIG DOPE WAS RIGHT!
MAMA MIA!
THE TRANSMITTER TOWER ON THE CHOPPER JAMMED ARNIE'S SIGNAL PERFECTLY!
WOO-HOO!
BEEP! BEEP!
AND ACCORDING TO THIS RAGE-O-GRAPH READER, ARNIE'S ANGER IS OFF THE CHARTS!

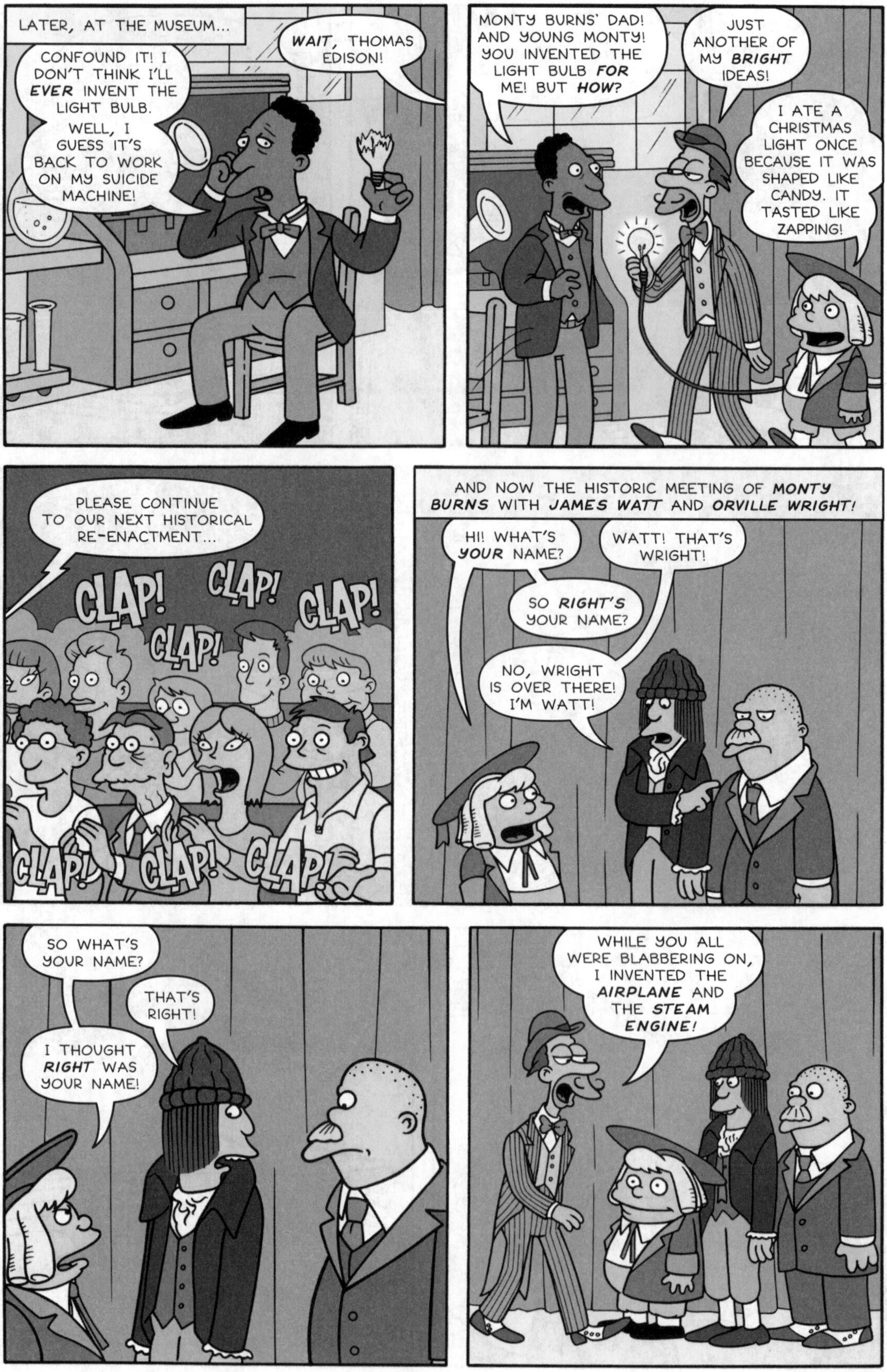

LATER, AT THE MUSEUM...
CONFOUND IT! I DON'T THINK I'LL *EVER* INVENT THE LIGHT BULB.
WELL, I GUESS IT'S BACK TO WORK ON MY SUICIDE MACHINE!
WAIT, THOMAS EDISON!
MONTY BURNS' DAD! AND YOUNG MONTY! YOU INVENTED THE LIGHT BULB *FOR* ME! BUT *HOW*?
JUST ANOTHER OF MY *BRIGHT* IDEAS!
I ATE A CHRISTMAS LIGHT ONCE BECAUSE IT WAS SHAPED LIKE CANDY. IT TASTED LIKE ZAPPING!
PLEASE CONTINUE TO OUR NEXT HISTORICAL RE-ENACTMENT...
CLAP! CLAP! CLAP! CLAP!
CLAP! CLAP! CLAP!
AND NOW THE HISTORIC MEETING OF *MONTY BURNS* WITH *JAMES WATT* AND *ORVILLE WRIGHT*!
HI! WHAT'S *YOUR* NAME?
WATT! THAT'S WRIGHT!
SO *RIGHT'S* YOUR NAME?
NO, WRIGHT IS OVER THERE! I'M WATT!
SO WHAT'S YOUR NAME?
THAT'S RIGHT!
I THOUGHT *RIGHT* WAS YOUR NAME!
WHILE YOU ALL WERE BLABBERING ON, I INVENTED THE *AIRPLANE* AND THE *STEAM ENGINE*!

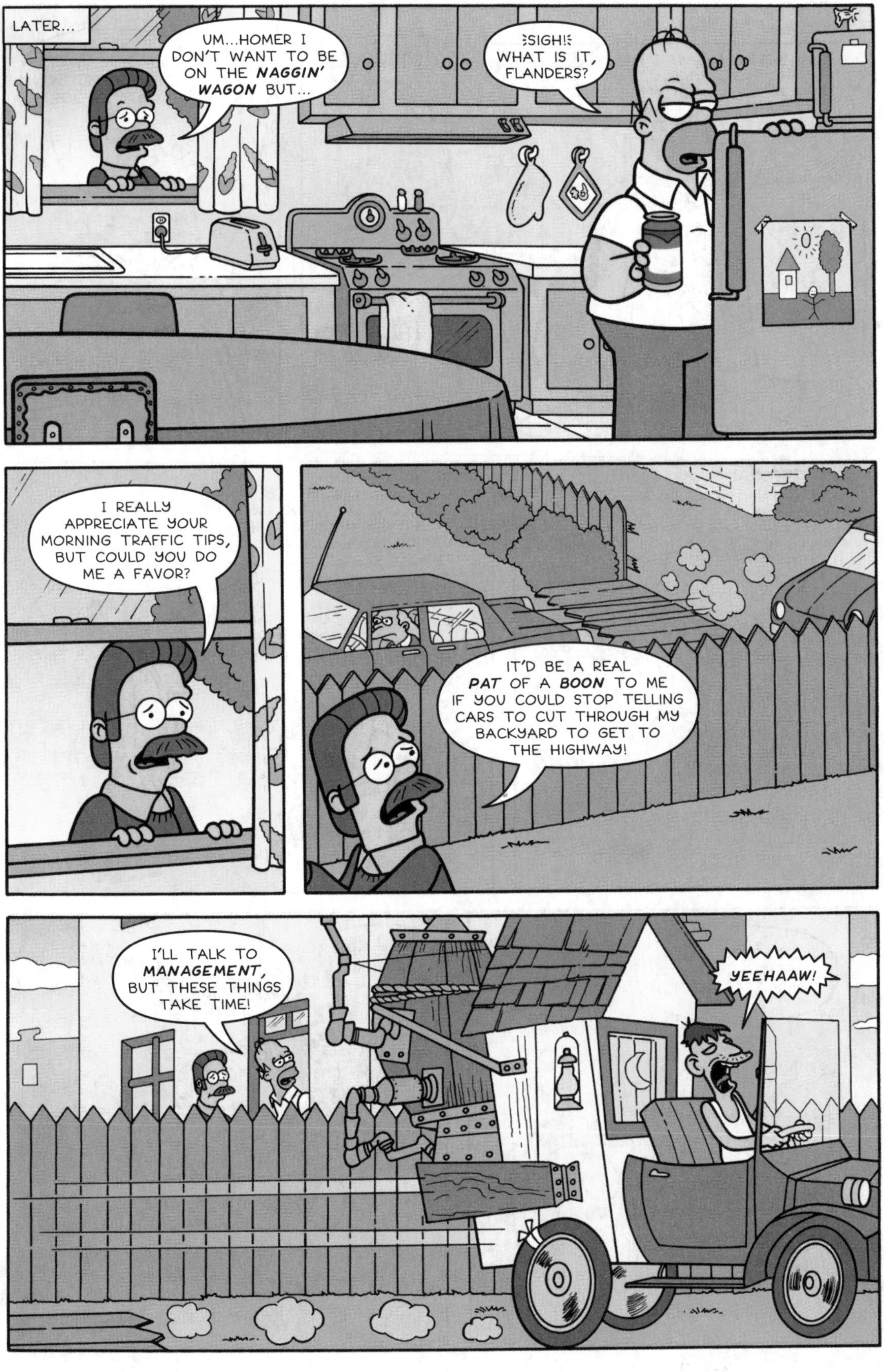
LATER...
UM...HOMER I DON'T WANT TO BE ON THE NAGGIN' WAGON BUT...
SIGH! WHAT IS IT, FLANDERS?
I REALLY APPRECIATE YOUR MORNING TRAFFIC TIPS, BUT COULD YOU DO ME A FAVOR?
IT'D BE A REAL PAT OF A BOON TO ME IF YOU COULD STOP TELLING CARS TO CUT THROUGH MY BACKYARD TO GET TO THE HIGHWAY!
I'LL TALK TO MANAGEMENT, BUT THESE THINGS TAKE TIME!
YEEHAAW!

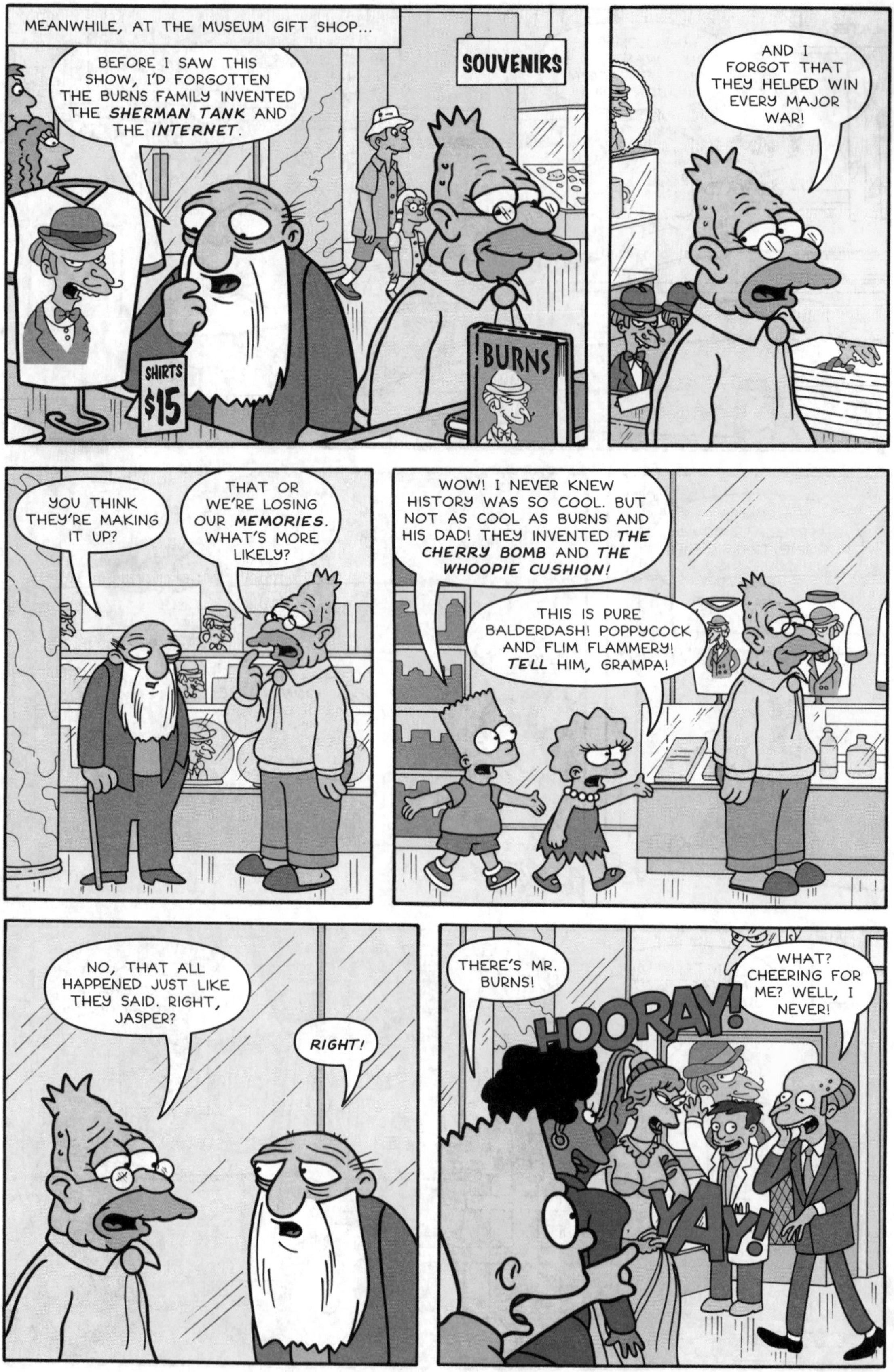

MEANWHILE, AT THE MUSEUM GIFT SHOP...
BEFORE I SAW THIS SHOW, I'D FORGOTTEN THE BURNS FAMILY INVENTED THE ***SHERMAN TANK*** AND THE ***INTERNET***.
SOUVENIRS
SHIRTS $15
BURNS
AND I FORGOT THAT THEY HELPED WIN EVERY MAJOR WAR!
YOU THINK THEY'RE MAKING IT UP?
THAT OR WE'RE LOSING OUR ***MEMORIES***. WHAT'S MORE LIKELY?
WOW! I NEVER KNEW HISTORY WAS SO COOL. BUT NOT AS COOL AS BURNS AND HIS DAD! THEY INVENTED ***THE CHERRY BOMB*** AND ***THE WHOOPIE CUSHION***!
THIS IS PURE BALDERDASH! POPPYCOCK AND FLIM FLAMMERY! ***TELL*** HIM, GRAMPA!
NO, THAT ALL HAPPENED JUST LIKE THEY SAID. RIGHT, JASPER?
RIGHT!
THERE'S MR. BURNS!
HOORAY!
WHAT? CHEERING FOR ME? WELL, I NEVER!
YAY!

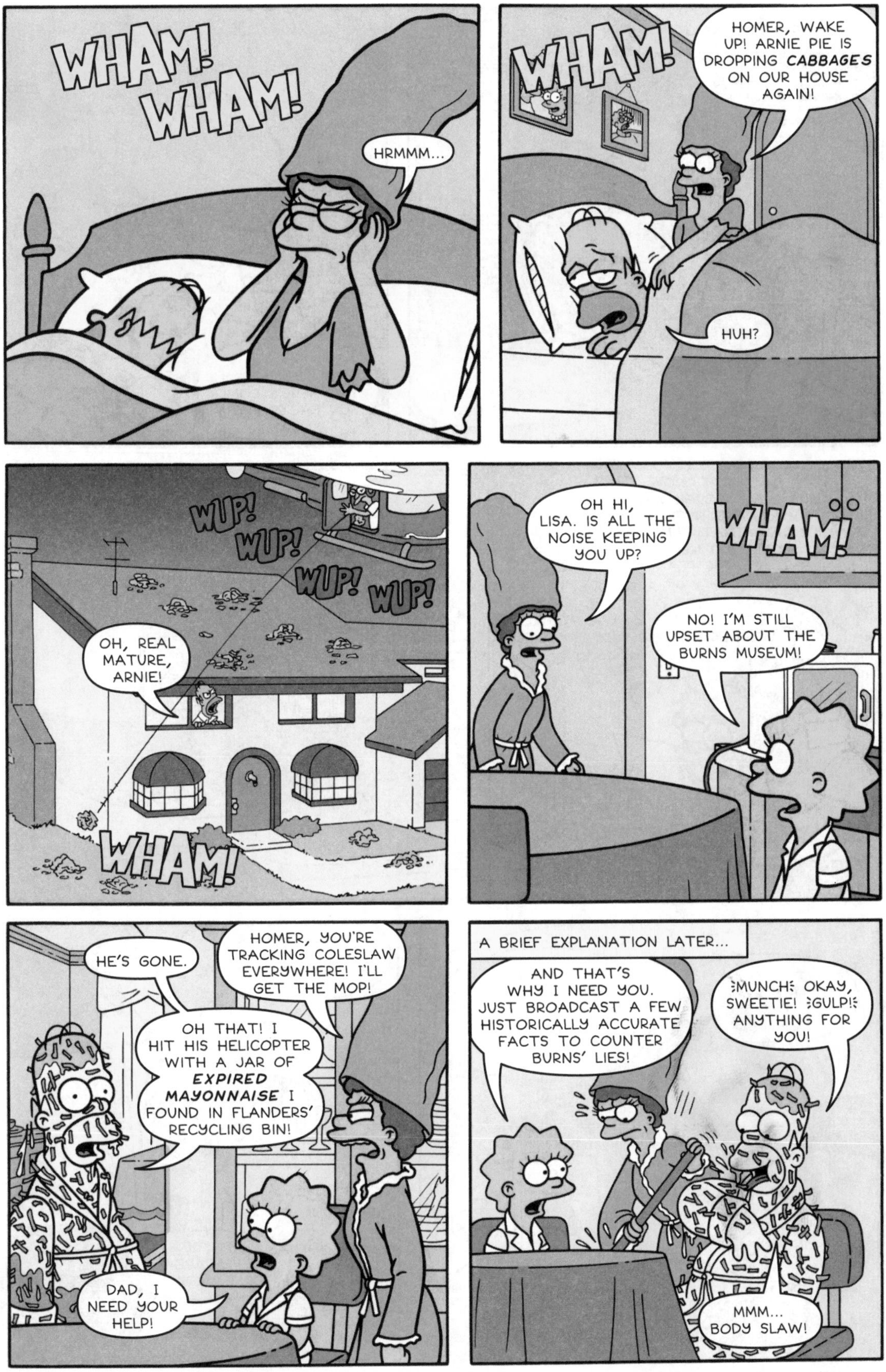
WHAM! WHAM!
HRMMM...
WHAM!
HOMER, WAKE UP! ARNIE PIE IS DROPPING CABBAGES ON OUR HOUSE AGAIN!
HUH?
WUP! WUP! WUP! WUP!
OH, REAL MATURE, ARNIE!
WHAM!
OH HI, LISA. IS ALL THE NOISE KEEPING YOU UP?
WHAM!
NO! I'M STILL UPSET ABOUT THE BURNS MUSEUM!
HE'S GONE.
HOMER, YOU'RE TRACKING COLESLAW EVERYWHERE! I'LL GET THE MOP!
OH THAT! I HIT HIS HELICOPTER WITH A JAR OF EXPIRED MAYONNAISE I FOUND IN FLANDERS' RECYCLING BIN!
DAD, I NEED YOUR HELP!
A BRIEF EXPLANATION LATER...
AND THAT'S WHY I NEED YOU. JUST BROADCAST A FEW HISTORICALLY ACCURATE FACTS TO COUNTER BURNS' LIES!
MUNCH OKAY, SWEETIE! GULP! ANYTHING FOR YOU!
MMM... BODY SLAW!

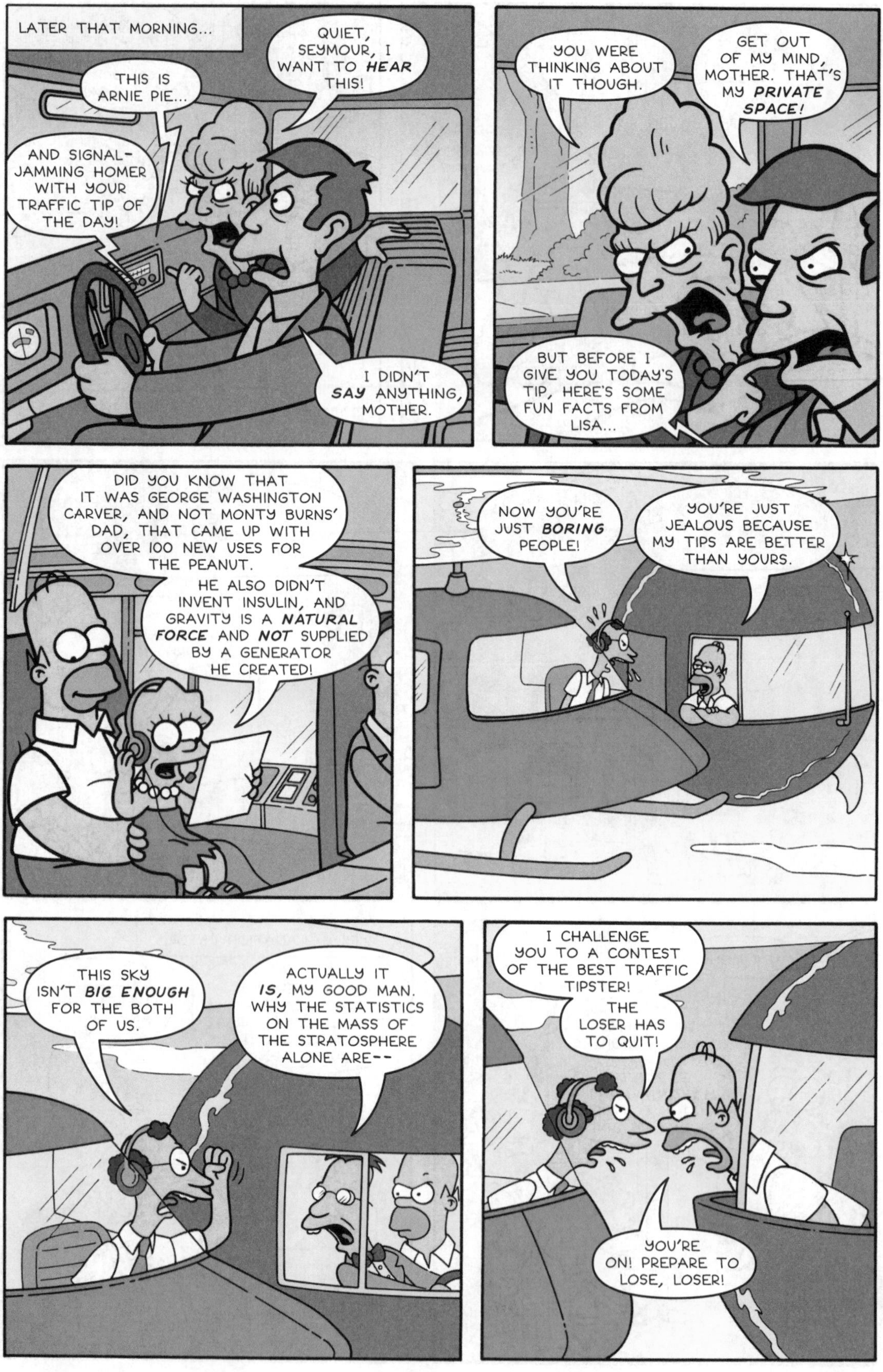

LATER THAT MORNING...
THIS IS ARNIE PIE...
QUIET, SEYMOUR, I WANT TO HEAR THIS!
AND SIGNAL-JAMMING HOMER WITH YOUR TRAFFIC TIP OF THE DAY!
I DIDN'T SAY ANYTHING, MOTHER.
YOU WERE THINKING ABOUT IT THOUGH.
GET OUT OF MY MIND, MOTHER. THAT'S MY PRIVATE SPACE!
BUT BEFORE I GIVE YOU TODAY'S TIP, HERE'S SOME FUN FACTS FROM LISA...
DID YOU KNOW THAT IT WAS GEORGE WASHINGTON CARVER, AND NOT MONTY BURNS' DAD, THAT CAME UP WITH OVER 100 NEW USES FOR THE PEANUT.
HE ALSO DIDN'T INVENT INSULIN, AND GRAVITY IS A NATURAL FORCE AND NOT SUPPLIED BY A GENERATOR HE CREATED!
NOW YOU'RE JUST BORING PEOPLE!
YOU'RE JUST JEALOUS BECAUSE MY TIPS ARE BETTER THAN YOURS.
THIS SKY ISN'T BIG ENOUGH FOR THE BOTH OF US.
ACTUALLY IT IS, MY GOOD MAN. WHY THE STATISTICS ON THE MASS OF THE STRATOSPHERE ALONE ARE--
I CHALLENGE YOU TO A CONTEST OF THE BEST TRAFFIC TIPSTER!
THE LOSER HAS TO QUIT!
YOU'RE ON! PREPARE TO LOSE, LOSER!

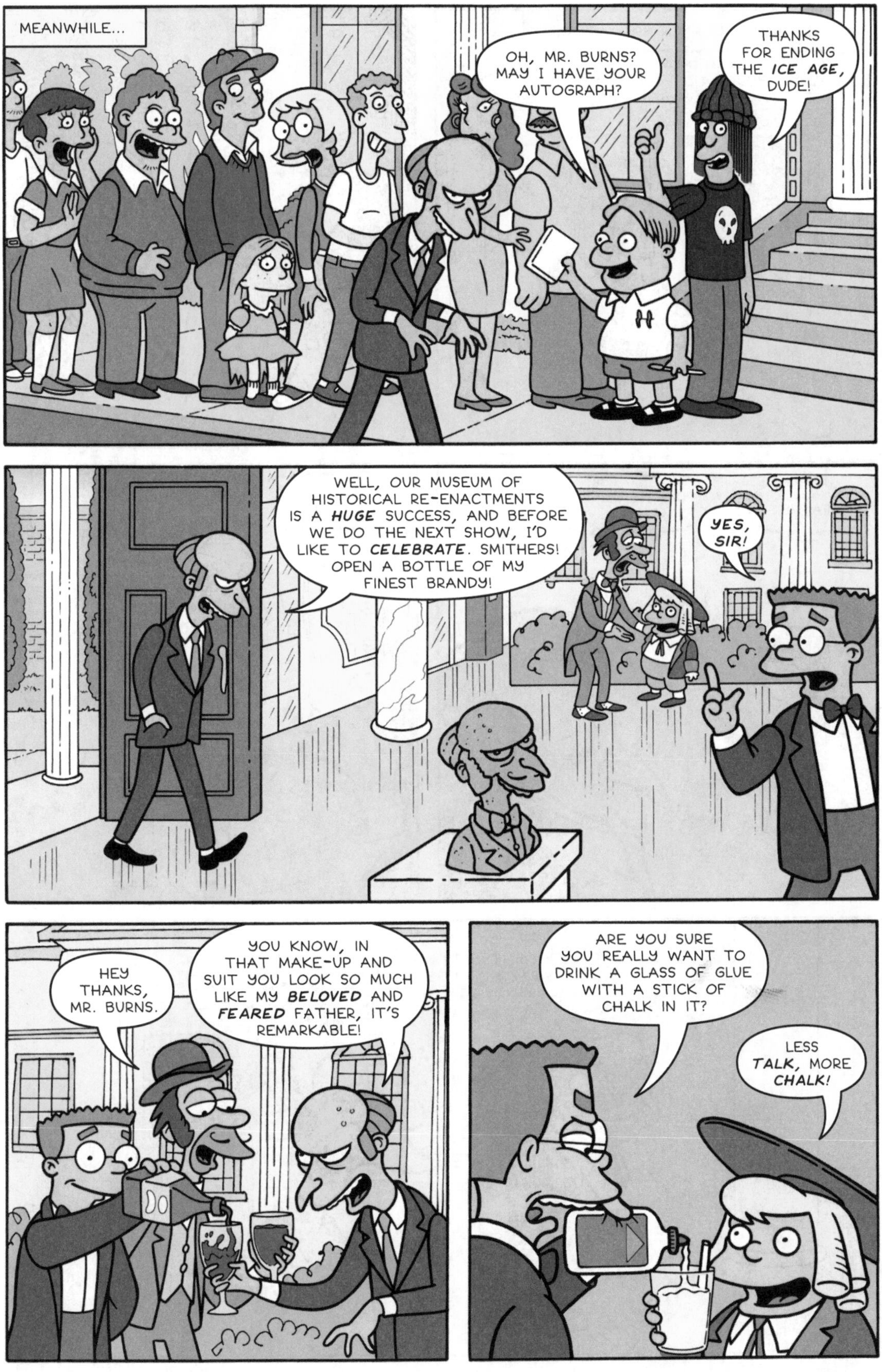
MEANWHILE...
OH, MR. BURNS? MAY I HAVE YOUR AUTOGRAPH?
THANKS FOR ENDING THE ICE AGE, DUDE!
WELL, OUR MUSEUM OF HISTORICAL RE-ENACTMENTS IS A HUGE SUCCESS, AND BEFORE WE DO THE NEXT SHOW, I'D LIKE TO CELEBRATE. SMITHERS! OPEN A BOTTLE OF MY FINEST BRANDY!
YES, SIR!
HEY THANKS, MR. BURNS.
YOU KNOW, IN THAT MAKE-UP AND SUIT YOU LOOK SO MUCH LIKE MY BELOVED AND FEARED FATHER, IT'S REMARKABLE!
ARE YOU SURE YOU REALLY WANT TO DRINK A GLASS OF GLUE WITH A STICK OF CHALK IN IT?
LESS TALK, MORE CHALK!

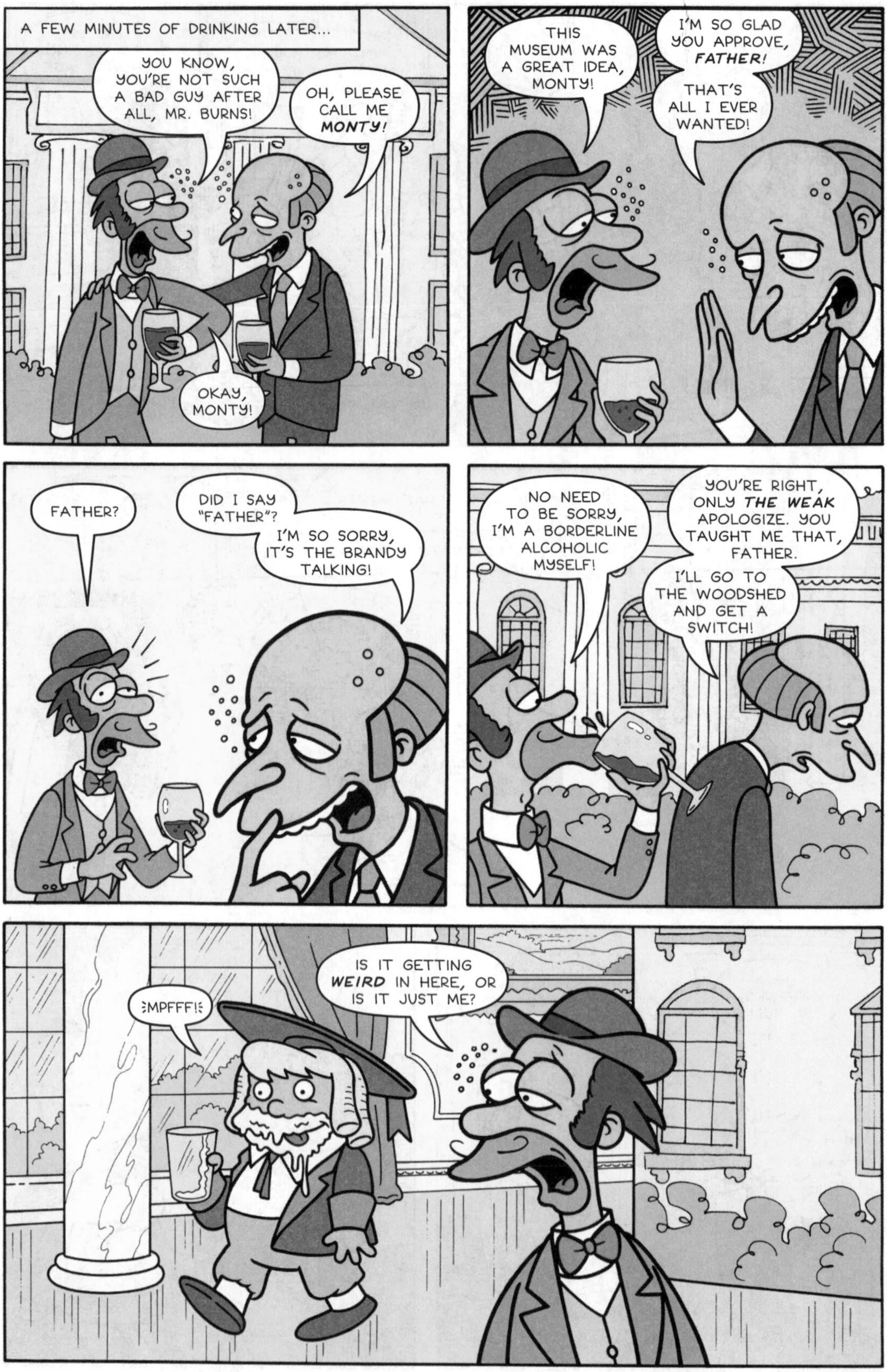

A FEW MINUTES OF DRINKING LATER...
YOU KNOW, YOU'RE NOT SUCH A BAD GUY AFTER ALL, MR. BURNS!
OH, PLEASE CALL ME *MONTY!*
OKAY, MONTY!
THIS MUSEUM WAS A GREAT IDEA, MONTY!
I'M SO GLAD YOU APPROVE, *FATHER!*
THAT'S ALL I EVER WANTED!
FATHER?
DID I SAY "FATHER"?
I'M SO SORRY, IT'S THE BRANDY TALKING!
NO NEED TO BE SORRY, I'M A BORDERLINE ALCOHOLIC MYSELF!
YOU'RE RIGHT, ONLY *THE WEAK* APOLOGIZE. YOU TAUGHT ME THAT, FATHER.
I'LL GO TO THE WOODSHED AND GET A SWITCH!
MPFFF!
IS IT GETTING *WEIRD* IN HERE, OR IS IT JUST ME?

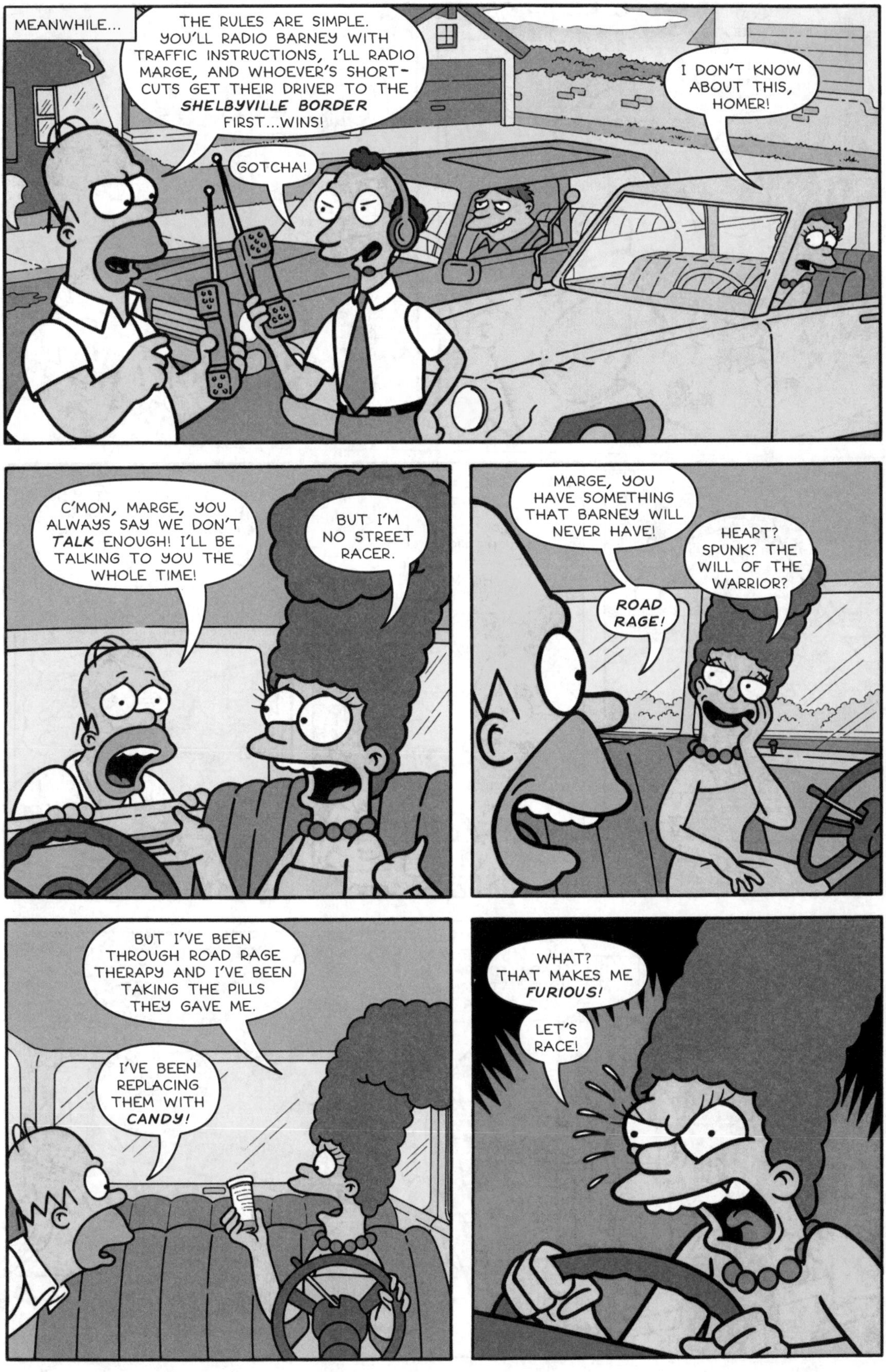
MEANWHILE...
THE RULES ARE SIMPLE. YOU'LL RADIO BARNEY WITH TRAFFIC INSTRUCTIONS, I'LL RADIO MARGE, AND WHOEVER'S SHORT-CUTS GET THEIR DRIVER TO THE **SHELBYVILLE BORDER** FIRST...WINS!
GOTCHA!
I DON'T KNOW ABOUT THIS, HOMER!
C'MON, MARGE, YOU ALWAYS SAY WE DON'T **TALK** ENOUGH! I'LL BE TALKING TO YOU THE WHOLE TIME!
BUT I'M NO STREET RACER.
MARGE, YOU HAVE SOMETHING THAT BARNEY WILL NEVER HAVE!
HEART? SPUNK? THE WILL OF THE WARRIOR?
ROAD RAGE!
BUT I'VE BEEN THROUGH ROAD RAGE THERAPY AND I'VE BEEN TAKING THE PILLS THEY GAVE ME.
I'VE BEEN REPLACING THEM WITH **CANDY!**
WHAT? THAT MAKES ME **FURIOUS!**
LET'S RACE!

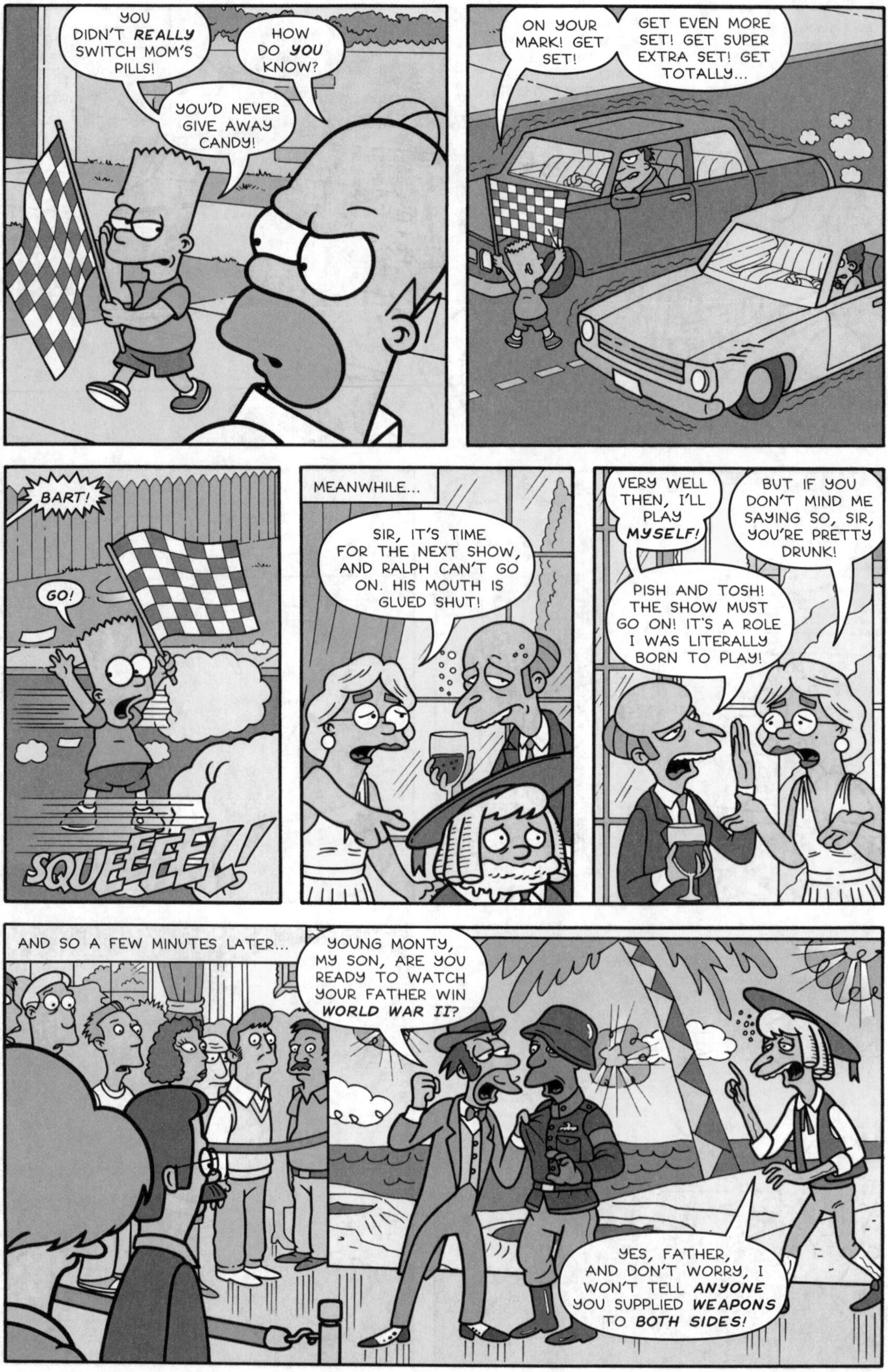

YOU DIDN'T REALLY SWITCH MOM'S PILLS!
HOW DO YOU KNOW?
YOU'D NEVER GIVE AWAY CANDY!
ON YOUR MARK! GET SET!
GET EVEN MORE SET! GET SUPER EXTRA SET! GET TOTALLY...
BART!
GO!
SQUEEEEEL!
MEANWHILE...
SIR, IT'S TIME FOR THE NEXT SHOW, AND RALPH CAN'T GO ON. HIS MOUTH IS GLUED SHUT!
VERY WELL THEN, I'LL PLAY MYSELF!
BUT IF YOU DON'T MIND ME SAYING SO, SIR, YOU'RE PRETTY DRUNK!
PISH AND TOSH! THE SHOW MUST GO ON! IT'S A ROLE I WAS LITERALLY BORN TO PLAY!
AND SO A FEW MINUTES LATER...
YOUNG MONTY, MY SON, ARE YOU READY TO WATCH YOUR FATHER WIN WORLD WAR II?
YES, FATHER, AND DON'T WORRY, I WON'T TELL ANYONE YOU SUPPLIED WEAPONS TO BOTH SIDES!

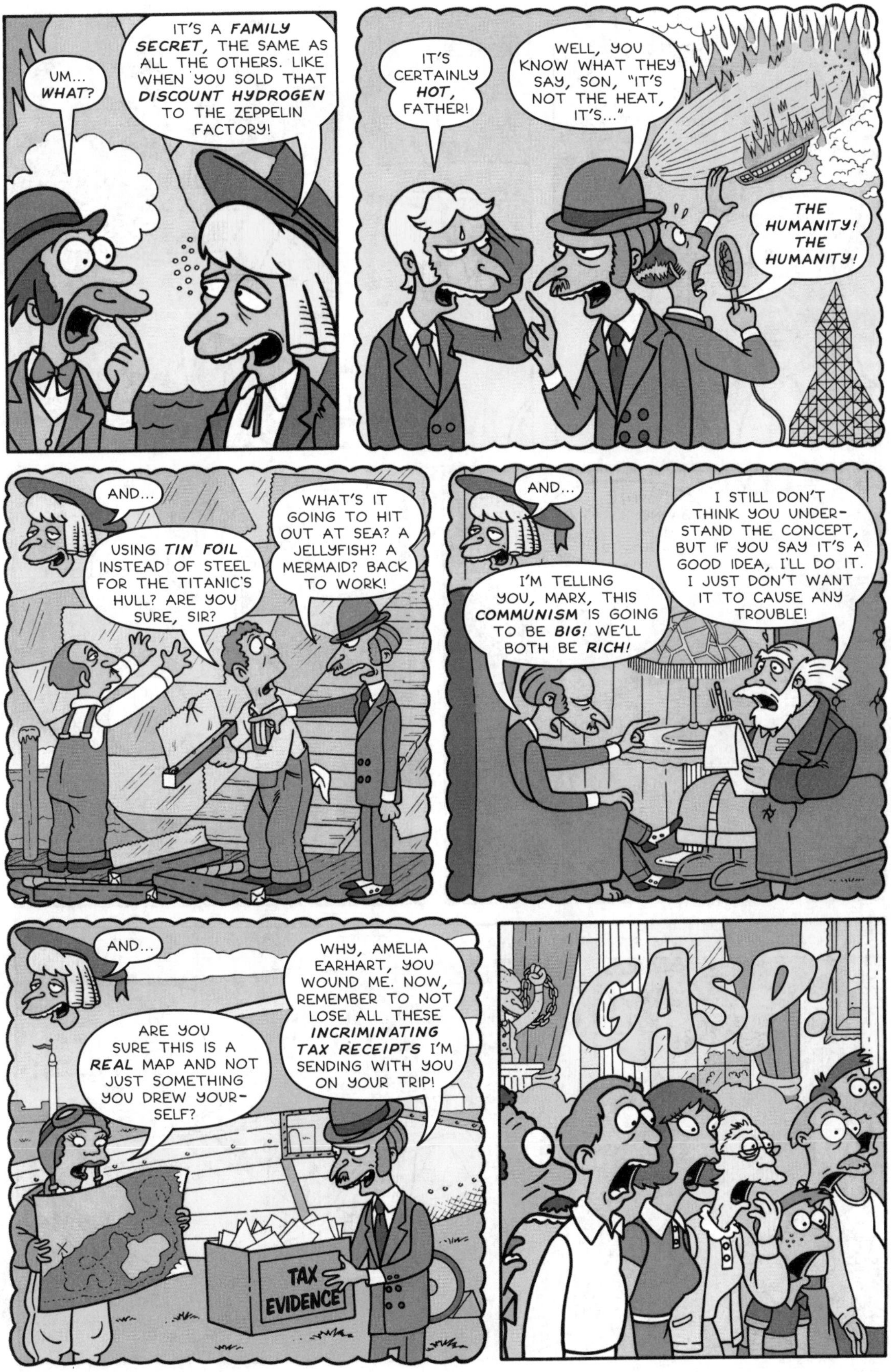
UM... WHAT?
IT'S A FAMILY SECRET, THE SAME AS ALL THE OTHERS. LIKE WHEN YOU SOLD THAT DISCOUNT HYDROGEN TO THE ZEPPELIN FACTORY!
IT'S CERTAINLY HOT, FATHER!
WELL, YOU KNOW WHAT THEY SAY, SON, "IT'S NOT THE HEAT, IT'S..."
THE HUMANITY! THE HUMANITY!
AND...
USING TIN FOIL INSTEAD OF STEEL FOR THE TITANIC'S HULL? ARE YOU SURE, SIR?
WHAT'S IT GOING TO HIT OUT AT SEA? A JELLYFISH? A MERMAID? BACK TO WORK!
AND...
I'M TELLING YOU, MARX, THIS COMMUNISM IS GOING TO BE BIG! WE'LL BOTH BE RICH!
I STILL DON'T THINK YOU UNDER-STAND THE CONCEPT, BUT IF YOU SAY IT'S A GOOD IDEA, I'LL DO IT. I JUST DON'T WANT IT TO CAUSE ANY TROUBLE!
AND...
ARE YOU SURE THIS IS A REAL MAP AND NOT JUST SOMETHING YOU DREW YOUR-SELF?
WHY, AMELIA EARHART, YOU WOUND ME. NOW, REMEMBER TO NOT LOSE ALL THESE INCRIMINATING TAX RECEIPTS I'M SENDING WITH YOU ON YOUR TRIP!
TAX EVIDENCE
GASP!

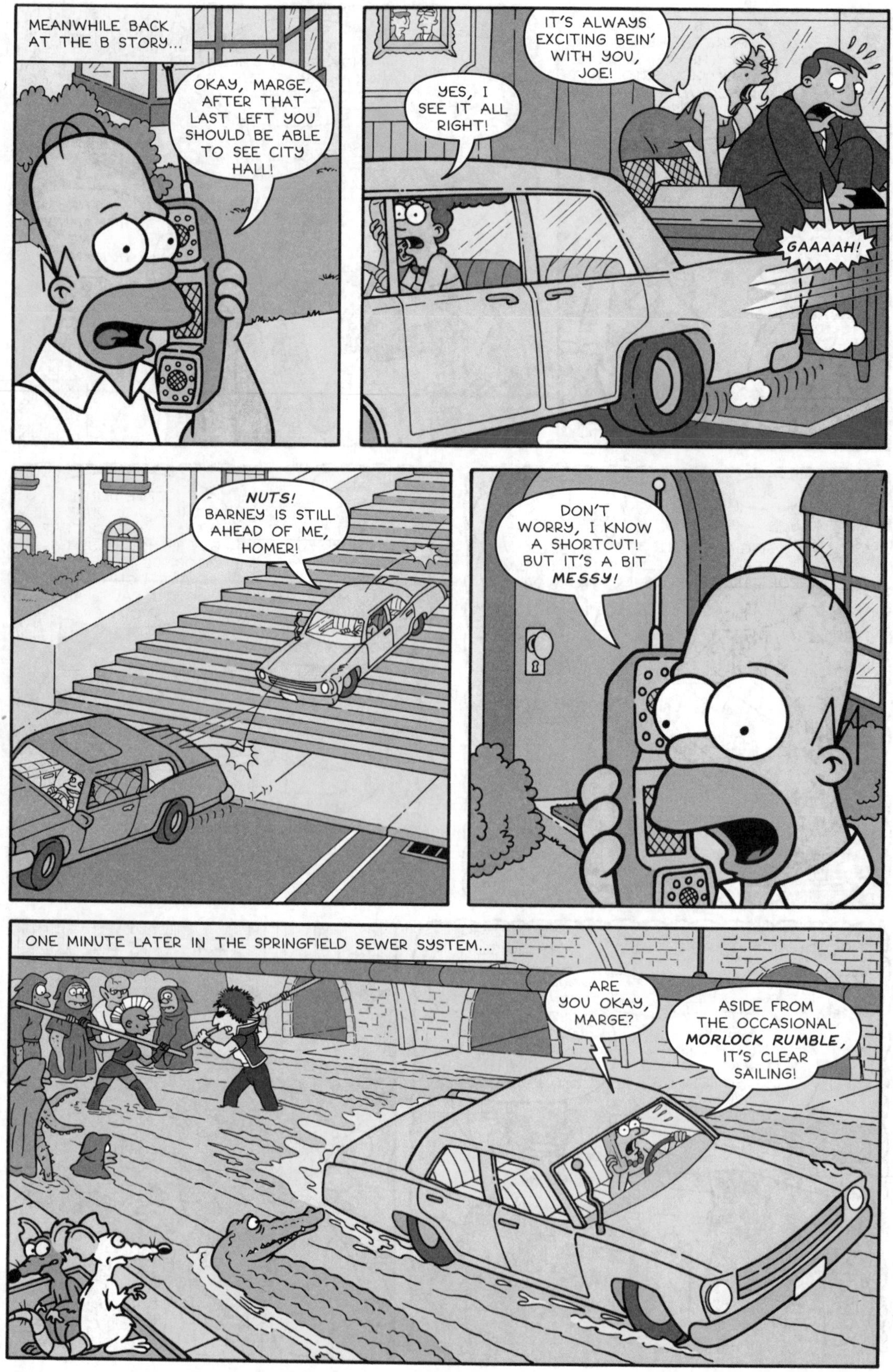
MEANWHILE BACK AT THE B STORY...
OKAY, MARGE, AFTER THAT LAST LEFT YOU SHOULD BE ABLE TO SEE CITY HALL!
YES, I SEE IT ALL RIGHT!
IT'S ALWAYS EXCITING BEIN' WITH YOU, JOE!
GAAAAH!
NUTS! BARNEY IS STILL AHEAD OF ME, HOMER!
DON'T WORRY, I KNOW A SHORTCUT! BUT IT'S A BIT MESSY!
ONE MINUTE LATER IN THE SPRINGFIELD SEWER SYSTEM...
ARE YOU OKAY, MARGE?
ASIDE FROM THE OCCASIONAL MORLOCK RUMBLE, IT'S CLEAR SAILING!

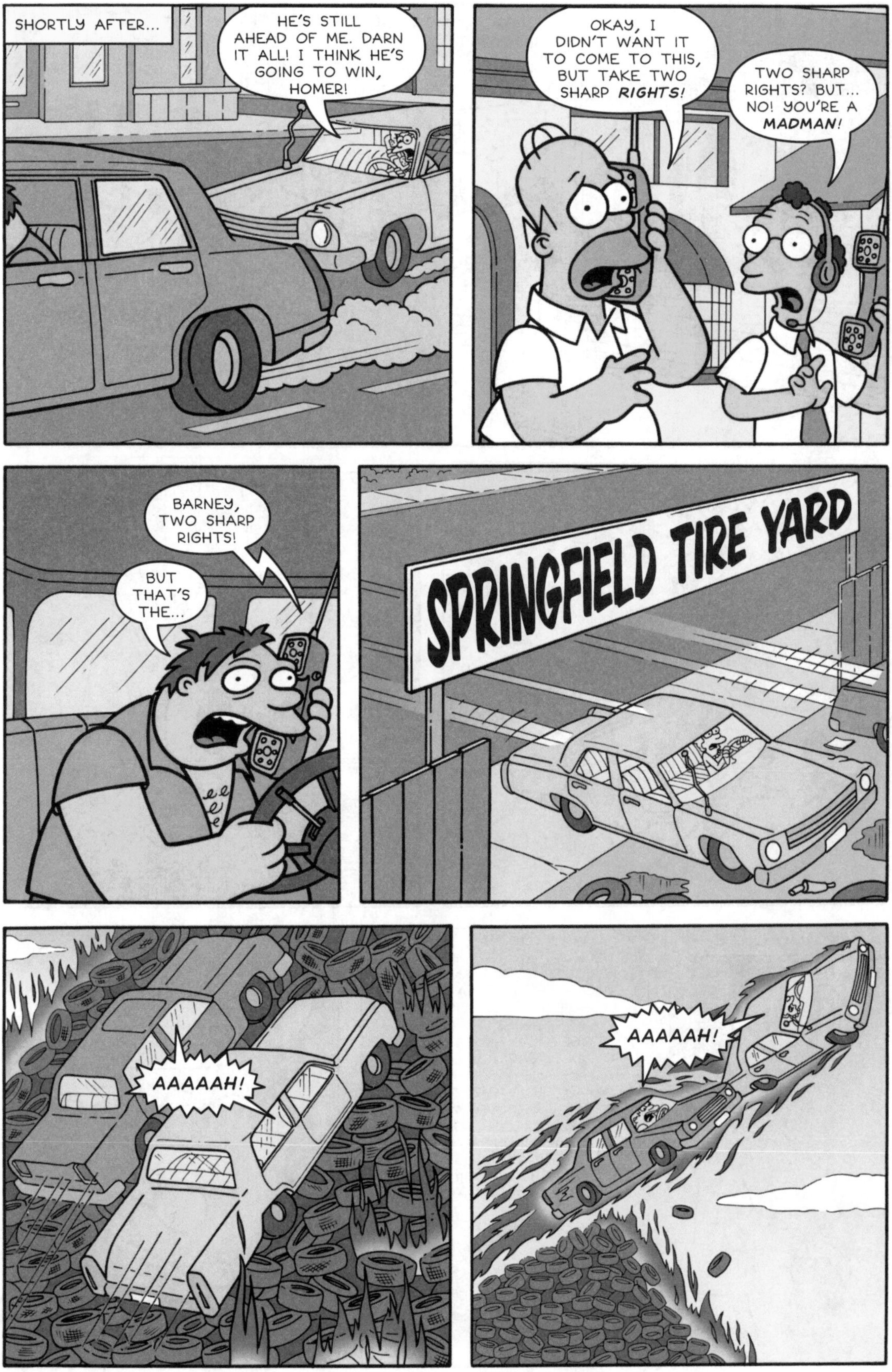
SHORTLY AFTER...
HE'S STILL AHEAD OF ME. DARN IT ALL! I THINK HE'S GOING TO WIN, HOMER!
OKAY, I DIDN'T WANT IT TO COME TO THIS, BUT TAKE TWO SHARP **RIGHTS!**
TWO SHARP RIGHTS? BUT... NO! YOU'RE A **MADMAN!**
BARNEY, TWO SHARP RIGHTS!
BUT THAT'S THE...
SPRINGFIELD TIRE YARD
AAAAAH!
AAAAAH!

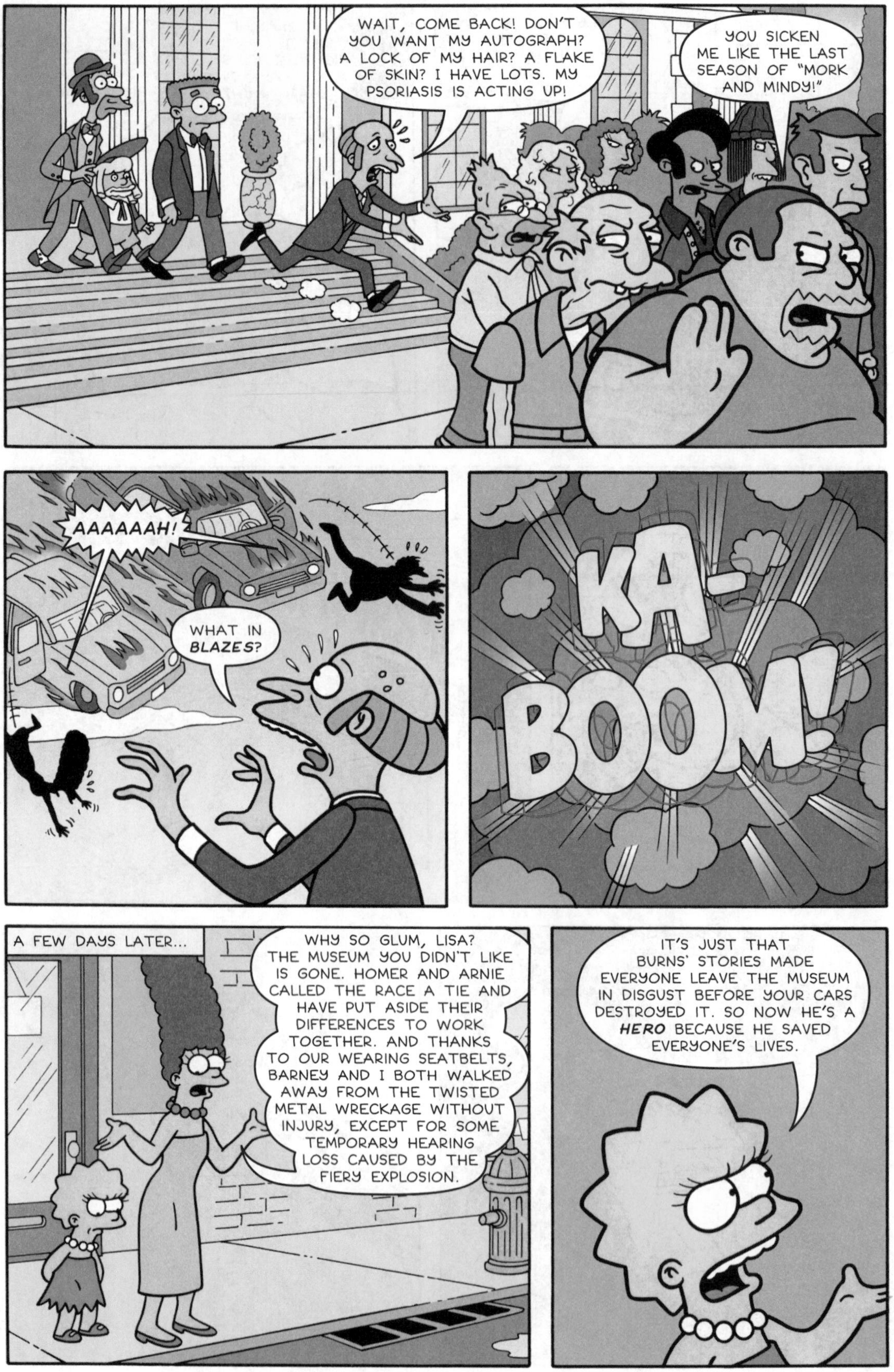

WAIT, COME BACK! DON'T YOU WANT MY AUTOGRAPH? A LOCK OF MY HAIR? A FLAKE OF SKIN? I HAVE LOTS. MY PSORIASIS IS ACTING UP!
YOU SICKEN ME LIKE THE LAST SEASON OF "MORK AND MINDY!"
AAAAAAH!
WHAT IN *BLAZES?*
KA-BOOM!
A FEW DAYS LATER...
WHY SO GLUM, LISA? THE MUSEUM YOU DIDN'T LIKE IS GONE. HOMER AND ARNIE CALLED THE RACE A TIE AND HAVE PUT ASIDE THEIR DIFFERENCES TO WORK TOGETHER. AND THANKS TO OUR WEARING SEATBELTS, BARNEY AND I BOTH WALKED AWAY FROM THE TWISTED METAL WRECKAGE WITHOUT INJURY, EXCEPT FOR SOME TEMPORARY HEARING LOSS CAUSED BY THE FIERY EXPLOSION.
IT'S JUST THAT BURNS' STORIES MADE EVERYONE LEAVE THE MUSEUM IN DISGUST BEFORE YOUR CARS DESTROYED IT. SO NOW HE'S A *HERO* BECAUSE HE SAVED EVERYONE'S LIVES.

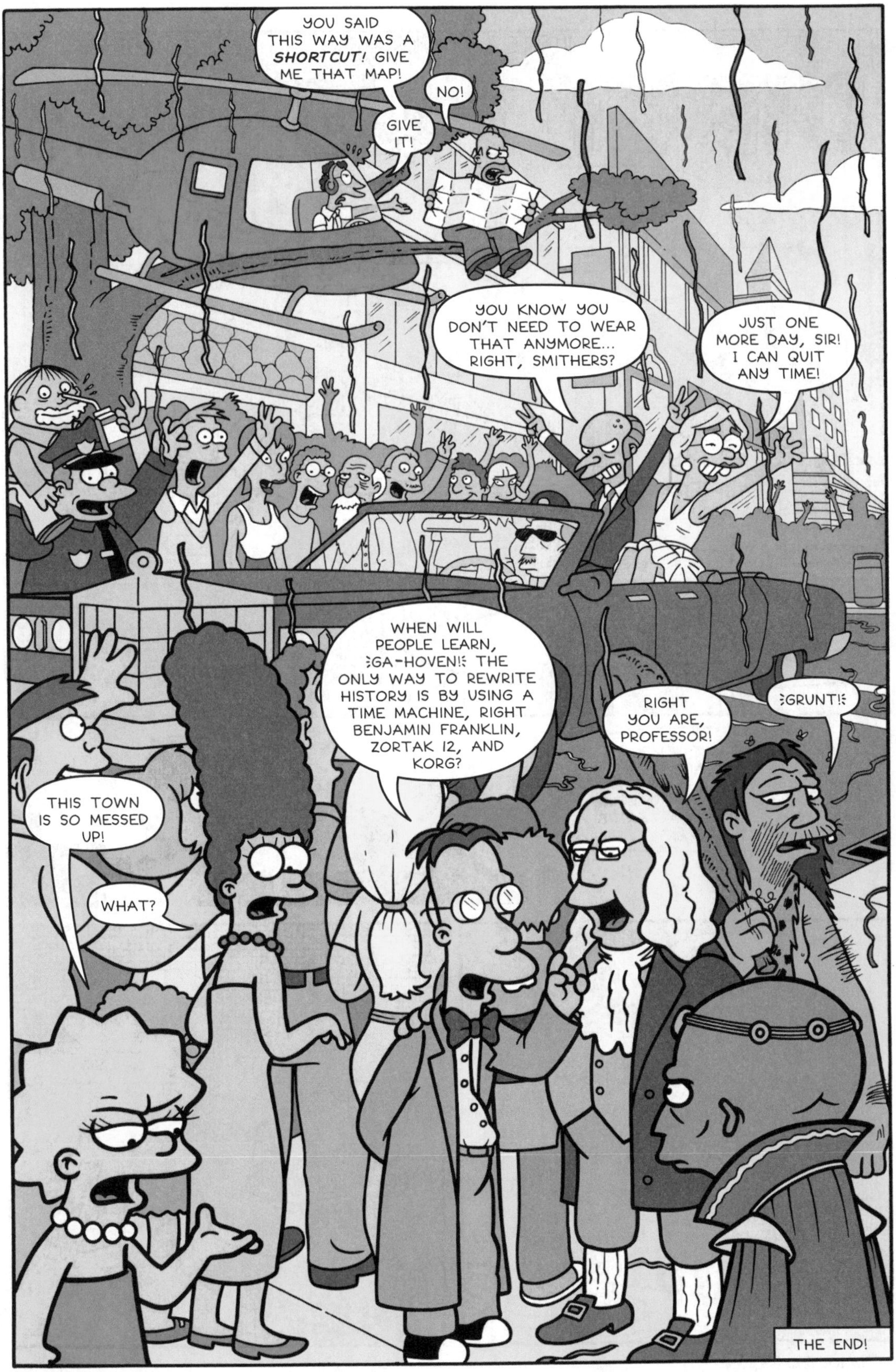
YOU SAID THIS WAY WAS A *SHORTCUT!* GIVE ME THAT MAP!
NO!
GIVE IT!
YOU KNOW YOU DON'T NEED TO WEAR THAT ANYMORE... RIGHT, SMITHERS?
JUST ONE MORE DAY, SIR! I CAN QUIT ANY TIME!
WHEN WILL PEOPLE LEARN, ⁝GA-HOVEN!⁝ THE ONLY WAY TO REWRITE HISTORY IS BY USING A TIME MACHINE, RIGHT BENJAMIN FRANKLIN, ZORTAK 12, AND KORG?
RIGHT YOU ARE, PROFESSOR!
⁝GRUNT!⁝
THIS TOWN IS SO MESSED UP!
WHAT?
THE END!

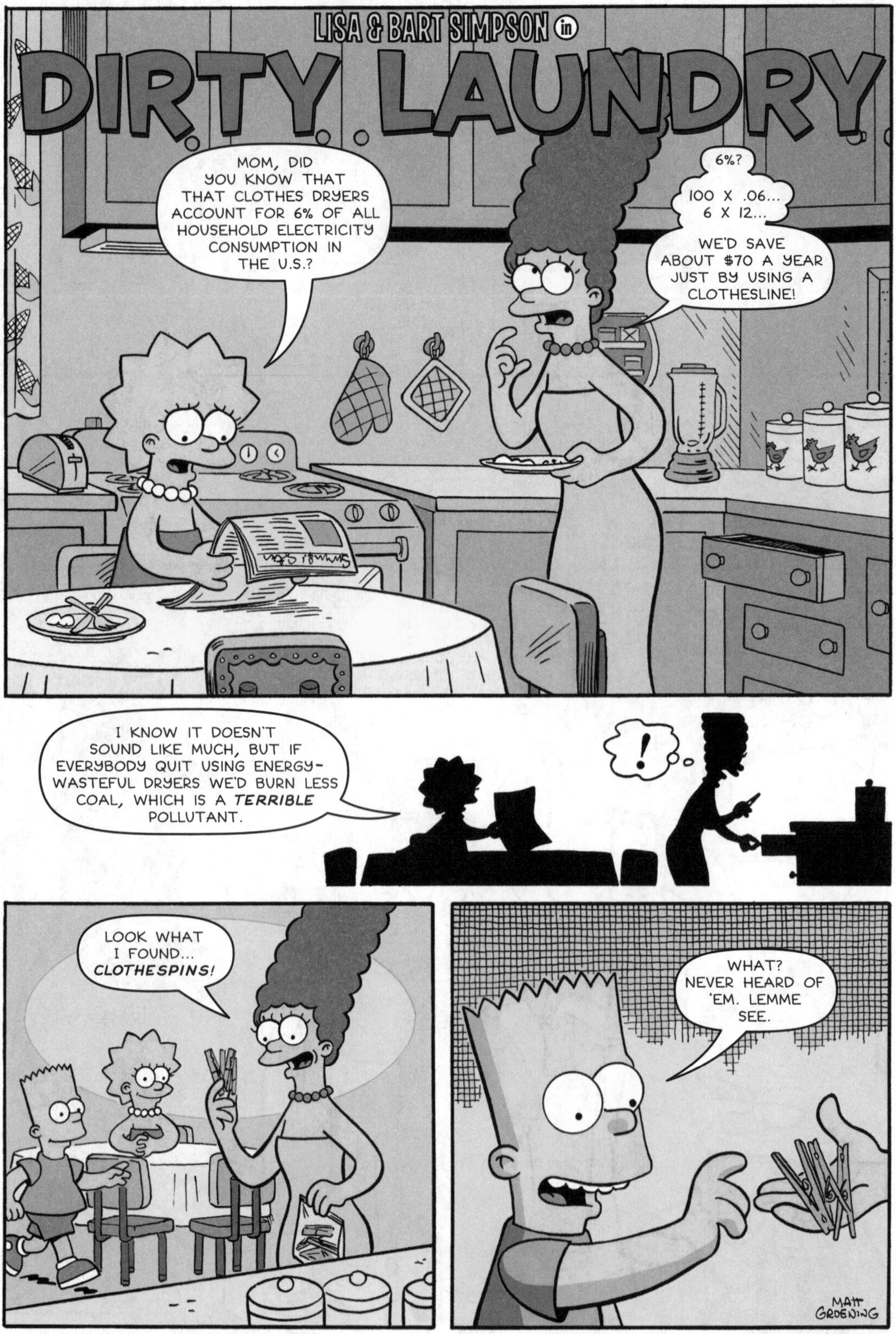
LISA & BART SIMPSON in
DIRTY LAUNDRY
MOM, DID YOU KNOW THAT THAT CLOTHES DRYERS ACCOUNT FOR 6% OF ALL HOUSEHOLD ELECTRICITY CONSUMPTION IN THE U.S.?
6%?
100 X .06... 6 X 12...
WE'D SAVE ABOUT $70 A YEAR JUST BY USING A CLOTHESLINE!
I KNOW IT DOESN'T SOUND LIKE MUCH, BUT IF EVERYBODY QUIT USING ENERGY-WASTEFUL DRYERS WE'D BURN LESS COAL, WHICH IS A TERRIBLE POLLUTANT.
!
LOOK WHAT I FOUND... CLOTHESPINS!
WHAT? NEVER HEARD OF 'EM. LEMME SEE.
MATT GROENING

CAROL LAY
STORY & ART

ALAN HELLARD
COLORS

KAREN BATES
LETTERS

BILL MORRISON
EDITOR

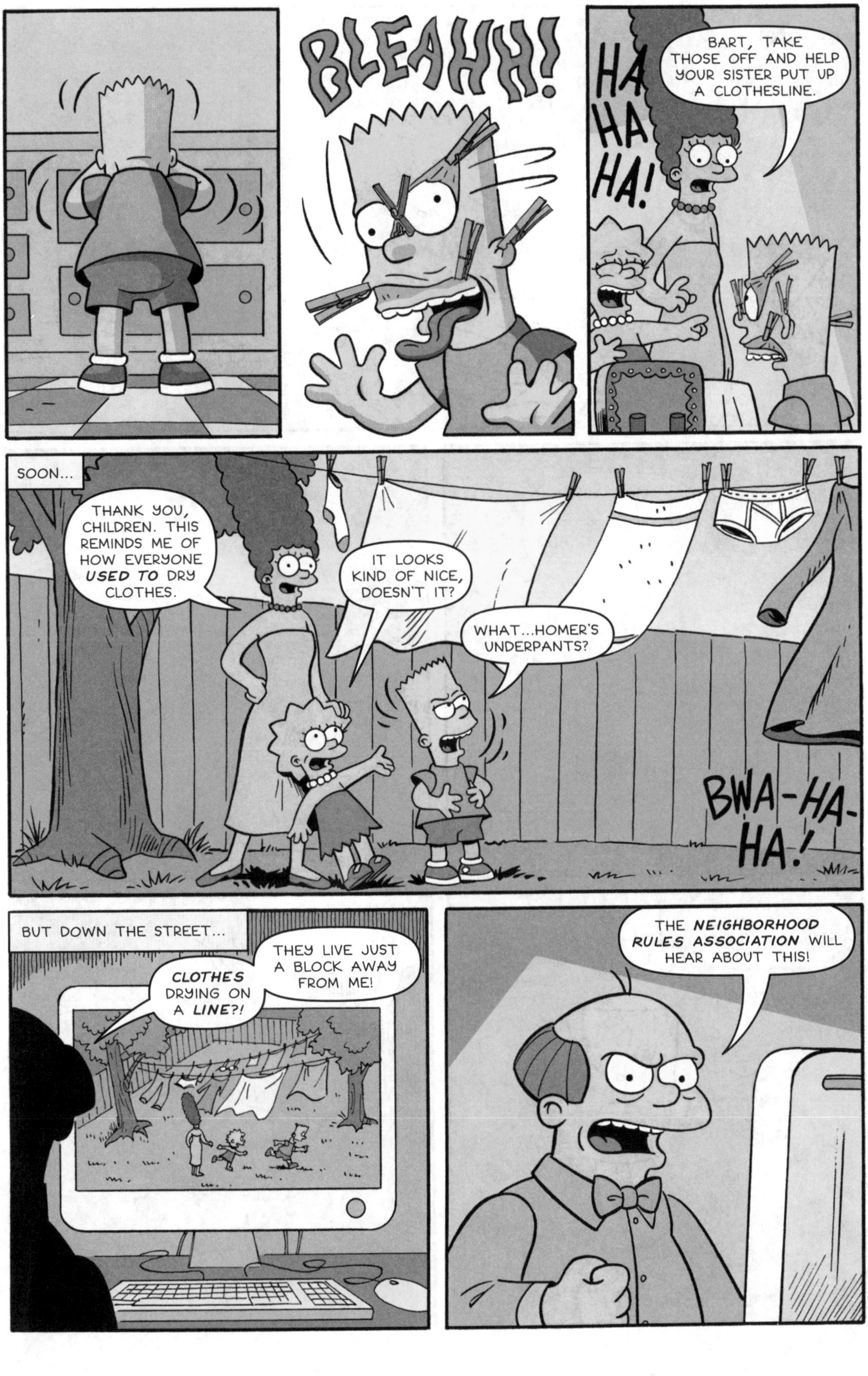

BLEAHH!
HA HA HA!
BART, TAKE THOSE OFF AND HELP YOUR SISTER PUT UP A CLOTHESLINE.
SOON...
THANK YOU, CHILDREN. THIS REMINDS ME OF HOW EVERYONE USED TO DRY CLOTHES.
IT LOOKS KIND OF NICE, DOESN'T IT?
WHAT...HOMER'S UNDERPANTS?
BWA-HA-HA!
BUT DOWN THE STREET...
CLOTHES DRYING ON A LINE?!
THEY LIVE JUST A BLOCK AWAY FROM ME!
THE NEIGHBORHOOD RULES ASSOCIATION WILL HEAR ABOUT THIS!

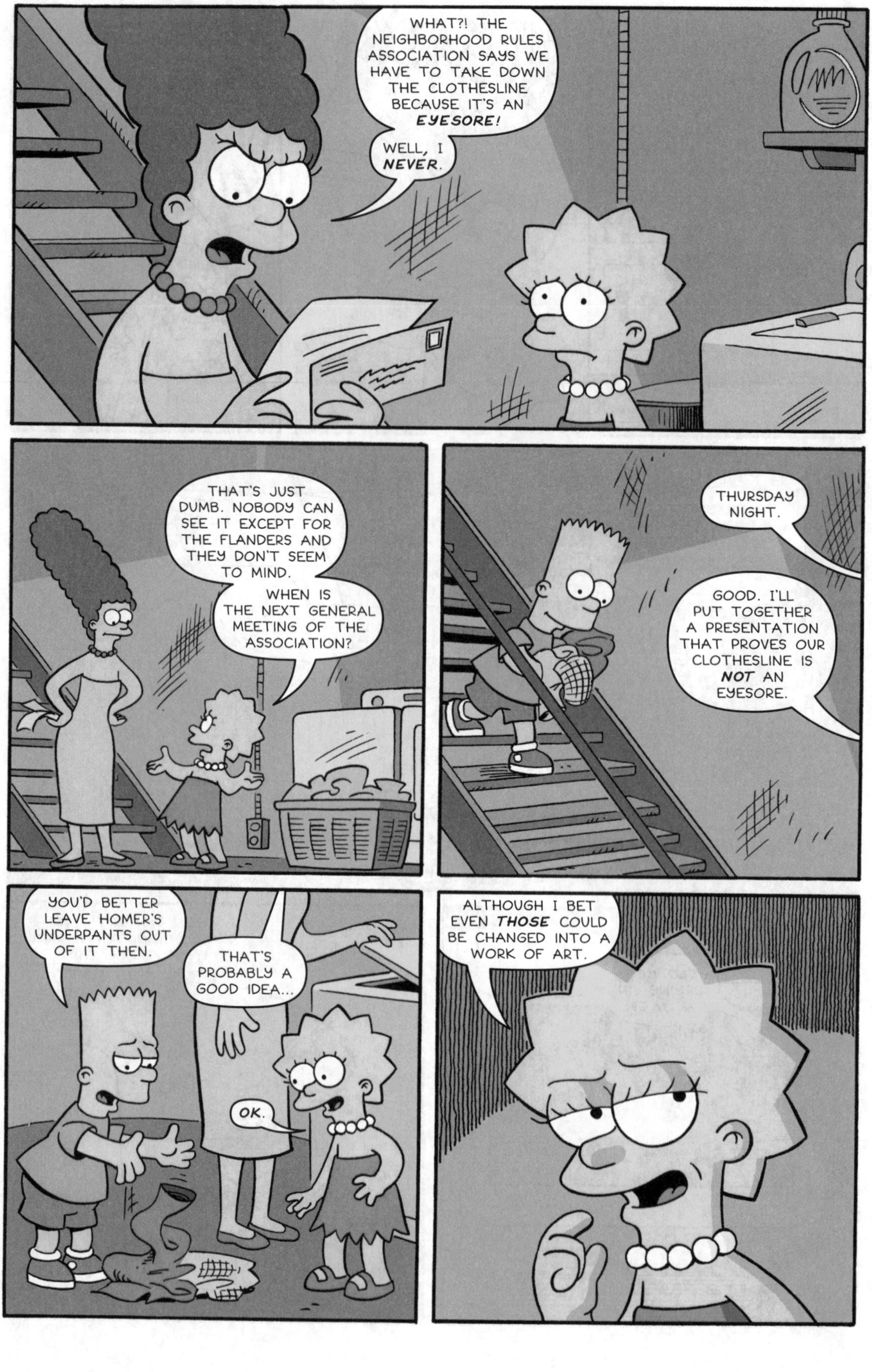
WHAT?! THE NEIGHBORHOOD RULES ASSOCIATION SAYS WE HAVE TO TAKE DOWN THE CLOTHESLINE BECAUSE IT'S AN EYESORE!
WELL, I NEVER.
THAT'S JUST DUMB. NOBODY CAN SEE IT EXCEPT FOR THE FLANDERS AND THEY DON'T SEEM TO MIND.
WHEN IS THE NEXT GENERAL MEETING OF THE ASSOCIATION?
THURSDAY NIGHT.
GOOD. I'LL PUT TOGETHER A PRESENTATION THAT PROVES OUR CLOTHESLINE IS NOT AN EYESORE.
YOU'D BETTER LEAVE HOMER'S UNDERPANTS OUT OF IT THEN.
THAT'S PROBABLY A GOOD IDEA...
OK.
ALTHOUGH I BET EVEN THOSE COULD BE CHANGED INTO A WORK OF ART.

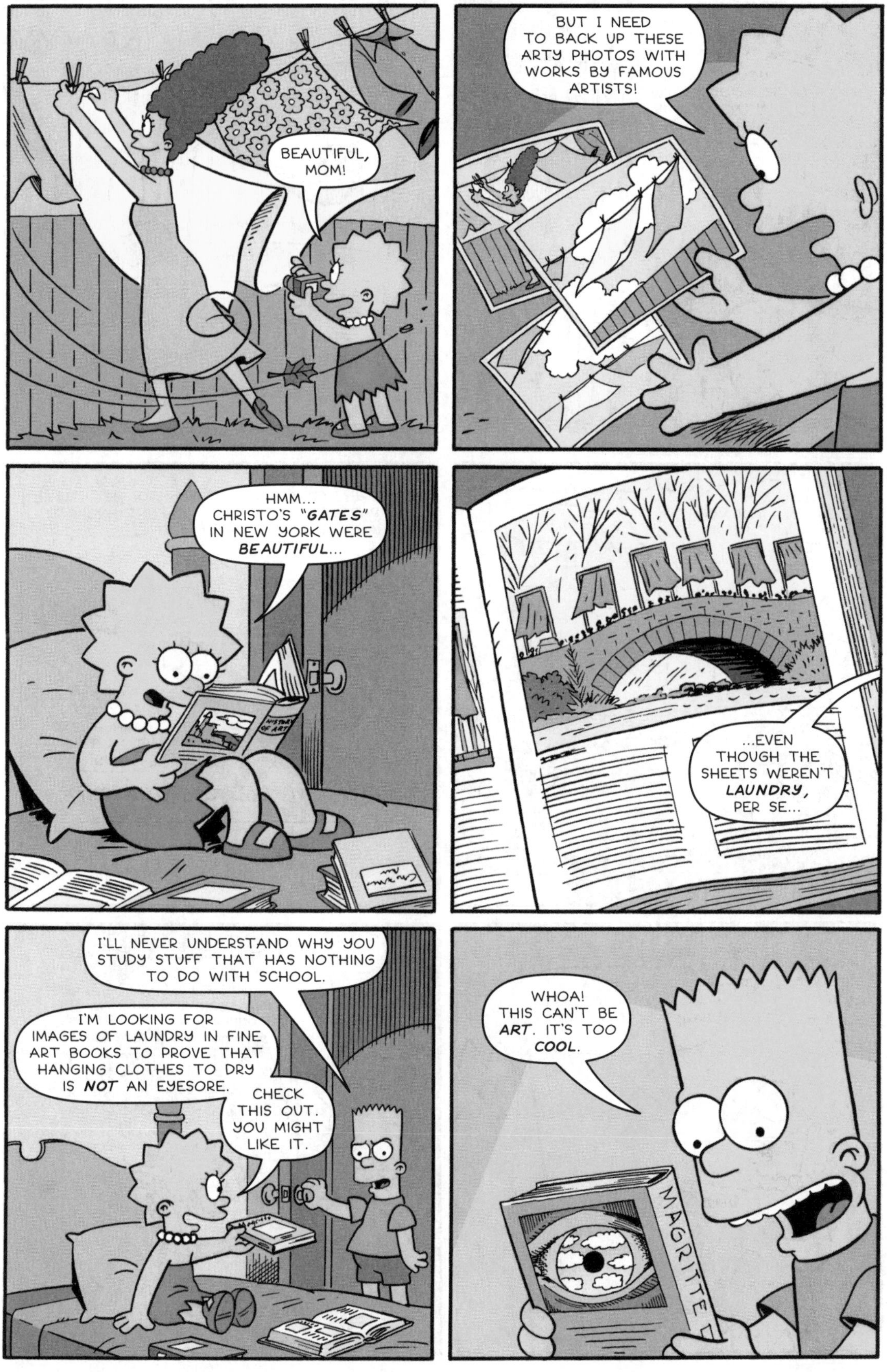
BEAUTIFUL, MOM!
BUT I NEED TO BACK UP THESE ARTY PHOTOS WITH WORKS BY FAMOUS ARTISTS!
HMM... CHRISTO'S "GATES" IN NEW YORK WERE BEAUTIFUL...
HISTORY OF ART
...EVEN THOUGH THE SHEETS WEREN'T LAUNDRY, PER SE...
I'LL NEVER UNDERSTAND WHY YOU STUDY STUFF THAT HAS NOTHING TO DO WITH SCHOOL.
I'M LOOKING FOR IMAGES OF LAUNDRY IN FINE ART BOOKS TO PROVE THAT HANGING CLOTHES TO DRY IS NOT AN EYESORE.
CHECK THIS OUT. YOU MIGHT LIKE IT.
WHOA! THIS CAN'T BE ART. IT'S TOO COOL.
MAGRITTE

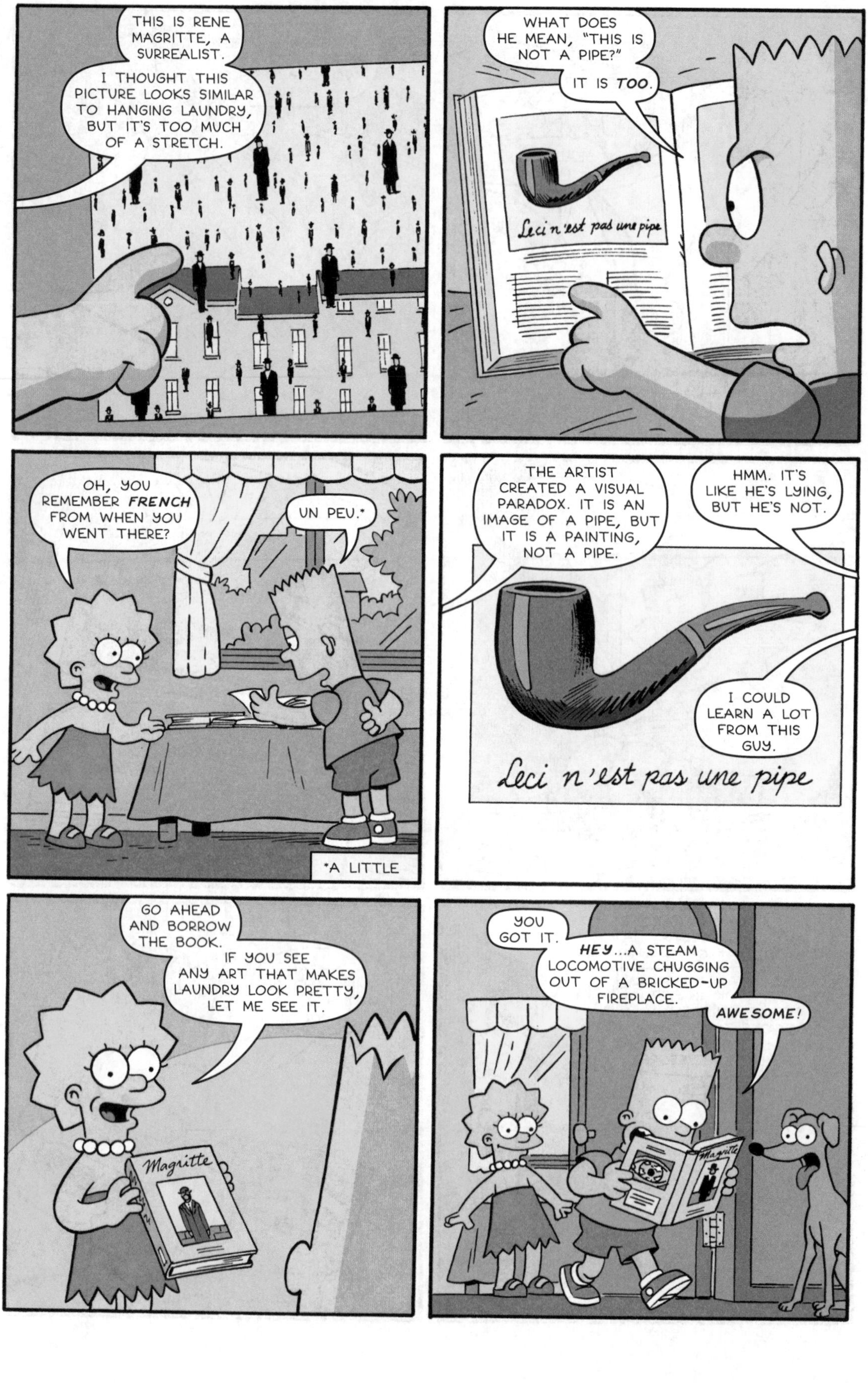

THIS IS RENE MAGRITTE, A SURREALIST.
I THOUGHT THIS PICTURE LOOKS SIMILAR TO HANGING LAUNDRY, BUT IT'S TOO MUCH OF A STRETCH.
WHAT DOES HE MEAN, "THIS IS NOT A PIPE?"
IT IS TOO.
Leci n'est pas une pipe
OH, YOU REMEMBER FRENCH FROM WHEN YOU WENT THERE?
UN PEU.*
*A LITTLE
THE ARTIST CREATED A VISUAL PARADOX. IT IS AN IMAGE OF A PIPE, BUT IT IS A PAINTING, NOT A PIPE.
HMM. IT'S LIKE HE'S LYING, BUT HE'S NOT.
I COULD LEARN A LOT FROM THIS GUY.
Leci n'est pas une pipe
GO AHEAD AND BORROW THE BOOK.
IF YOU SEE ANY ART THAT MAKES LAUNDRY LOOK PRETTY, LET ME SEE IT.
Magritte
YOU GOT IT.
HEY...A STEAM LOCOMOTIVE CHUGGING OUT OF A BRICKED-UP FIREPLACE.
AWESOME!
Magritte

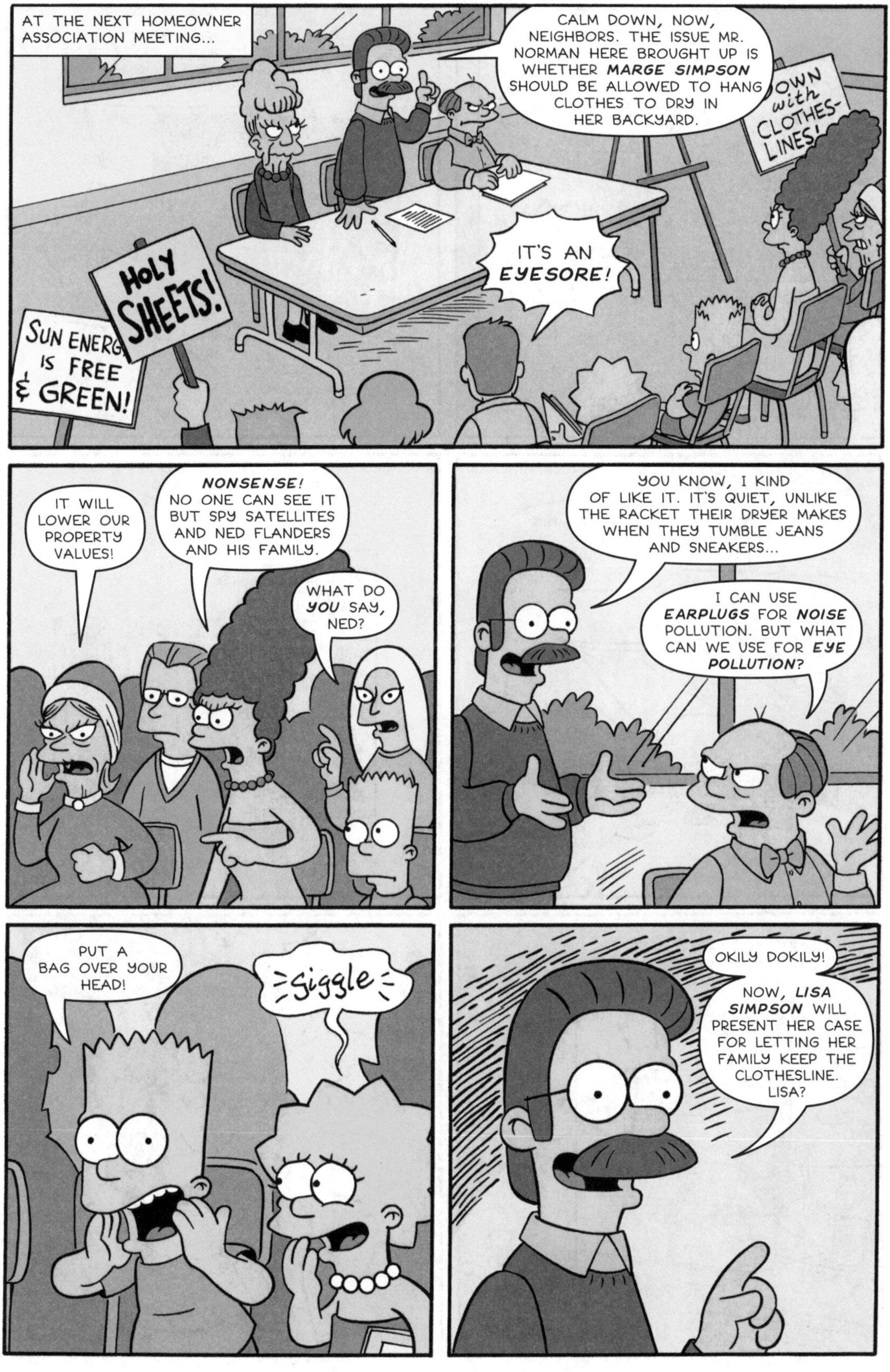
AT THE NEXT HOMEOWNER ASSOCIATION MEETING...
CALM DOWN, NOW, NEIGHBORS. THE ISSUE MR. NORMAN HERE BROUGHT UP IS WHETHER MARGE SIMPSON SHOULD BE ALLOWED TO HANG CLOTHES TO DRY IN HER BACKYARD.
DOWN with CLOTHES-LINES!
HOLY SHEETS!
SUN ENERG IS FREE & GREEN!
IT'S AN EYESORE!
IT WILL LOWER OUR PROPERTY VALUES!
NONSENSE! NO ONE CAN SEE IT BUT SPY SATELLITES AND NED FLANDERS AND HIS FAMILY.
WHAT DO YOU SAY, NED?
YOU KNOW, I KIND OF LIKE IT. IT'S QUIET, UNLIKE THE RACKET THEIR DRYER MAKES WHEN THEY TUMBLE JEANS AND SNEAKERS...
I CAN USE EARPLUGS FOR NOISE POLLUTION. BUT WHAT CAN WE USE FOR EYE POLLUTION?
PUT A BAG OVER YOUR HEAD!
Giggle
OKILY DOKILY!
NOW, LISA SIMPSON WILL PRESENT HER CASE FOR LETTING HER FAMILY KEEP THE CLOTHESLINE. LISA?

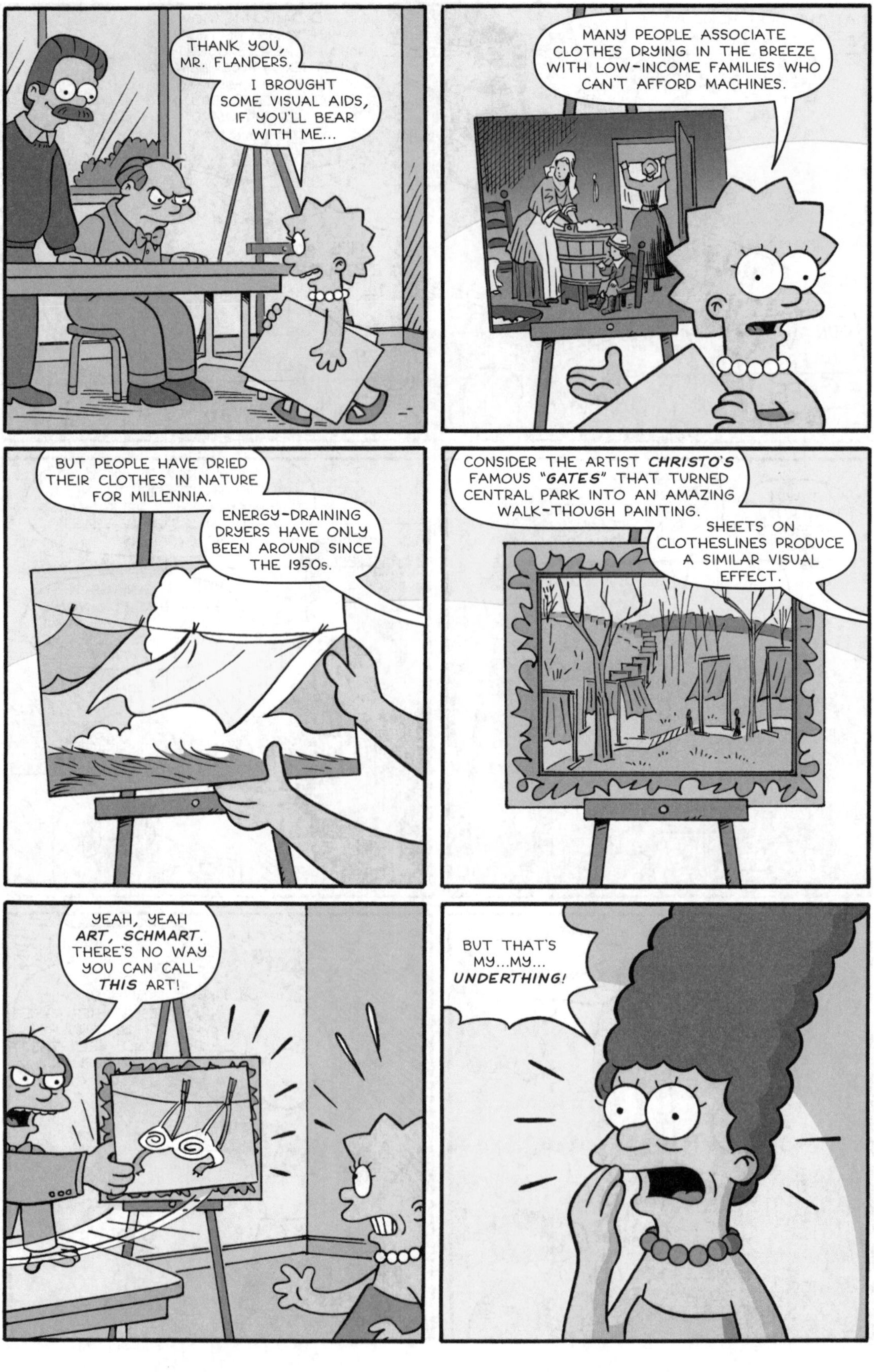
THANK YOU, MR. FLANDERS.
I BROUGHT SOME VISUAL AIDS, IF YOU'LL BEAR WITH ME...
MANY PEOPLE ASSOCIATE CLOTHES DRYING IN THE BREEZE WITH LOW-INCOME FAMILIES WHO CAN'T AFFORD MACHINES.
BUT PEOPLE HAVE DRIED THEIR CLOTHES IN NATURE FOR MILLENNIA.
ENERGY-DRAINING DRYERS HAVE ONLY BEEN AROUND SINCE THE 1950s.
CONSIDER THE ARTIST ***CHRISTO'S*** FAMOUS "***GATES***" THAT TURNED CENTRAL PARK INTO AN AMAZING WALK-THOUGH PAINTING.
SHEETS ON CLOTHESLINES PRODUCE A SIMILAR VISUAL EFFECT.
YEAH, YEAH ***ART, SCHMART***. THERE'S NO WAY YOU CAN CALL ***THIS*** ART!
BUT THAT'S MY...MY... ***UNDERTHING!***

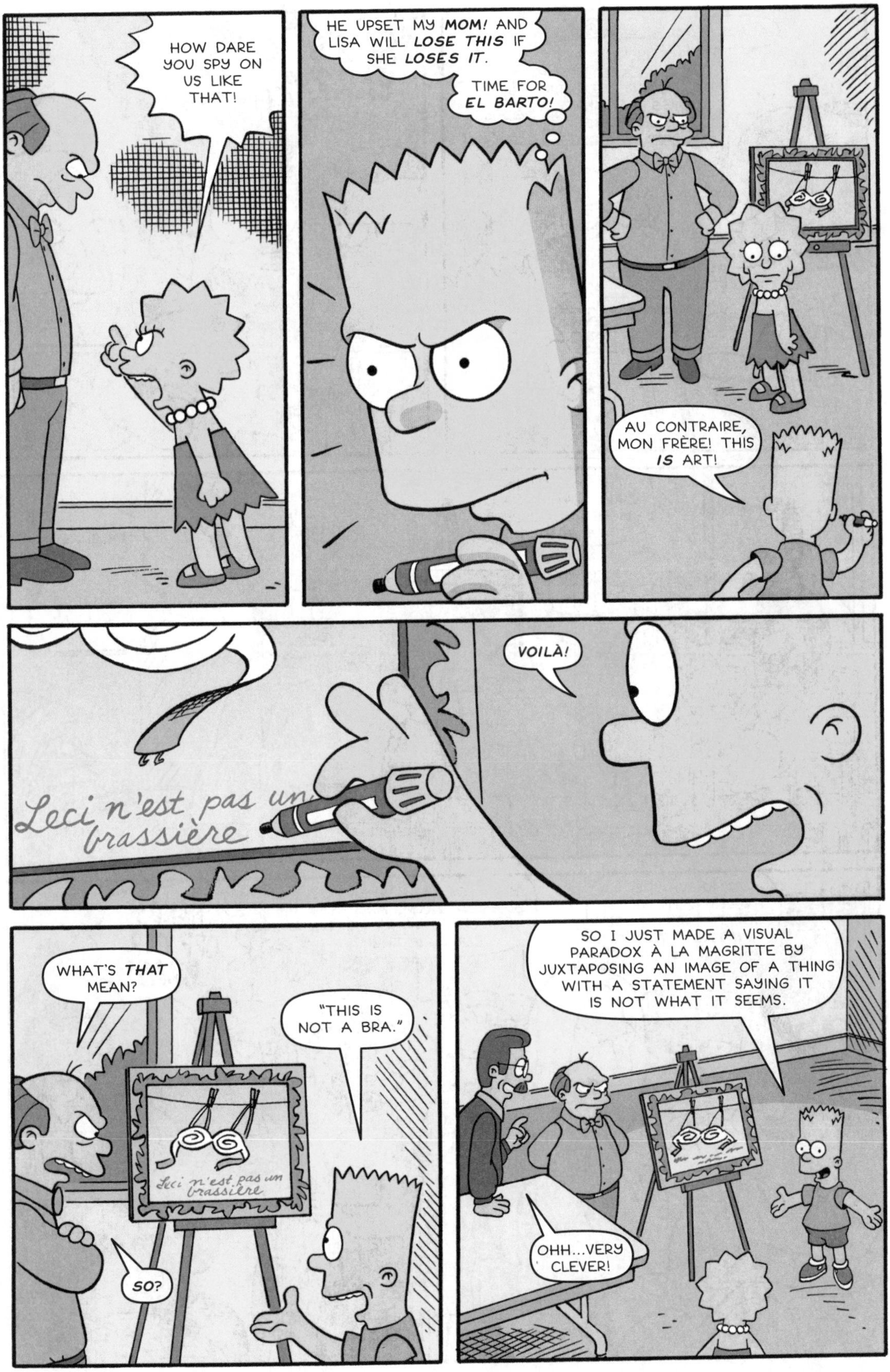

HOW DARE YOU SPY ON US LIKE THAT!
HE UPSET MY MOM! AND LISA WILL LOSE THIS IF SHE LOSES IT.
TIME FOR EL BARTO!
AU CONTRAIRE, MON FRÈRE! THIS IS ART!
Leci n'est pas un brassière
VOILÀ!
WHAT'S THAT MEAN?
"THIS IS NOT A BRA."
SO?
SO I JUST MADE A VISUAL PARADOX À LA MAGRITTE BY JUXTAPOSING AN IMAGE OF A THING WITH A STATEMENT SAYING IT IS NOT WHAT IT SEEMS.
OHH...VERY CLEVER!

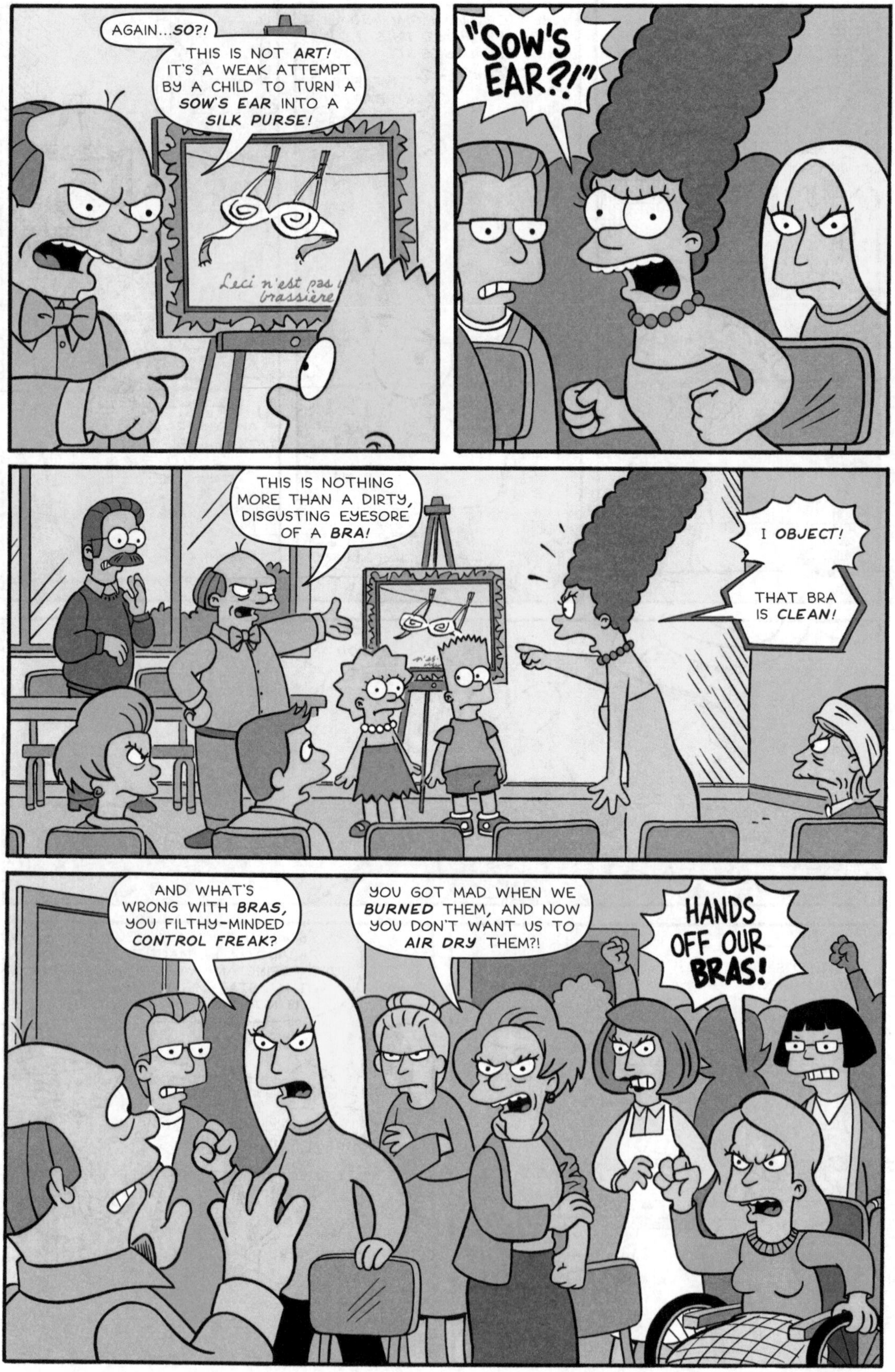

AGAIN...SO?!
THIS IS NOT ART! IT'S A WEAK ATTEMPT BY A CHILD TO TURN A SOW'S EAR INTO A SILK PURSE!
"SOW'S EAR?!"
THIS IS NOTHING MORE THAN A DIRTY, DISGUSTING EYESORE OF A BRA!
I OBJECT!
THAT BRA IS CLEAN!
AND WHAT'S WRONG WITH BRAS, YOU FILTHY-MINDED CONTROL FREAK?
YOU GOT MAD WHEN WE BURNED THEM, AND NOW YOU DON'T WANT US TO AIR DRY THEM?!
HANDS OFF OUR BRAS!

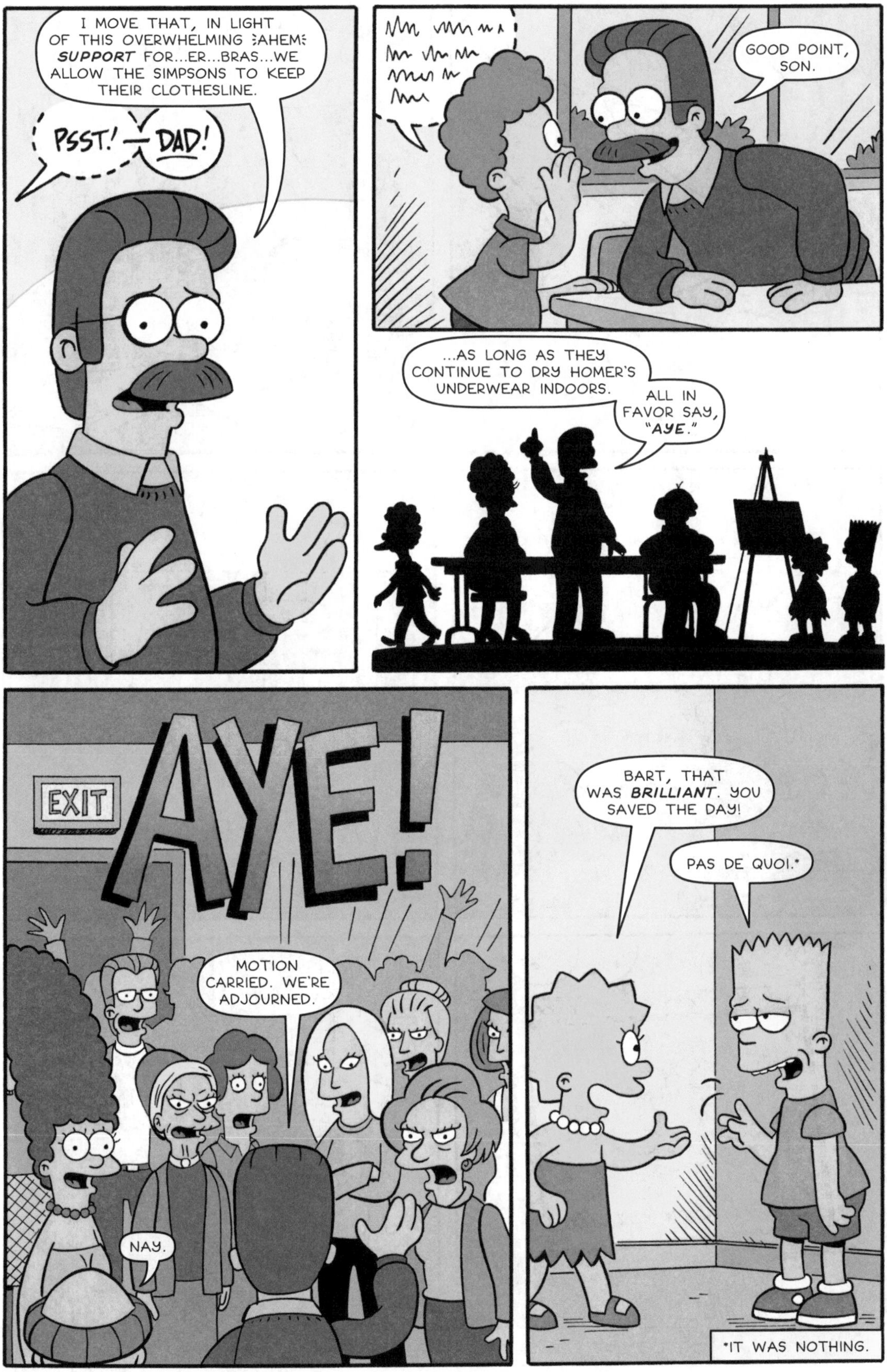
I MOVE THAT, IN LIGHT OF THIS OVERWHELMING :AHEM: SUPPORT FOR...ER...BRAS...WE ALLOW THE SIMPSONS TO KEEP THEIR CLOTHESLINE.
PSST! DAD!
GOOD POINT, SON.
...AS LONG AS THEY CONTINUE TO DRY HOMER'S UNDERWEAR INDOORS.
ALL IN FAVOR SAY, "AYE."
EXIT
AYE!
MOTION CARRIED. WE'RE ADJOURNED.
NAY.
BART, THAT WAS BRILLIANT. YOU SAVED THE DAY!
PAS DE QUOI.*
*IT WAS NOTHING.

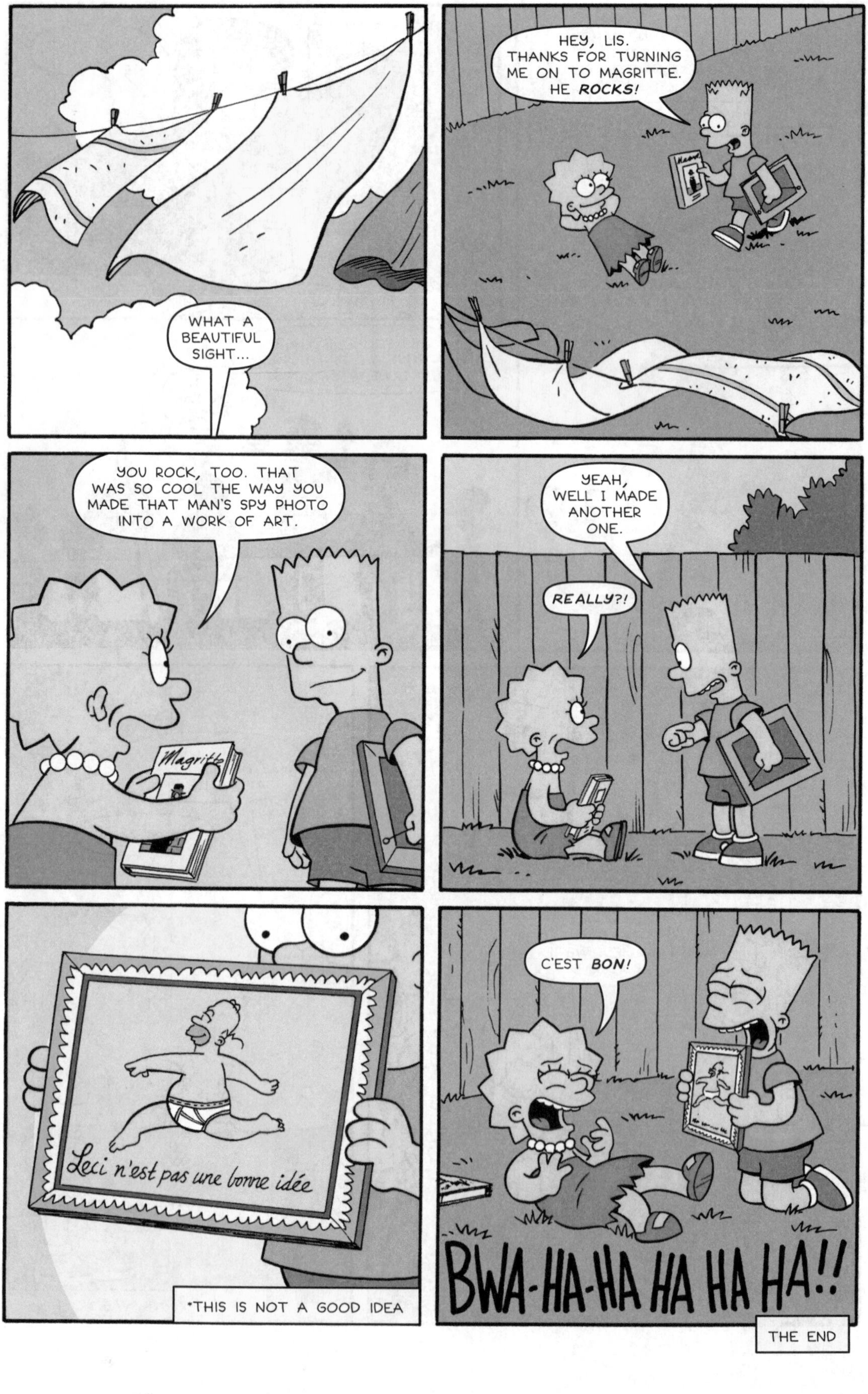
WHAT A BEAUTIFUL SIGHT...
HEY, LIS. THANKS FOR TURNING ME ON TO MAGRITTE. HE ROCKS!
YOU ROCK, TOO. THAT WAS SO COOL THE WAY YOU MADE THAT MAN'S SPY PHOTO INTO A WORK OF ART.
Magritte
YEAH, WELL I MADE ANOTHER ONE.
REALLY?!
Ceci n'est pas une bonne idée
*THIS IS NOT A GOOD IDEA
C'EST BON!
BWA-HA-HA HA HA HA!!
THE END

FUR 'N' HATE 451

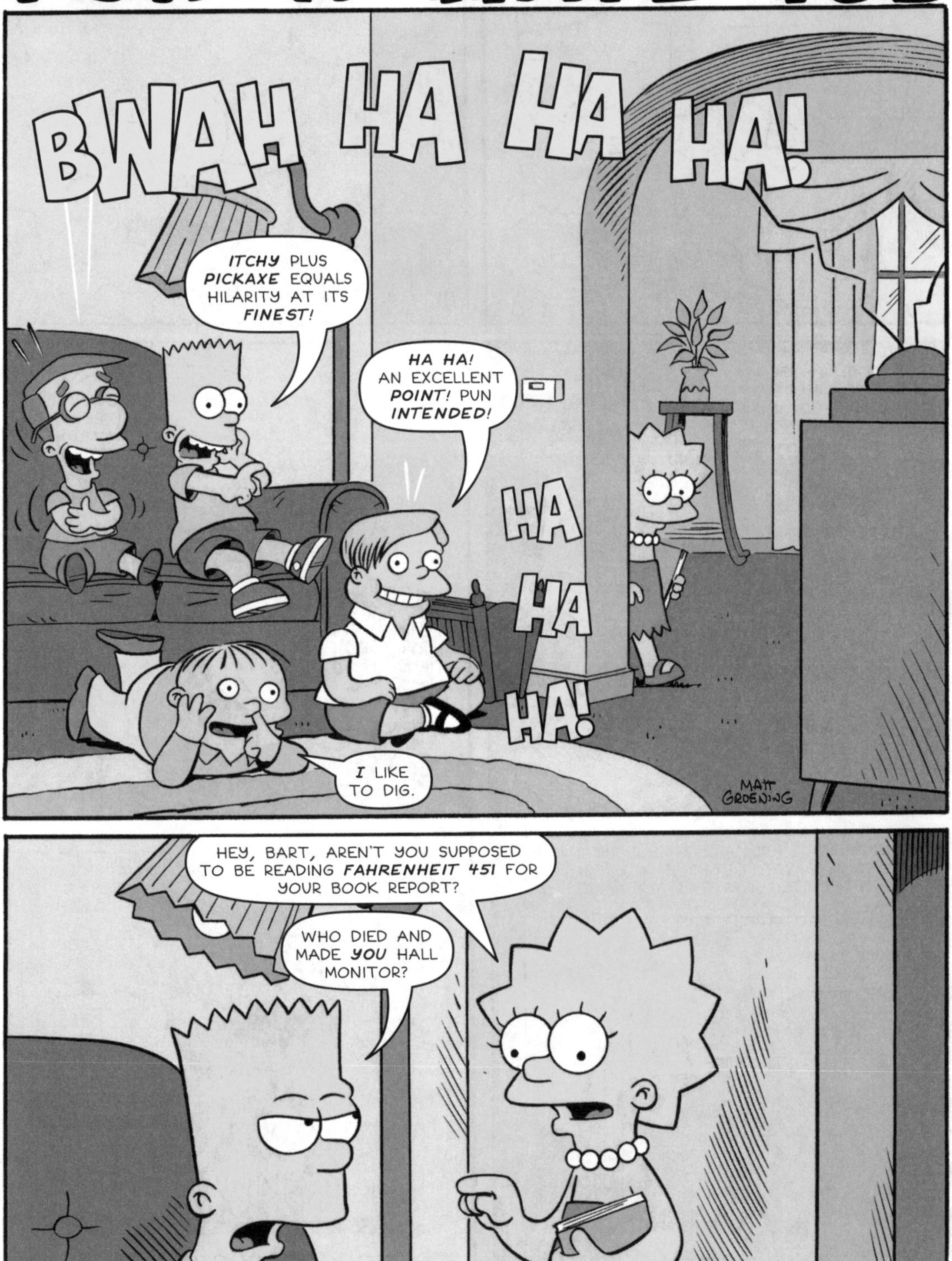
BWAH HA HA HA!
ITCHY PLUS PICKAXE EQUALS HILARITY AT ITS FINEST!
HA HA! AN EXCELLENT POINT! PUN INTENDED!
HA HA HA!
I LIKE TO DIG.
MATT GROENING
HEY, BART, AREN'T YOU SUPPOSED TO BE READING FAHRENHEIT 451 FOR YOUR BOOK REPORT?
WHO DIED AND MADE YOU HALL MONITOR?

CAROL LAY	***NATHAN HAMILL***	***KAREN BATES***	***BILL MORRISON***
STORY & ART	COLORS	LETTERS	EDITOR

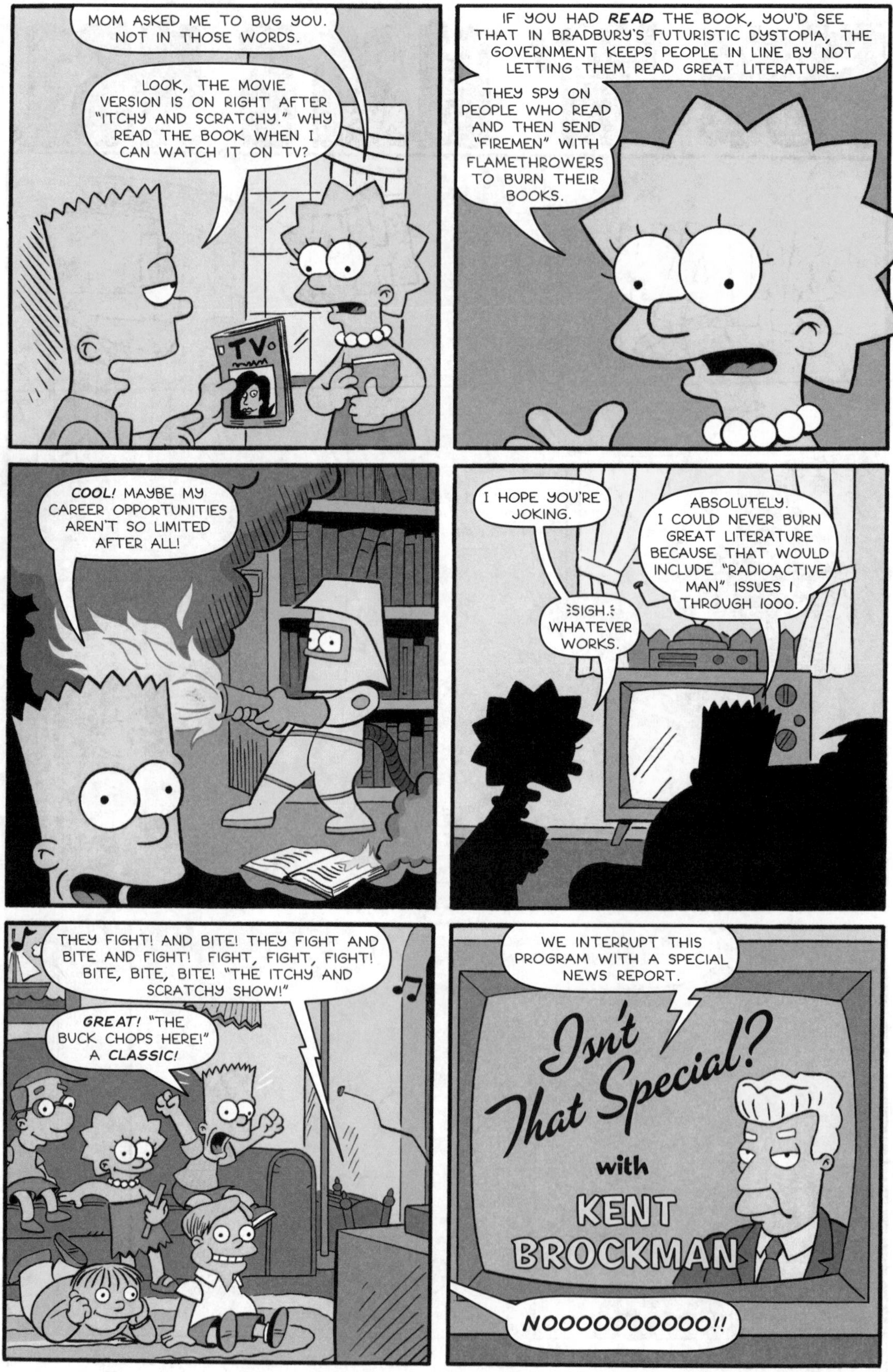

MOM ASKED ME TO BUG YOU. NOT IN THOSE WORDS.
LOOK, THE MOVIE VERSION IS ON RIGHT AFTER "ITCHY AND SCRATCHY." WHY READ THE BOOK WHEN I CAN WATCH IT ON TV?
TV
IF YOU HAD READ THE BOOK, YOU'D SEE THAT IN BRADBURY'S FUTURISTIC DYSTOPIA, THE GOVERNMENT KEEPS PEOPLE IN LINE BY NOT LETTING THEM READ GREAT LITERATURE.
THEY SPY ON PEOPLE WHO READ AND THEN SEND "FIREMEN" WITH FLAMETHROWERS TO BURN THEIR BOOKS.
COOL! MAYBE MY CAREER OPPORTUNITIES AREN'T SO LIMITED AFTER ALL!
I HOPE YOU'RE JOKING.
ABSOLUTELY. I COULD NEVER BURN GREAT LITERATURE BECAUSE THAT WOULD INCLUDE "RADIOACTIVE MAN" ISSUES 1 THROUGH 1000.
SIGH. WHATEVER WORKS.
THEY FIGHT! AND BITE! THEY FIGHT AND BITE AND FIGHT! FIGHT, FIGHT, FIGHT! BITE, BITE, BITE! "THE ITCHY AND SCRATCHY SHOW!"
GREAT! "THE BUCK CHOPS HERE!" A CLASSIC!
WE INTERRUPT THIS PROGRAM WITH A SPECIAL NEWS REPORT.
Isn't That Special?
with
KENT BROCKMAN
NOOOOOOOOOO!!

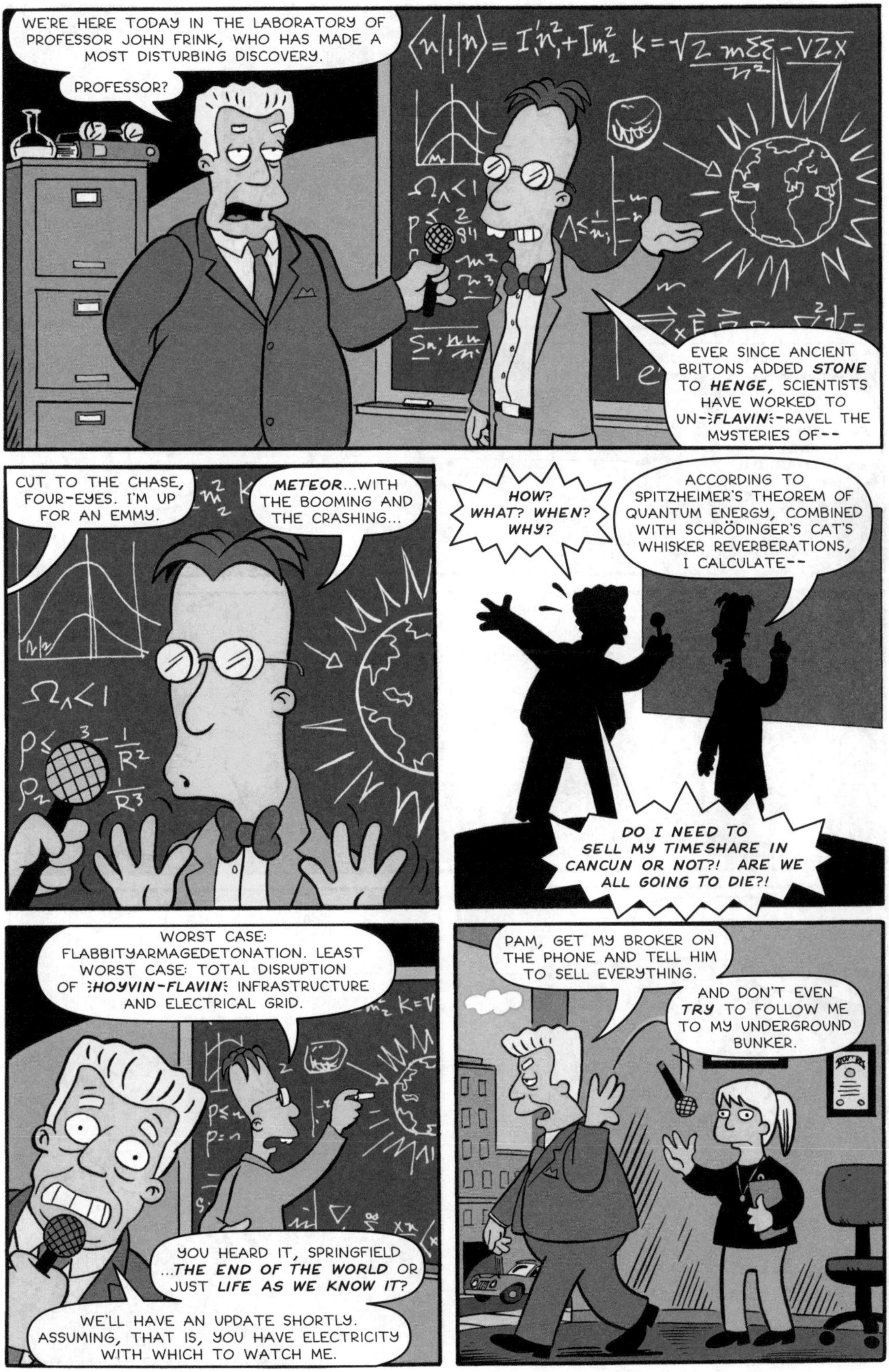
WE'RE HERE TODAY IN THE LABORATORY OF PROFESSOR JOHN FRINK, WHO HAS MADE A MOST DISTURBING DISCOVERY.
PROFESSOR?
EVER SINCE ANCIENT BRITONS ADDED STONE TO HENGE, SCIENTISTS HAVE WORKED TO UN-FLAVIN-RAVEL THE MYSTERIES OF--
CUT TO THE CHASE, FOUR-EYES. I'M UP FOR AN EMMY.
METEOR...WITH THE BOOMING AND THE CRASHING...
HOW? WHAT? WHEN? WHY?
ACCORDING TO SPITZHEIMER'S THEOREM OF QUANTUM ENERGY, COMBINED WITH SCHRÖDINGER'S CAT'S WHISKER REVERBERATIONS, I CALCULATE--
DO I NEED TO SELL MY TIMESHARE IN CANCUN OR NOT?! ARE WE ALL GOING TO DIE?!
WORST CASE: FLABBITYARMAGEDETONATION. LEAST WORST CASE: TOTAL DISRUPTION OF HOYVIN-FLAVIN INFRASTRUCTURE AND ELECTRICAL GRID.
YOU HEARD IT, SPRINGFIELD ...THE END OF THE WORLD OR JUST LIFE AS WE KNOW IT?
WE'LL HAVE AN UPDATE SHORTLY. ASSUMING, THAT IS, YOU HAVE ELECTRICITY WITH WHICH TO WATCH ME.
PAM, GET MY BROKER ON THE PHONE AND TELL HIM TO SELL EVERYTHING.
AND DON'T EVEN TRY TO FOLLOW ME TO MY UNDERGROUND BUNKER.

IS THIS... THE END?

WE'RE BEING PRANKED.

I HOPE.

BART, MILHOUSE...YOUR MOVIE IS ON.

WHAT'S THE POINT OF *BOOK REPORTS* IF THE WORLD WILL SOON BE A *CHARCOAL BRIQUET*?!

WHAT IF WE ALL DIE?!

THEN WE WON'T HAVE TO WORRY ANYMORE.

WHAT IF WE DON'T DIE, BUT THERE'S *NO ELECTRICITY*?!

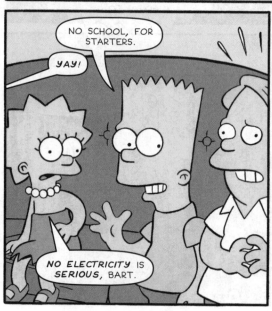

NO SCHOOL, FOR STARTERS.

YAY!

NO ELECTRICITY IS *SERIOUS*, BART.

WE WOULD HAVE NO INTERNET, TV, RADIO, AIR TRAVEL, LIGHTS, REFRIGERATION... SOCIETY WOULD *MELT DOWN*! WE'D BE THROWN BACK TO THE DARK AGES! LITERALLY. RIOTS! MURDER! ANARCHY! FAMINE!

WHADDYA MEAN, *NO TV*?

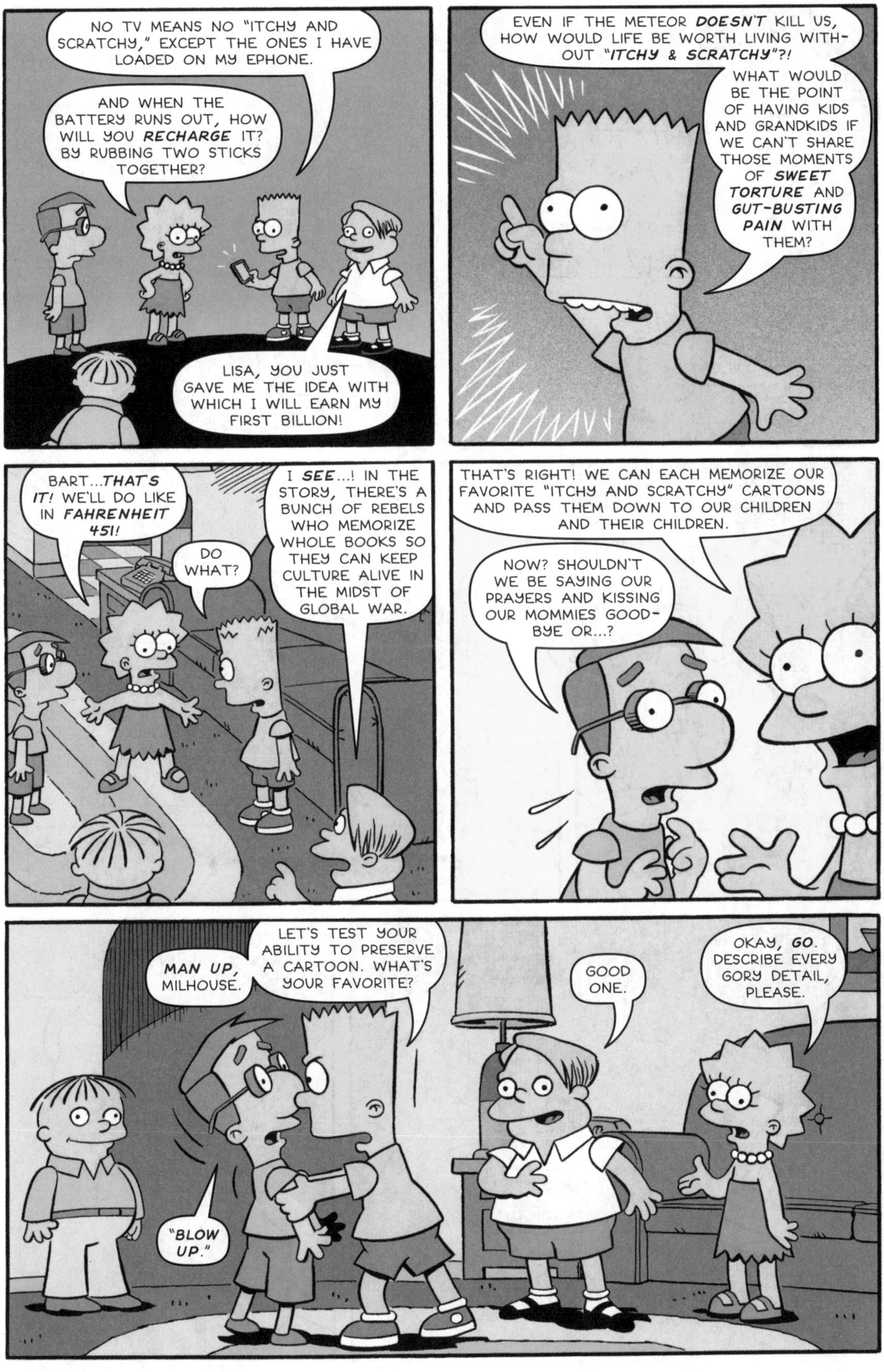
NO TV MEANS NO "ITCHY AND SCRATCHY," EXCEPT THE ONES I HAVE LOADED ON MY EPHONE.
AND WHEN THE BATTERY RUNS OUT, HOW WILL YOU RECHARGE IT? BY RUBBING TWO STICKS TOGETHER?
LISA, YOU JUST GAVE ME THE IDEA WITH WHICH I WILL EARN MY FIRST BILLION!
EVEN IF THE METEOR DOESN'T KILL US, HOW WOULD LIFE BE WORTH LIVING WITH-OUT "ITCHY & SCRATCHY"?!
WHAT WOULD BE THE POINT OF HAVING KIDS AND GRANDKIDS IF WE CAN'T SHARE THOSE MOMENTS OF SWEET TORTURE AND GUT-BUSTING PAIN WITH THEM?
BART...THAT'S IT! WE'LL DO LIKE IN FAHRENHEIT 451!
DO WHAT?
I SEE...! IN THE STORY, THERE'S A BUNCH OF REBELS WHO MEMORIZE WHOLE BOOKS SO THEY CAN KEEP CULTURE ALIVE IN THE MIDST OF GLOBAL WAR.
THAT'S RIGHT! WE CAN EACH MEMORIZE OUR FAVORITE "ITCHY AND SCRATCHY" CARTOONS AND PASS THEM DOWN TO OUR CHILDREN AND THEIR CHILDREN.
NOW? SHOULDN'T WE BE SAYING OUR PRAYERS AND KISSING OUR MOMMIES GOOD-BYE OR...?
MAN UP, MILHOUSE.
LET'S TEST YOUR ABILITY TO PRESERVE A CARTOON. WHAT'S YOUR FAVORITE?
"BLOW UP."
GOOD ONE.
OKAY, GO. DESCRIBE EVERY GORY DETAIL, PLEASE.

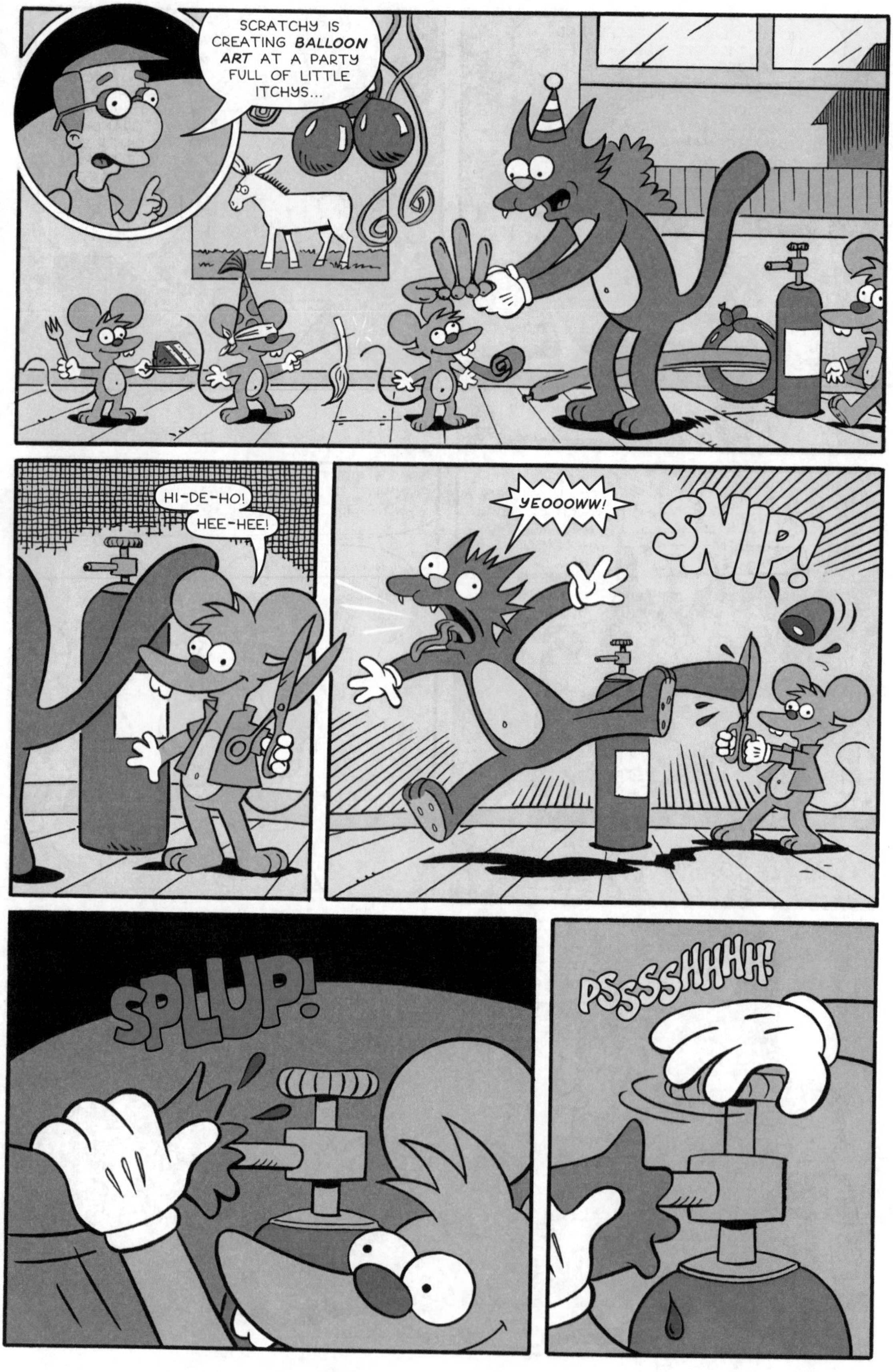

SCRATCHY IS CREATING BALLOON ART AT A PARTY FULL OF LITTLE ITCHYS...
HI-DE-HO!
HEE-HEE!
YEOOOWW!
SNIP!
SPLUP!
PSSSSHHHH!

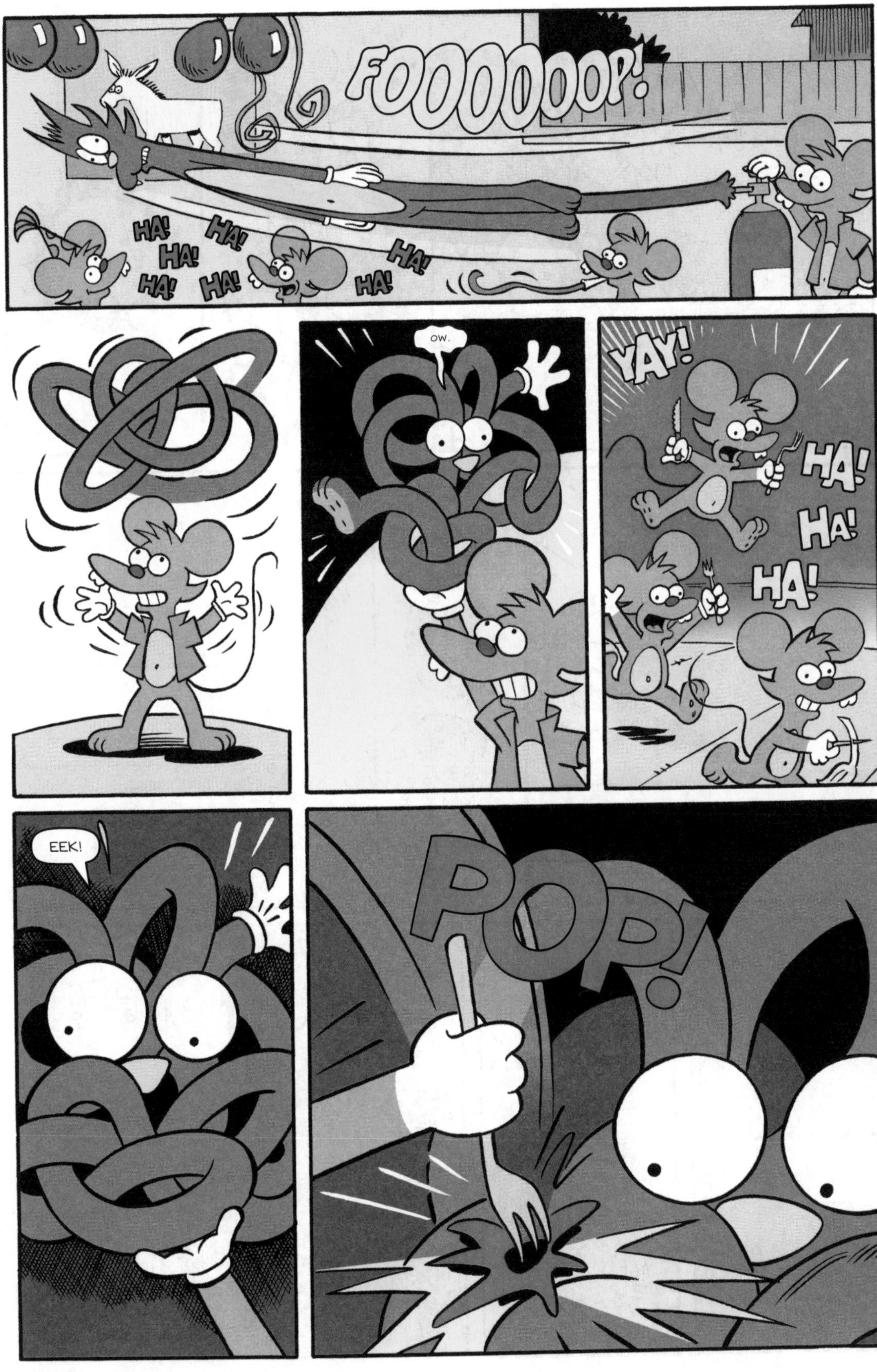
FOOOOOOP!
HA!
HA!
HA!
HA!
HA!
HA!
HA!
OW.
YAY!
HA!
HA!
HA!
EEK!
POP!

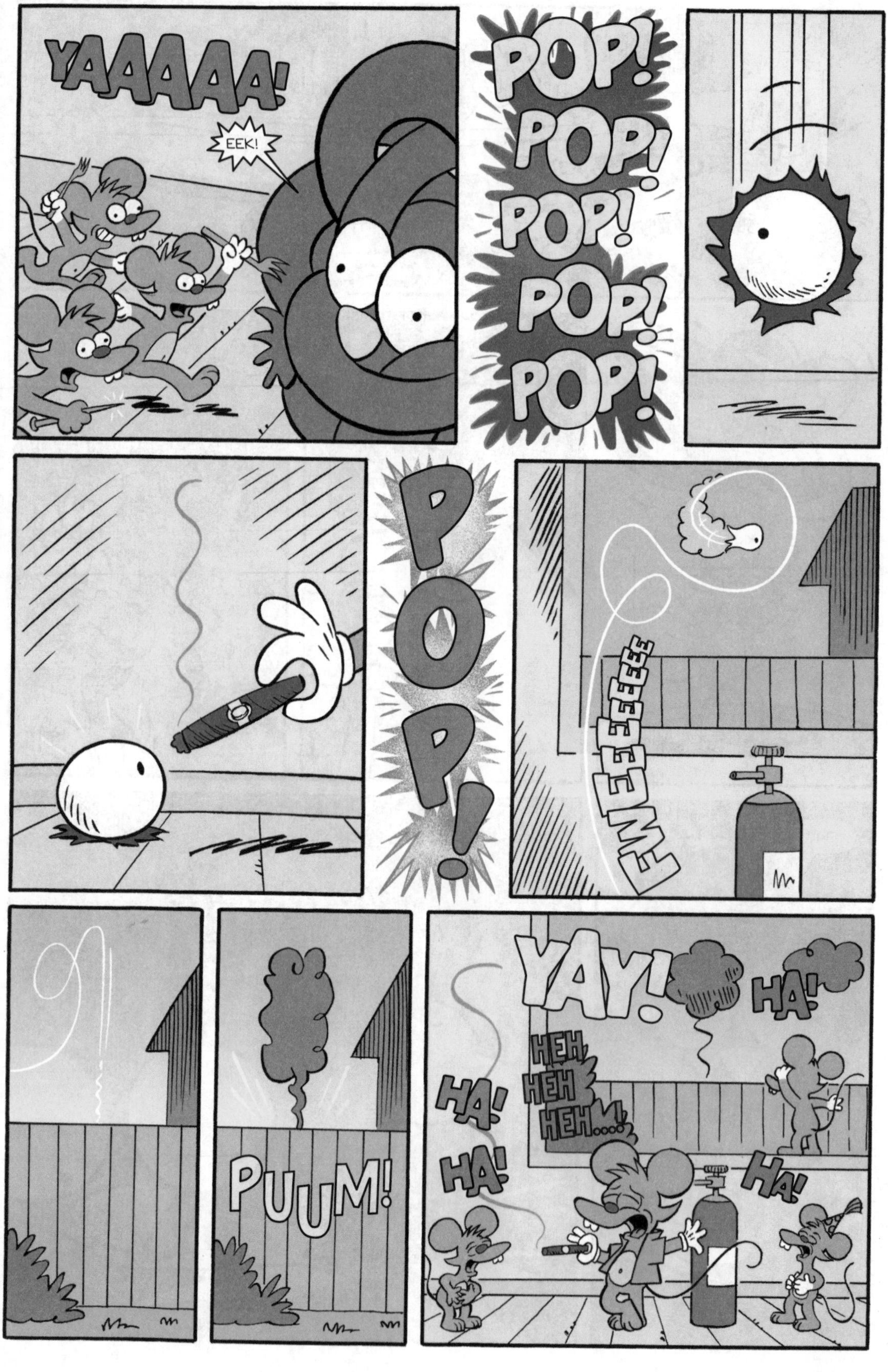

YAAAAA!
EEK!
POP!
POP!
POP!
POP!
POP!
POP!
FWEEEEEEEE
PUUUM!
YAY!
HA!
HEH HEH HEH...!
HA!
HA!
HA!

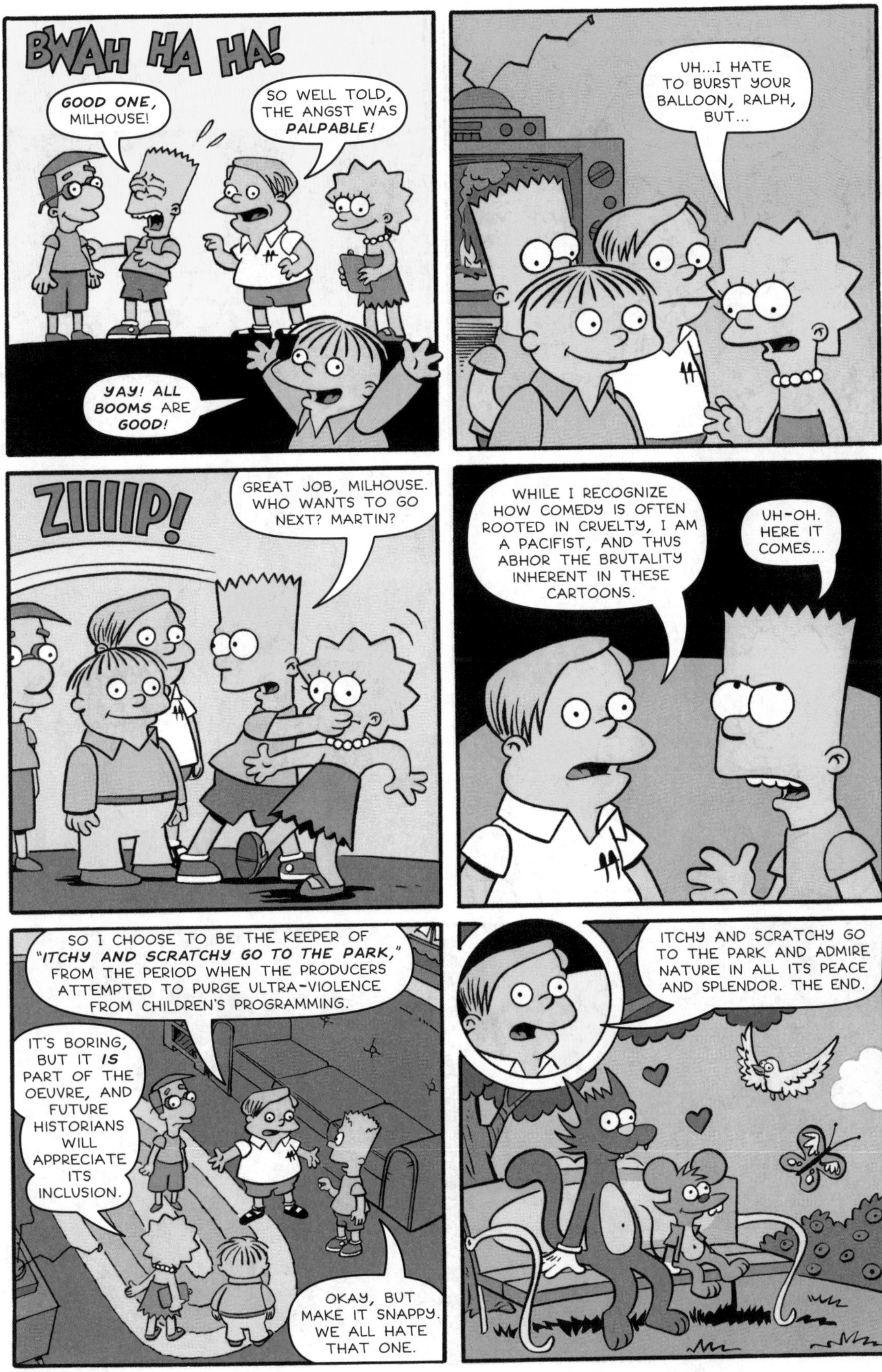
BWAH HA HA!
GOOD ONE, MILHOUSE!
SO WELL TOLD, THE ANGST WAS PALPABLE!
YAY! ALL BOOMS ARE GOOD!
UH...I HATE TO BURST YOUR BALLOON, RALPH, BUT...
ZIIIIP!
GREAT JOB, MILHOUSE. WHO WANTS TO GO NEXT? MARTIN?
WHILE I RECOGNIZE HOW COMEDY IS OFTEN ROOTED IN CRUELTY, I AM A PACIFIST, AND THUS ABHOR THE BRUTALITY INHERENT IN THESE CARTOONS.
UH-OH. HERE IT COMES...
SO I CHOOSE TO BE THE KEEPER OF "ITCHY AND SCRATCHY GO TO THE PARK," FROM THE PERIOD WHEN THE PRODUCERS ATTEMPTED TO PURGE ULTRA-VIOLENCE FROM CHILDREN'S PROGRAMMING.
IT'S BORING, BUT IT IS PART OF THE OEUVRE, AND FUTURE HISTORIANS WILL APPRECIATE ITS INCLUSION.
OKAY, BUT MAKE IT SNAPPY. WE ALL HATE THAT ONE.
ITCHY AND SCRATCHY GO TO THE PARK AND ADMIRE NATURE IN ALL ITS PEACE AND SPLENDOR. THE END.

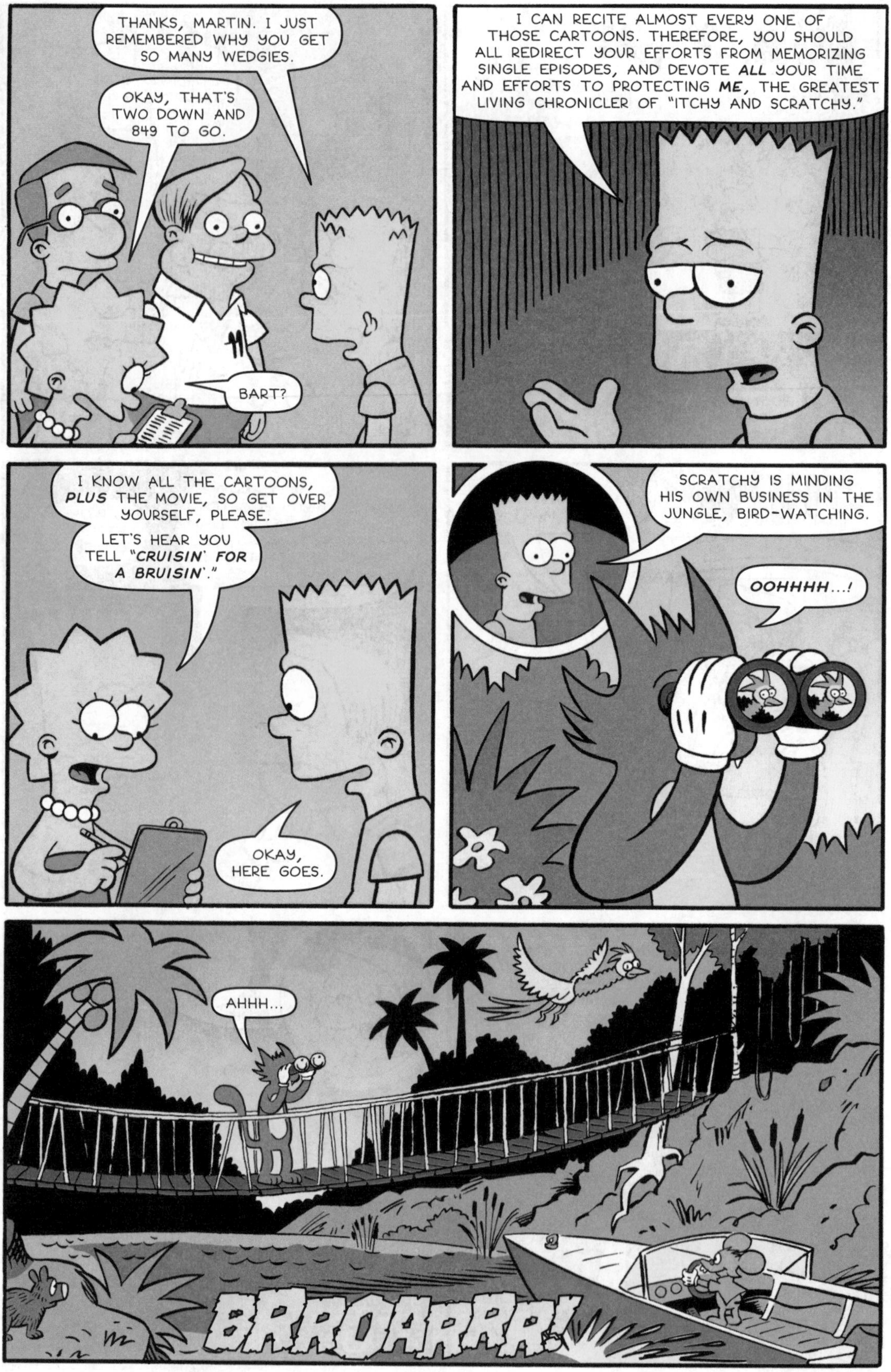
THANKS, MARTIN. I JUST REMEMBERED WHY YOU GET SO MANY WEDGIES.
OKAY, THAT'S TWO DOWN AND 849 TO GO.
BART?
I CAN RECITE ALMOST EVERY ONE OF THOSE CARTOONS. THEREFORE, YOU SHOULD ALL REDIRECT YOUR EFFORTS FROM MEMORIZING SINGLE EPISODES, AND DEVOTE ALL YOUR TIME AND EFFORTS TO PROTECTING ME, THE GREATEST LIVING CHRONICLER OF "ITCHY AND SCRATCHY."
I KNOW ALL THE CARTOONS, PLUS THE MOVIE, SO GET OVER YOURSELF, PLEASE.
LET'S HEAR YOU TELL "CRUISIN' FOR A BRUISIN'."
OKAY, HERE GOES.
SCRATCHY IS MINDING HIS OWN BUSINESS IN THE JUNGLE, BIRD-WATCHING.
OOHHHH...!
AHHH...
BRROARRR!

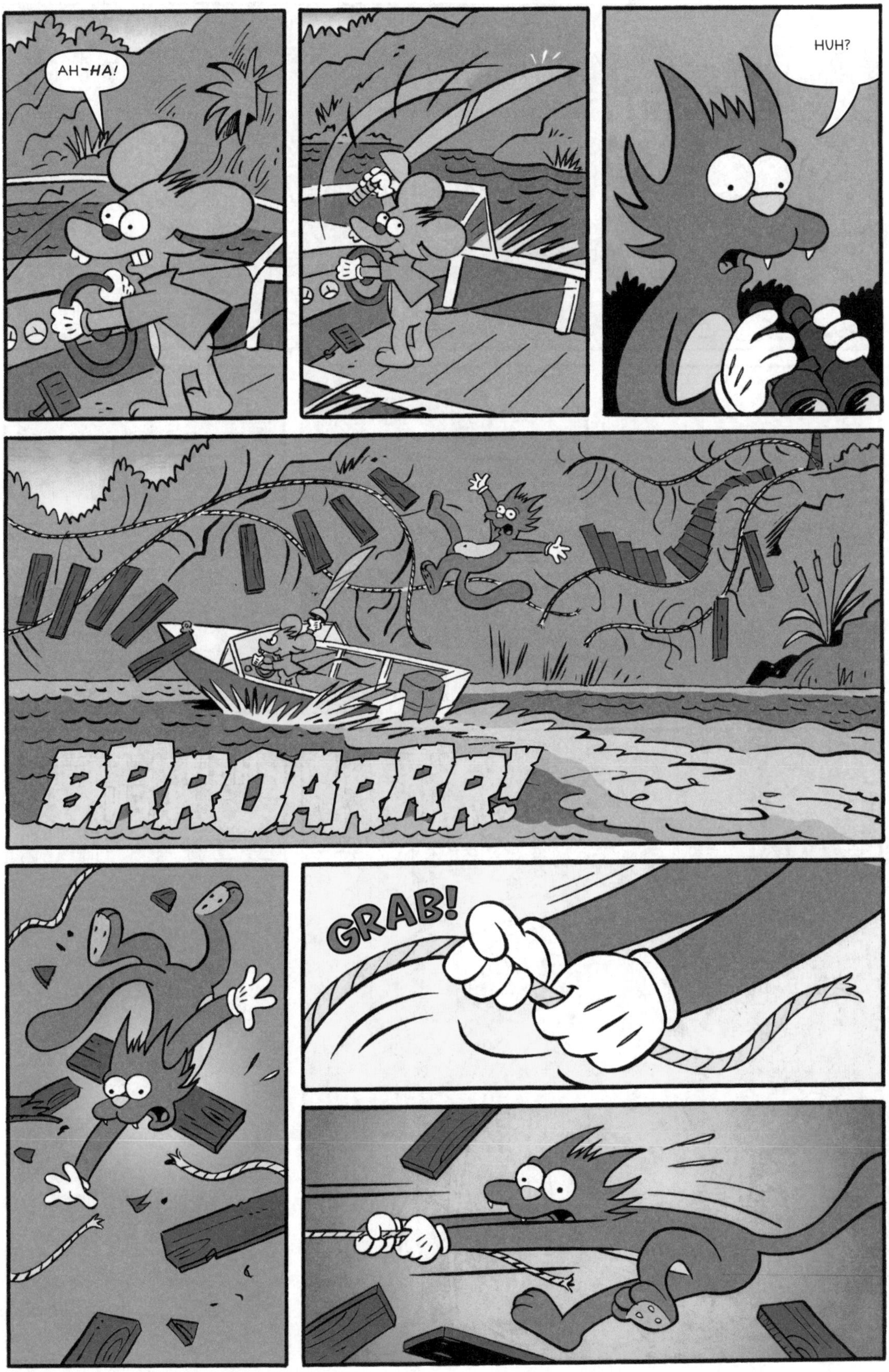
AH-HA!
HUH?
BRROARRR!
GRAB!

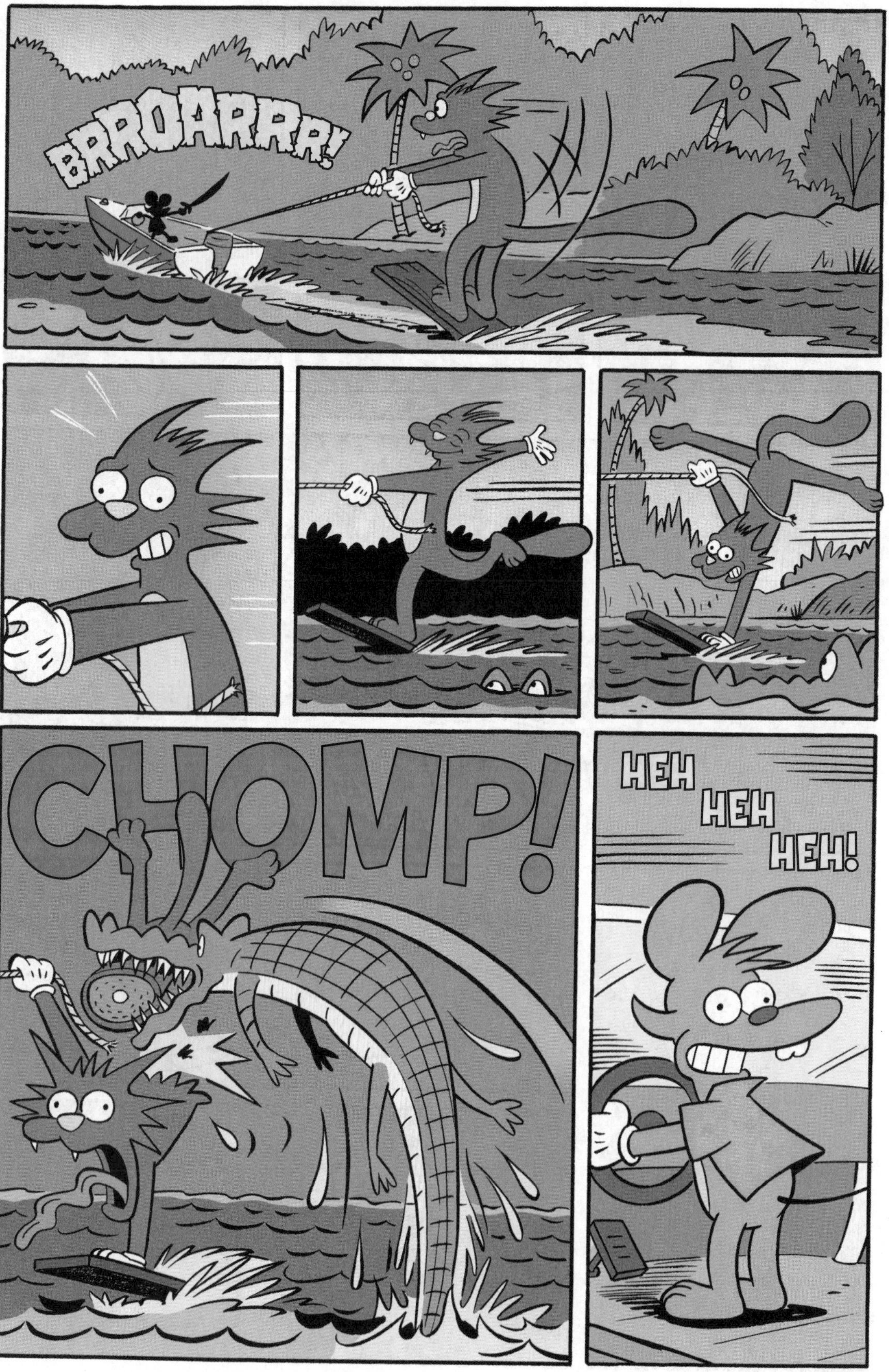
BRROARRRR!
CHOMP!
HEH
HEH
HEH!

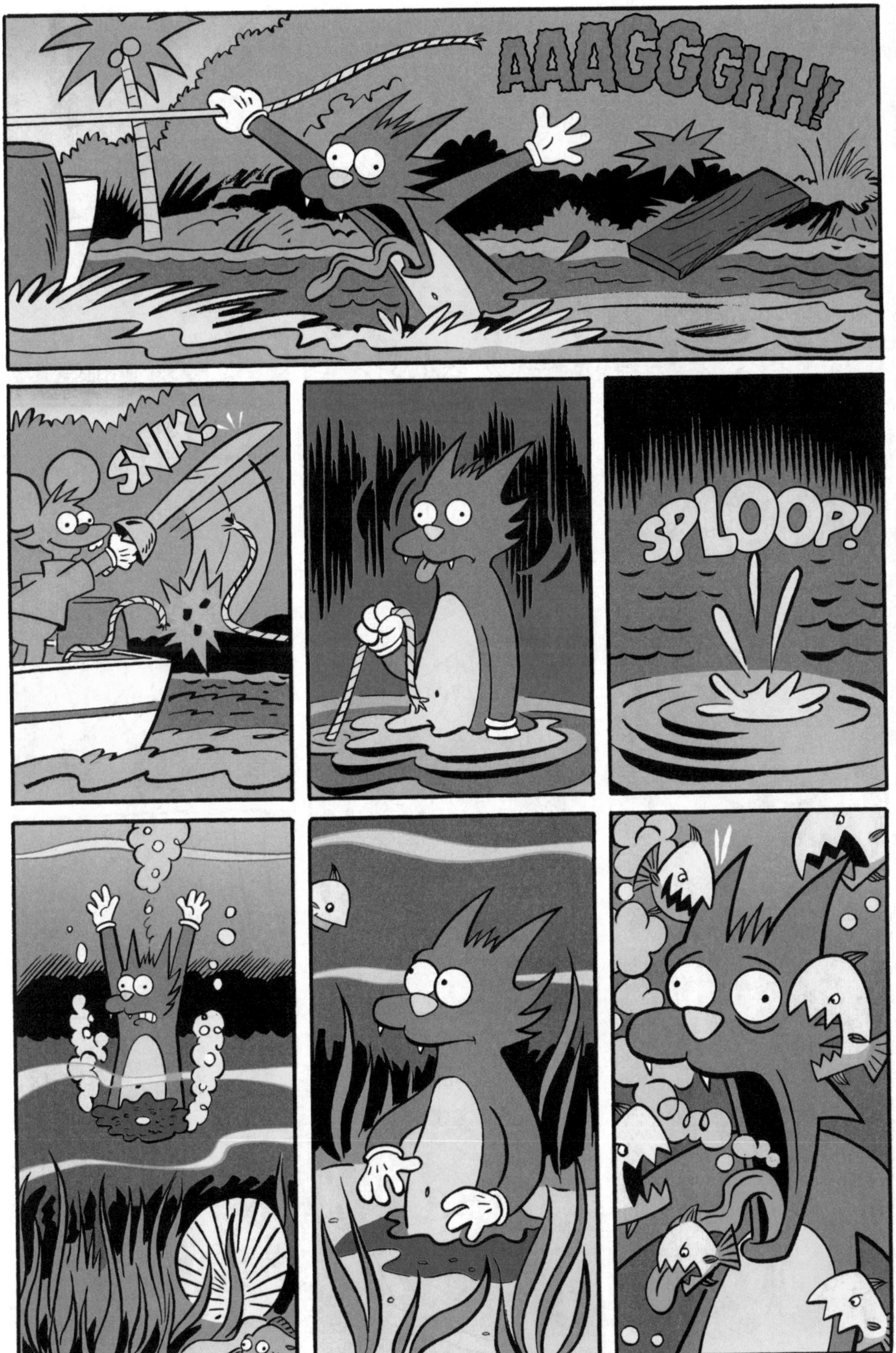
AAAGGGHH!
SNIK!
SPLOOP!

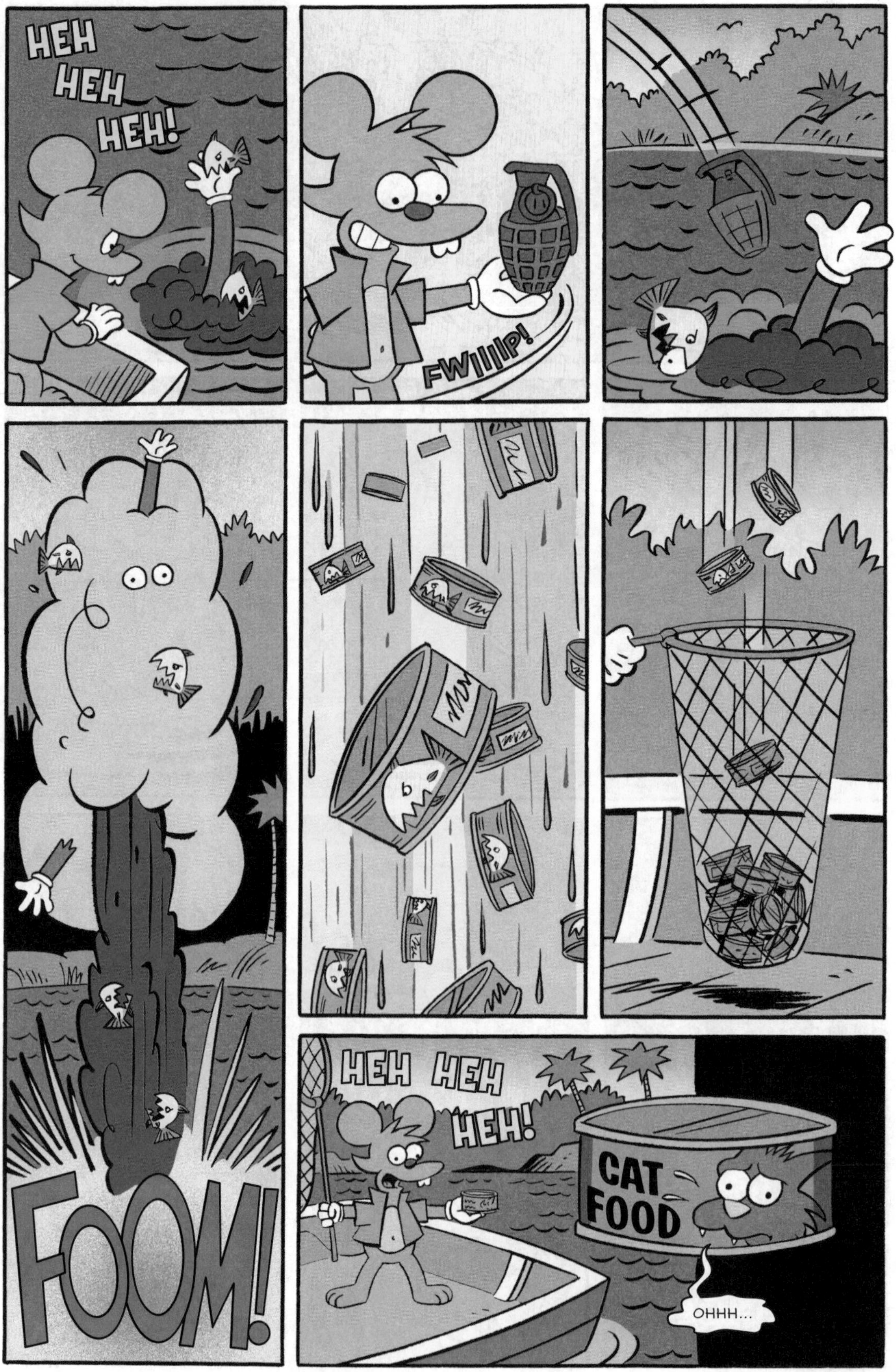
HEH HEH HEH!
FWIIIIP!
FOOM!
HEH HEH HEH!
CAT FOOD
OHHH...

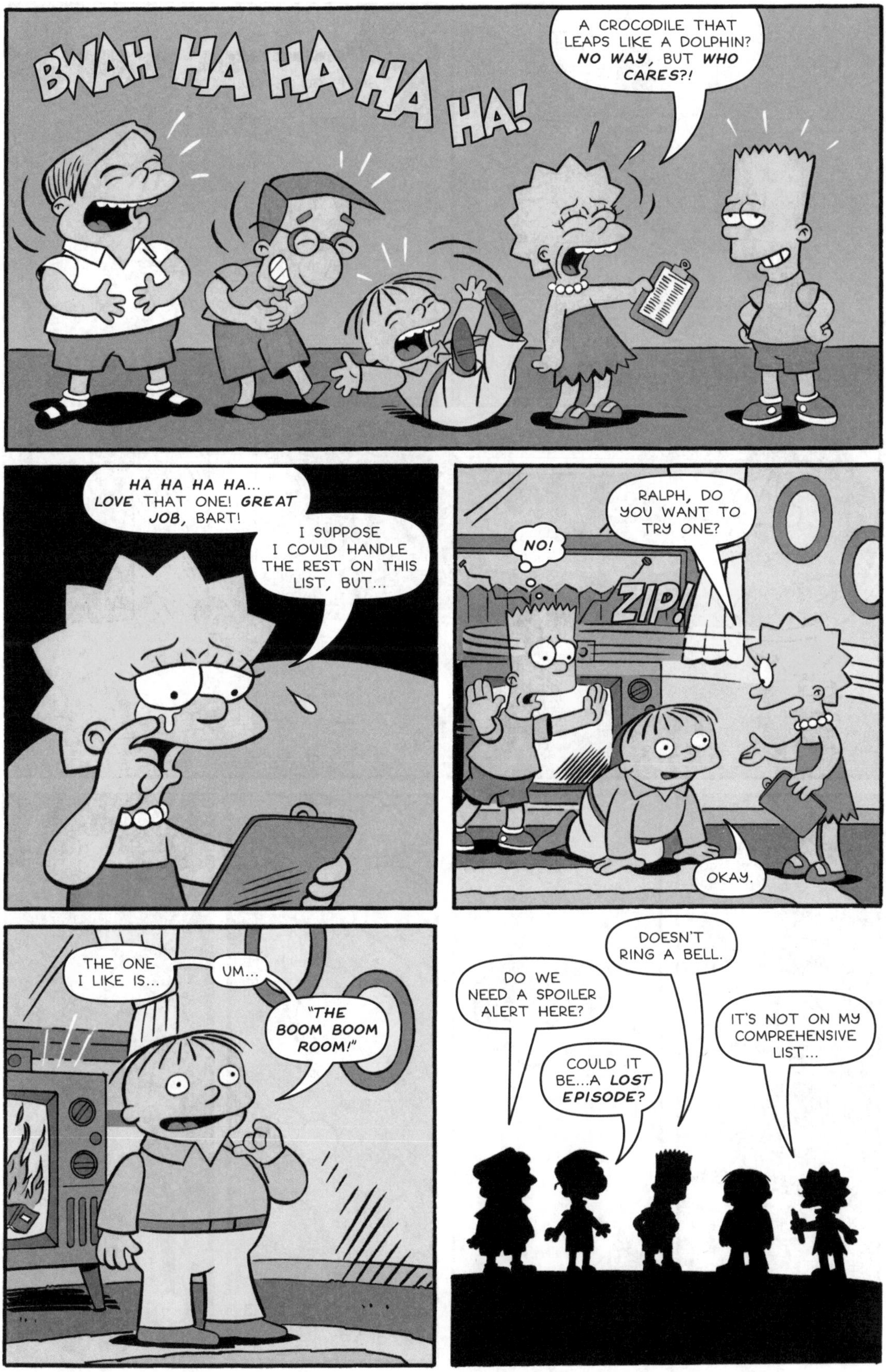
BWAH HA HA HA HA!
A CROCODILE THAT LEAPS LIKE A DOLPHIN? NO WAY, BUT WHO CARES?!
HA HA HA HA... LOVE THAT ONE! GREAT JOB, BART!
I SUPPOSE I COULD HANDLE THE REST ON THIS LIST, BUT...
RALPH, DO YOU WANT TO TRY ONE?
NO!
ZIP!
OKAY.
THE ONE I LIKE IS...
UM...
"THE BOOM BOOM ROOM!"
DO WE NEED A SPOILER ALERT HERE?
DOESN'T RING A BELL.
COULD IT BE...A LOST EPISODE?
IT'S NOT ON MY COMPREHENSIVE LIST...

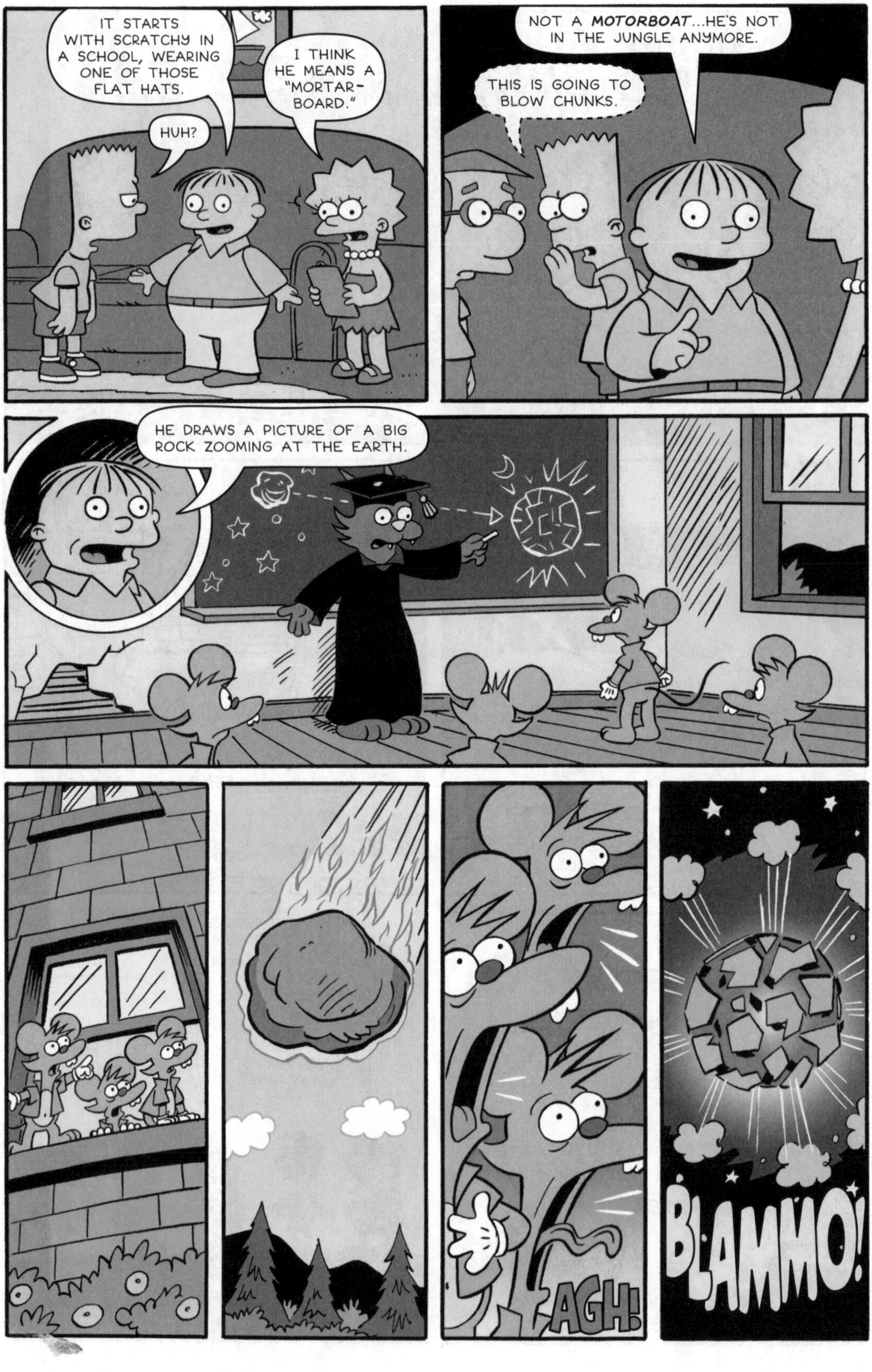
IT STARTS WITH SCRATCHY IN A SCHOOL, WEARING ONE OF THOSE FLAT HATS.
HUH?
I THINK HE MEANS A "MORTAR-BOARD."
NOT A **MOTORBOAT**...HE'S NOT IN THE JUNGLE ANYMORE.
THIS IS GOING TO BLOW CHUNKS.
HE DRAWS A PICTURE OF A BIG ROCK ZOOMING AT THE EARTH.
AGH!
BLAMMO!

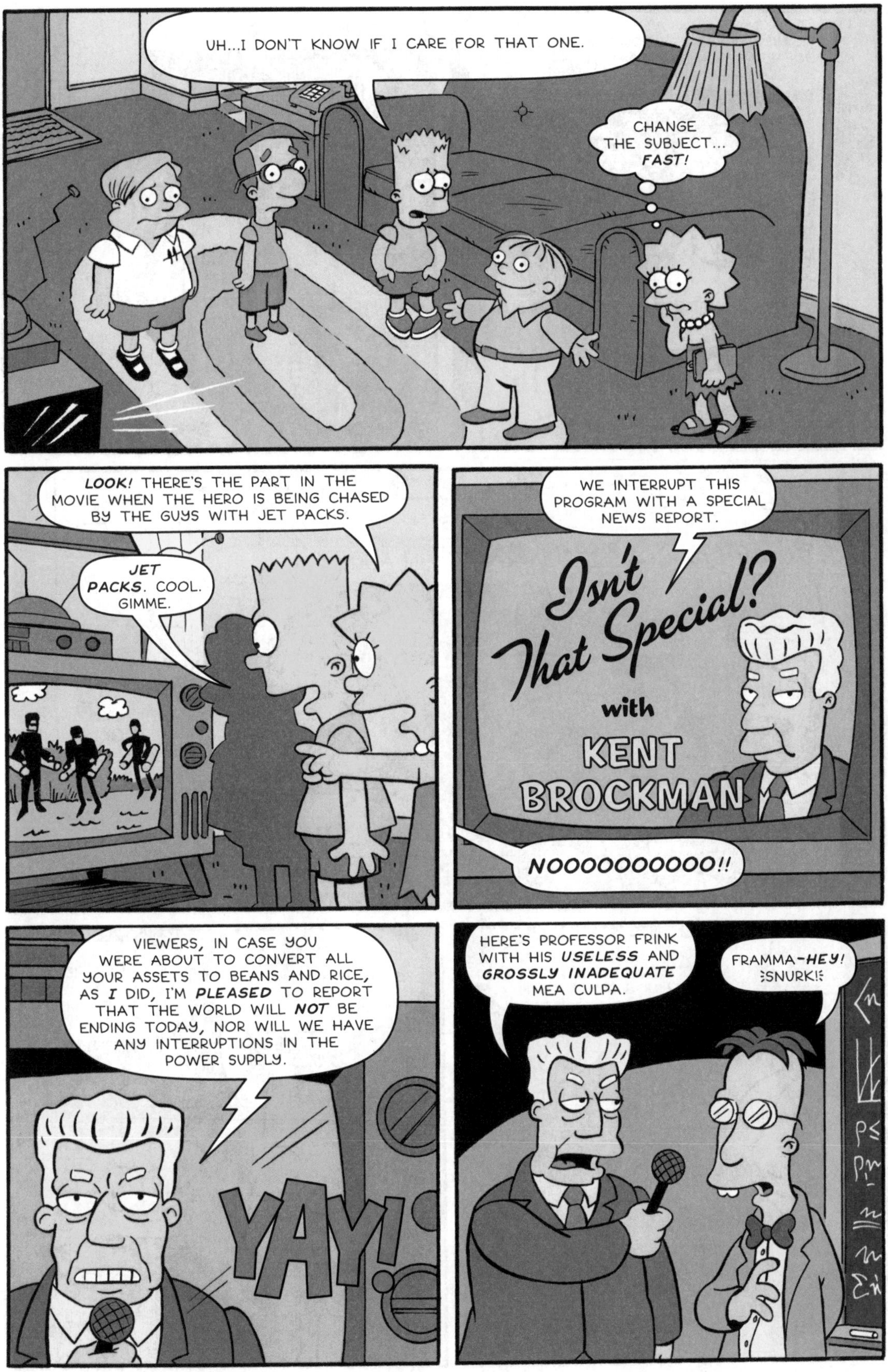
UH...I DON'T KNOW IF I CARE FOR THAT ONE.
CHANGE THE SUBJECT... FAST!
LOOK! THERE'S THE PART IN THE MOVIE WHEN THE HERO IS BEING CHASED BY THE GUYS WITH JET PACKS.
JET PACKS. COOL. GIMME.
WE INTERRUPT THIS PROGRAM WITH A SPECIAL NEWS REPORT.
Isn't That Special? with KENT BROCKMAN
NOOOOOOOOOO!!
VIEWERS, IN CASE YOU WERE ABOUT TO CONVERT ALL YOUR ASSETS TO BEANS AND RICE, AS I DID, I'M PLEASED TO REPORT THAT THE WORLD WILL NOT BE ENDING TODAY, NOR WILL WE HAVE ANY INTERRUPTIONS IN THE POWER SUPPLY.
YAY!
HERE'S PROFESSOR FRINK WITH HIS USELESS AND GROSSLY INADEQUATE MEA CULPA.
FRAMMA-HEY! SNURK!

DUE TO INCLEMENT WEATHER IDIOSYNCRASIES IN THE NORTHEAST CORRIDOR, A LEAK FROM MY ROOF ERASED A DIGIT ON THE FABBERJAY BLANKETY-BLANK. IN SHORT, I MADE A BOO-BOO...

$\sum = 2x^1$

$\leq \frac{1}{x_i}$

$\sqrt{2x\cdot x_i}$

THERE YOU HAVE IT...HE "MADE A BOO-BOO."

I'D LIKE TO BOO-BOO HIS BUTT STRAIGHT INTO *COURT*.

WOW! WHAT A *RELIEF!*

I, FOR ONE, NEVER BELIEVED IT FOR A SECOND!

OHYEAHRIGHT.

NO BOOM BOOM ROOM!

⊱WHEW⊰

OKAY, SO *NOW* WHAT ABOUT YOUR BOOK REPORT, BART? YOU DIDN'T EVEN WATCH THE MOVIE.

WELL, WE STILL HAVE ELECTRICITY, SO I'LL FIND SOMETHING ON THE INTERNET TO CLUE ME IN.

I DON'T THINK THE WORLD WIDE WEB IS BIG ENOUGH FOR THAT.

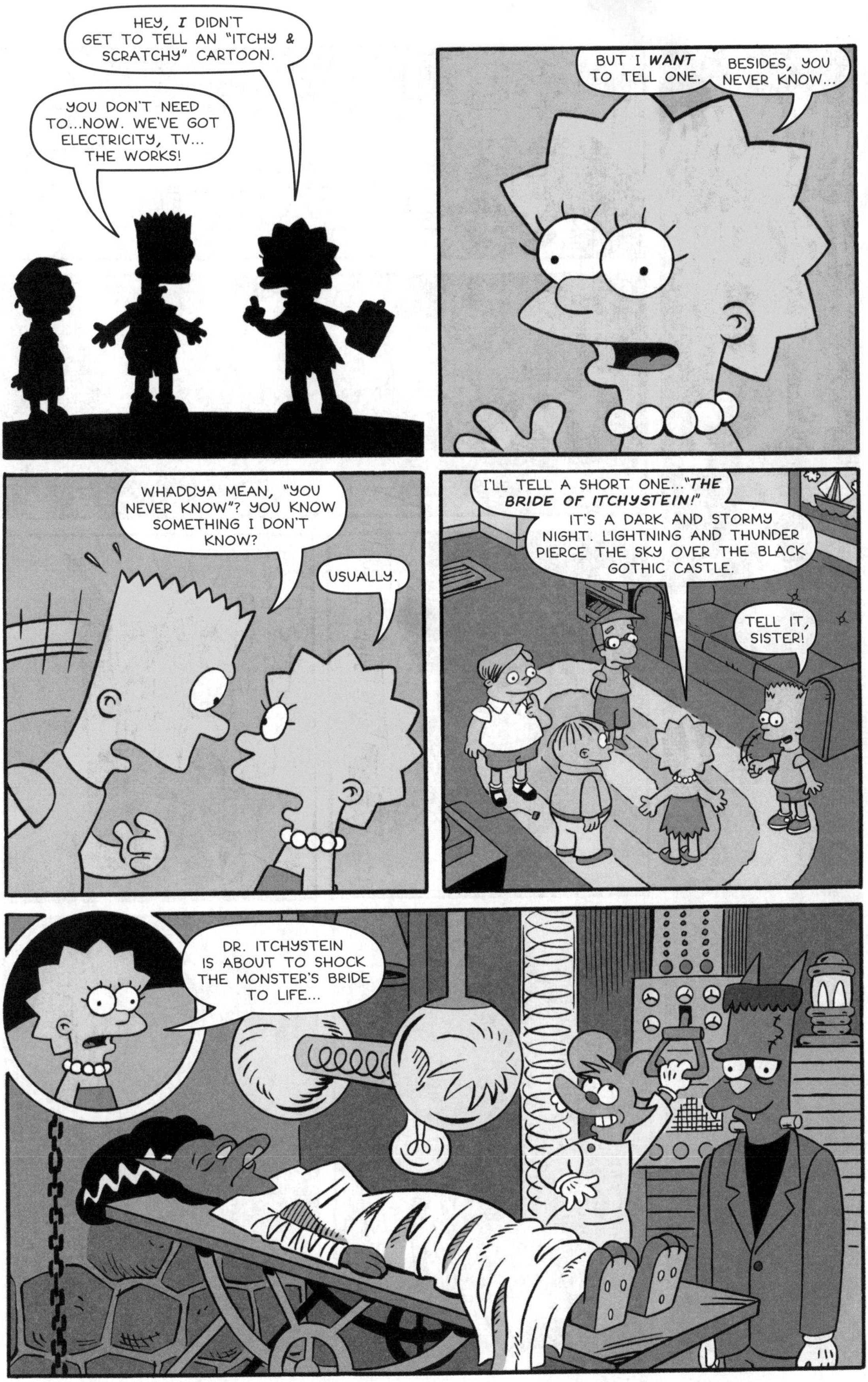

HEY, *I* DIDN'T GET TO TELL AN "ITCHY & SCRATCHY" CARTOON.
YOU DON'T NEED TO...NOW. WE'VE GOT ELECTRICITY, TV... THE WORKS!
BUT I *WANT* TO TELL ONE.
BESIDES, YOU NEVER KNOW...
WHADDYA MEAN, "YOU NEVER KNOW"? YOU KNOW SOMETHING I DON'T KNOW?
USUALLY.
I'LL TELL A SHORT ONE..."*THE BRIDE OF ITCHYSTEIN!*"
IT'S A DARK AND STORMY NIGHT. LIGHTNING AND THUNDER PIERCE THE SKY OVER THE BLACK GOTHIC CASTLE.
TELL IT, SISTER!
DR. ITCHYSTEIN IS ABOUT TO SHOCK THE MONSTER'S BRIDE TO LIFE...

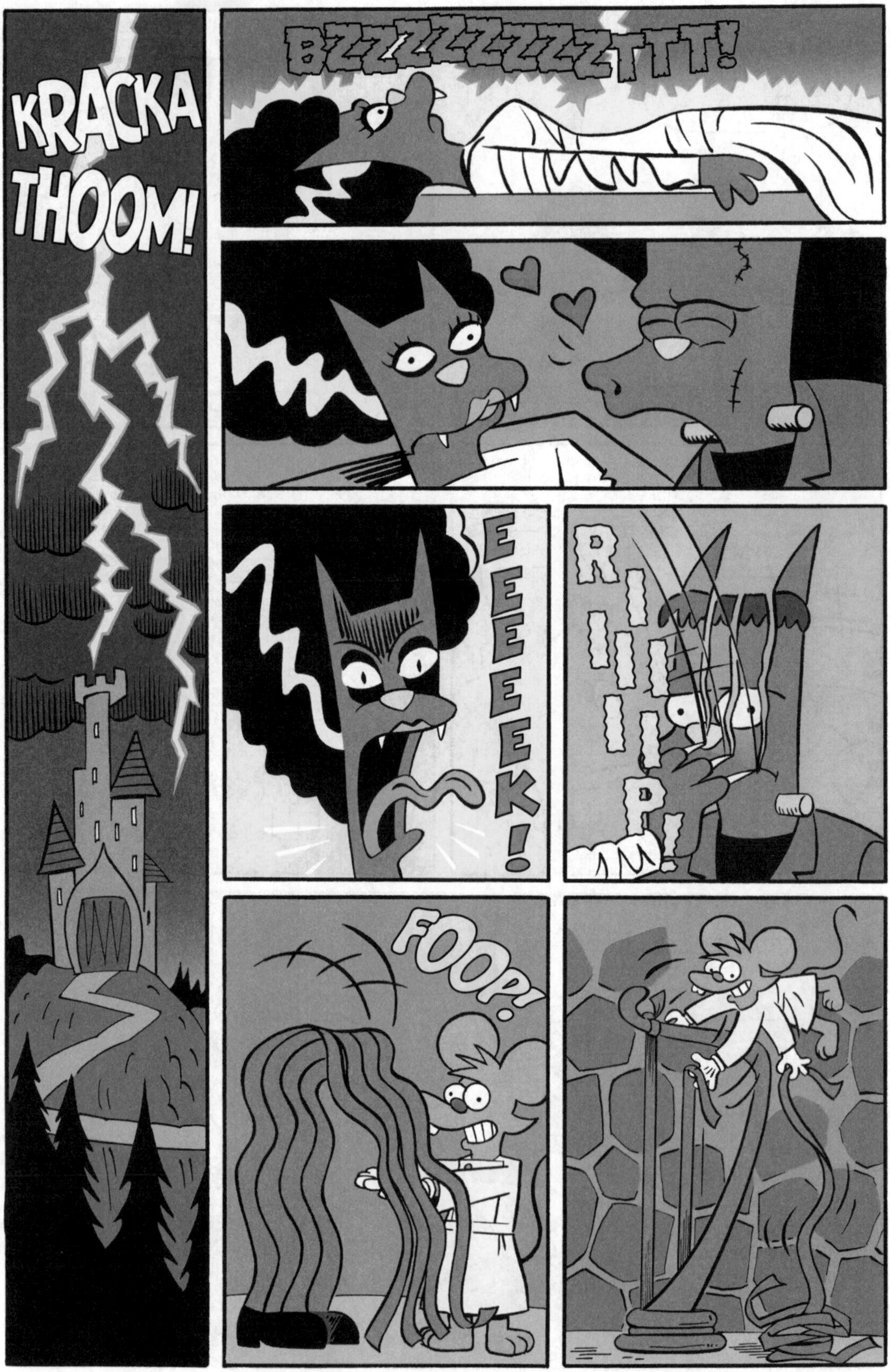

KRACKA THOOM!
BZZZZZZZZZZTTT!
EEEEEEK!
RIIIIIIP!
FOOP!

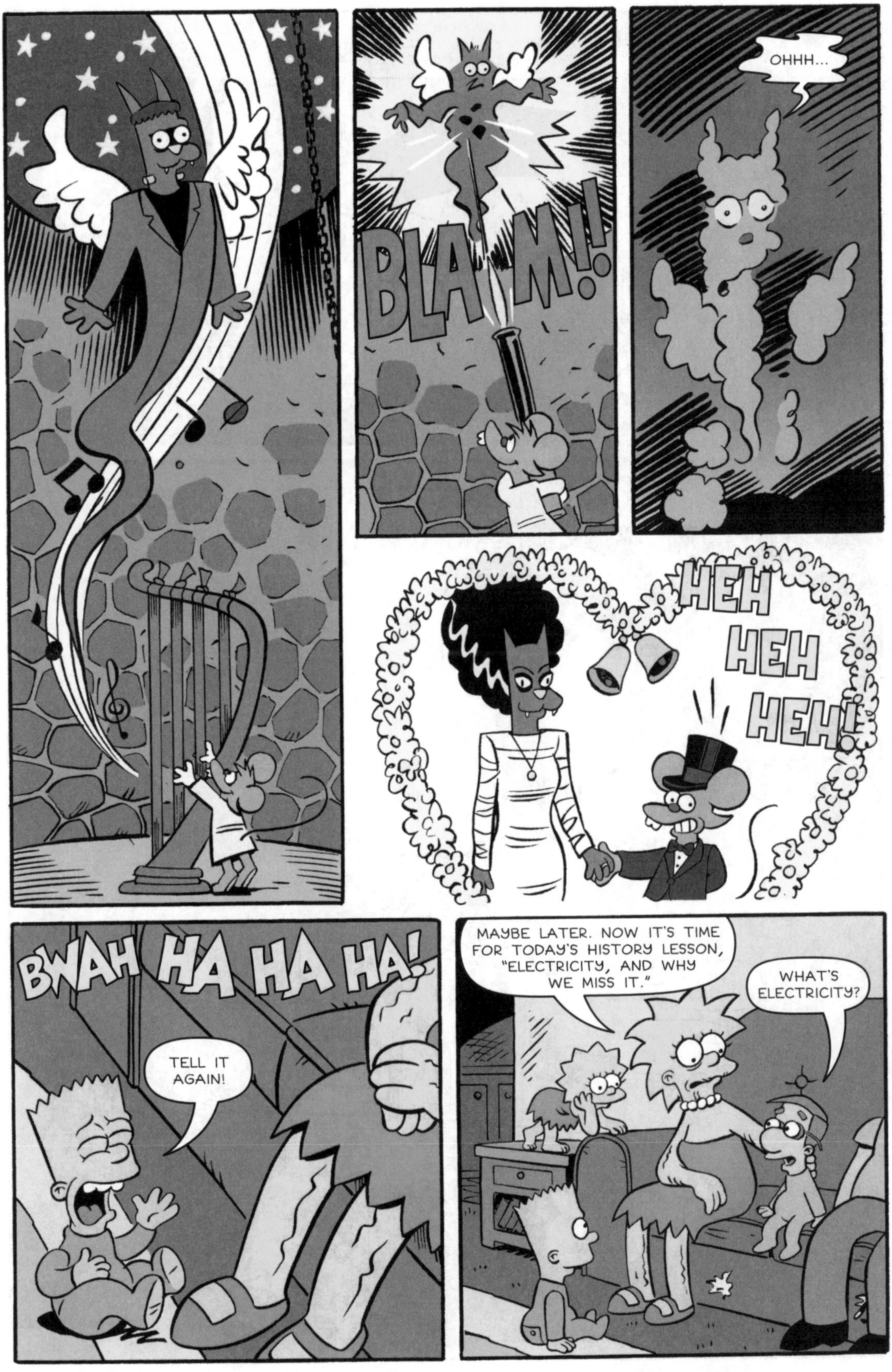

BLAM!!
OHHH...
HEH HEH HEH!
BWAH HA HA HA!
TELL IT AGAIN!
MAYBE LATER. NOW IT'S TIME FOR TODAY'S HISTORY LESSON, "ELECTRICITY, AND WHY WE MISS IT."
WHAT'S ELECTRICITY?

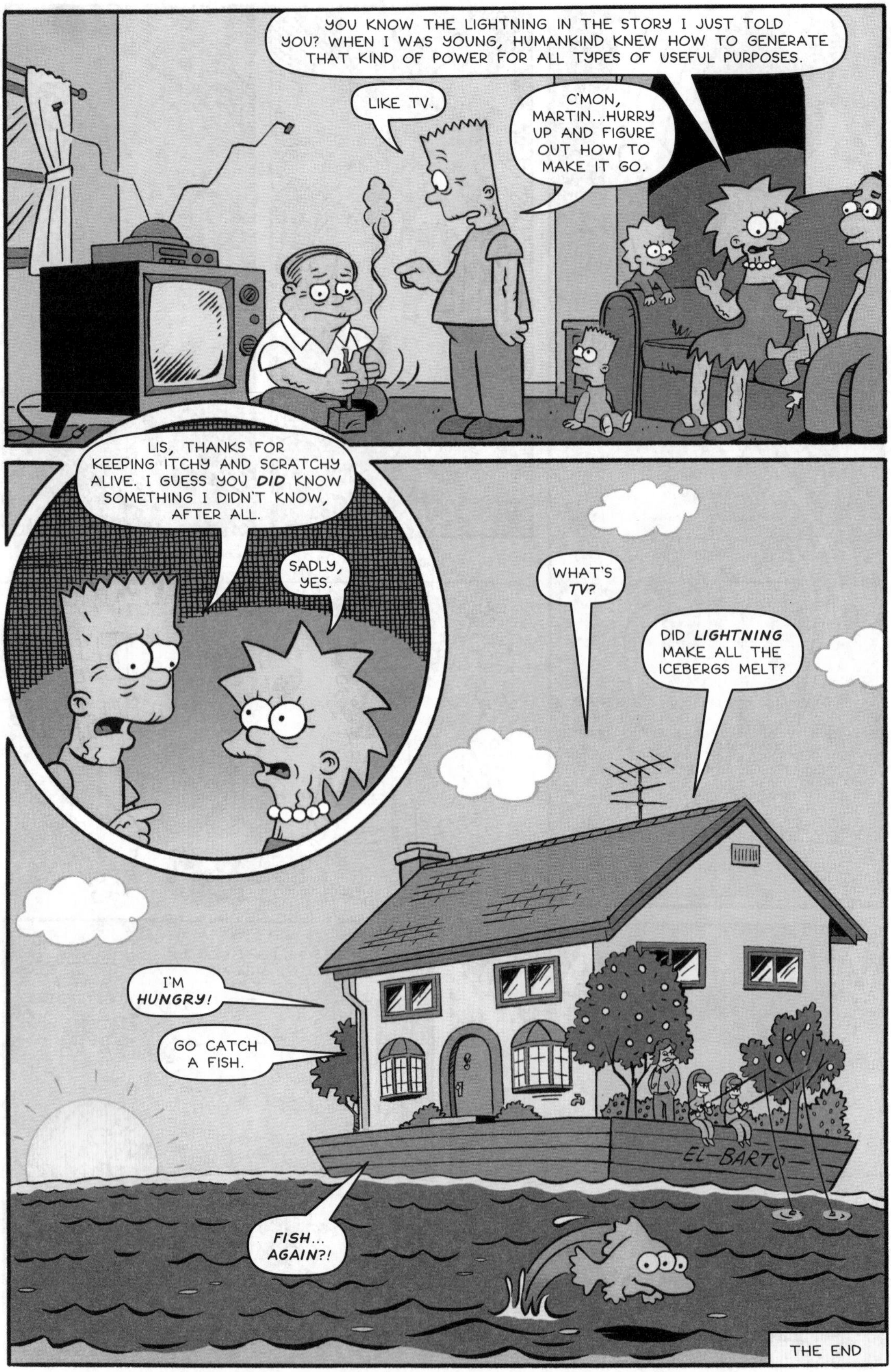
YOU KNOW THE LIGHTNING IN THE STORY I JUST TOLD YOU? WHEN I WAS YOUNG, HUMANKIND KNEW HOW TO GENERATE THAT KIND OF POWER FOR ALL TYPES OF USEFUL PURPOSES.
LIKE TV.
C'MON, MARTIN...HURRY UP AND FIGURE OUT HOW TO MAKE IT GO.
LIS, THANKS FOR KEEPING ITCHY AND SCRATCHY ALIVE. I GUESS YOU *DID* KNOW SOMETHING I DIDN'T KNOW, AFTER ALL.
SADLY, YES.
WHAT'S *TV*?
DID *LIGHTNING* MAKE ALL THE ICEBERGS MELT?
I'M *HUNGRY!*
GO CATCH A FISH.
FISH... AGAIN?!
EL-BARTO
THE END

MATT GROENING presents

KNOW IT ALL IN THE FAMILY

IT'S LIKE LOOKING IN A *FUNHOUSE MIRROR!*

IAN BOOTHBY	PHIL ORTIZ	PHYLLIS NOVIN	ART VILLANUEVA	KAREN BATES	BILL MORRISON
SCRIPT	PENCILS	INKS	COLORS	LETTERS	EDITOR

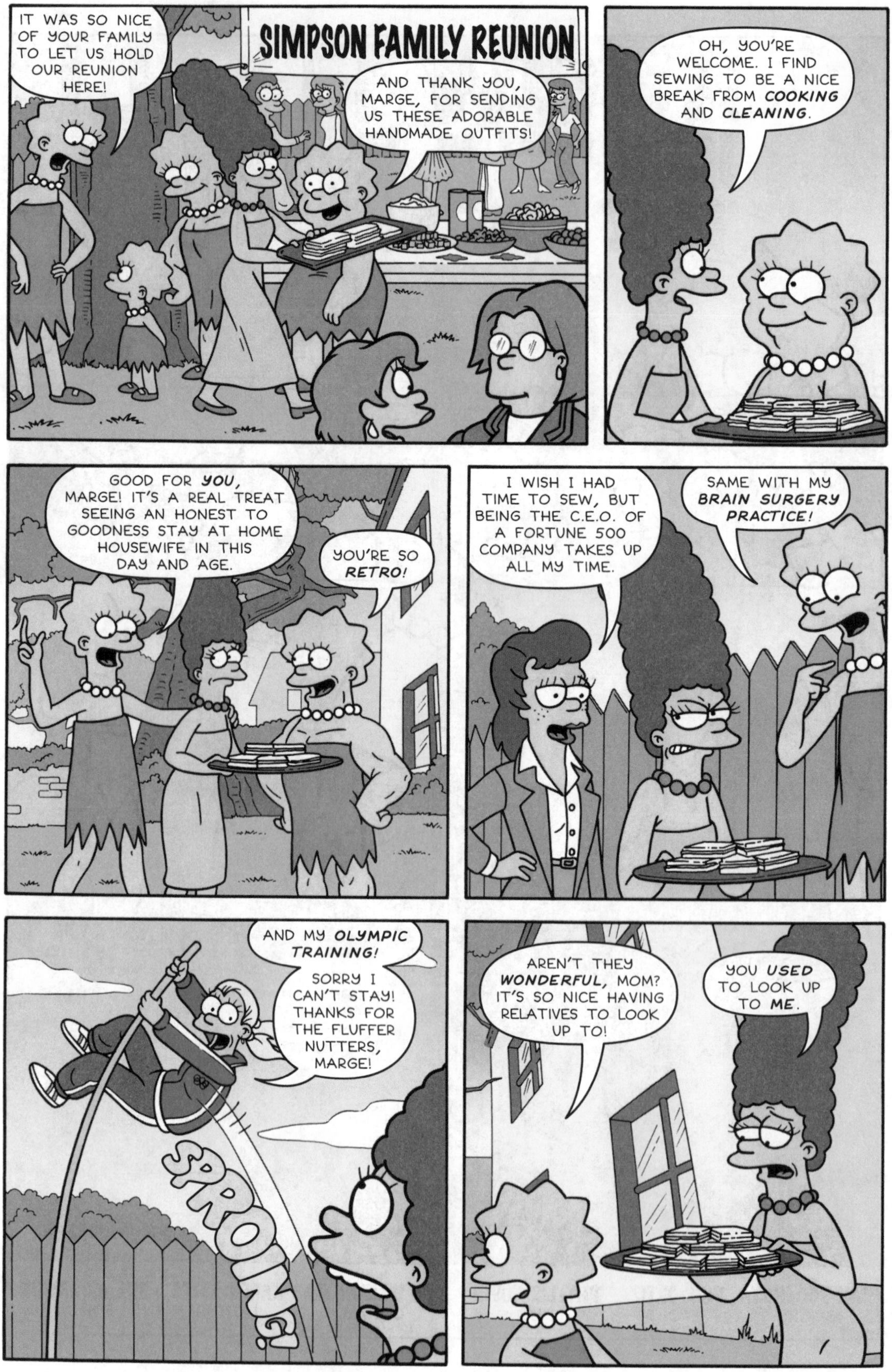

IT WAS SO NICE OF YOUR FAMILY TO LET US HOLD OUR REUNION HERE!
SIMPSON FAMILY REUNION
AND THANK YOU, MARGE, FOR SENDING US THESE ADORABLE HANDMADE OUTFITS!
OH, YOU'RE WELCOME. I FIND SEWING TO BE A NICE BREAK FROM COOKING AND CLEANING.
GOOD FOR YOU, MARGE! IT'S A REAL TREAT SEEING AN HONEST TO GOODNESS STAY AT HOME HOUSEWIFE IN THIS DAY AND AGE.
YOU'RE SO RETRO!
I WISH I HAD TIME TO SEW, BUT BEING THE C.E.O. OF A FORTUNE 500 COMPANY TAKES UP ALL MY TIME.
SAME WITH MY BRAIN SURGERY PRACTICE!
AND MY OLYMPIC TRAINING!
SORRY I CAN'T STAY! THANKS FOR THE FLUFFER NUTTERS, MARGE!
SPROING!
AREN'T THEY WONDERFUL, MOM? IT'S SO NICE HAVING RELATIVES TO LOOK UP TO!
YOU USED TO LOOK UP TO ME.

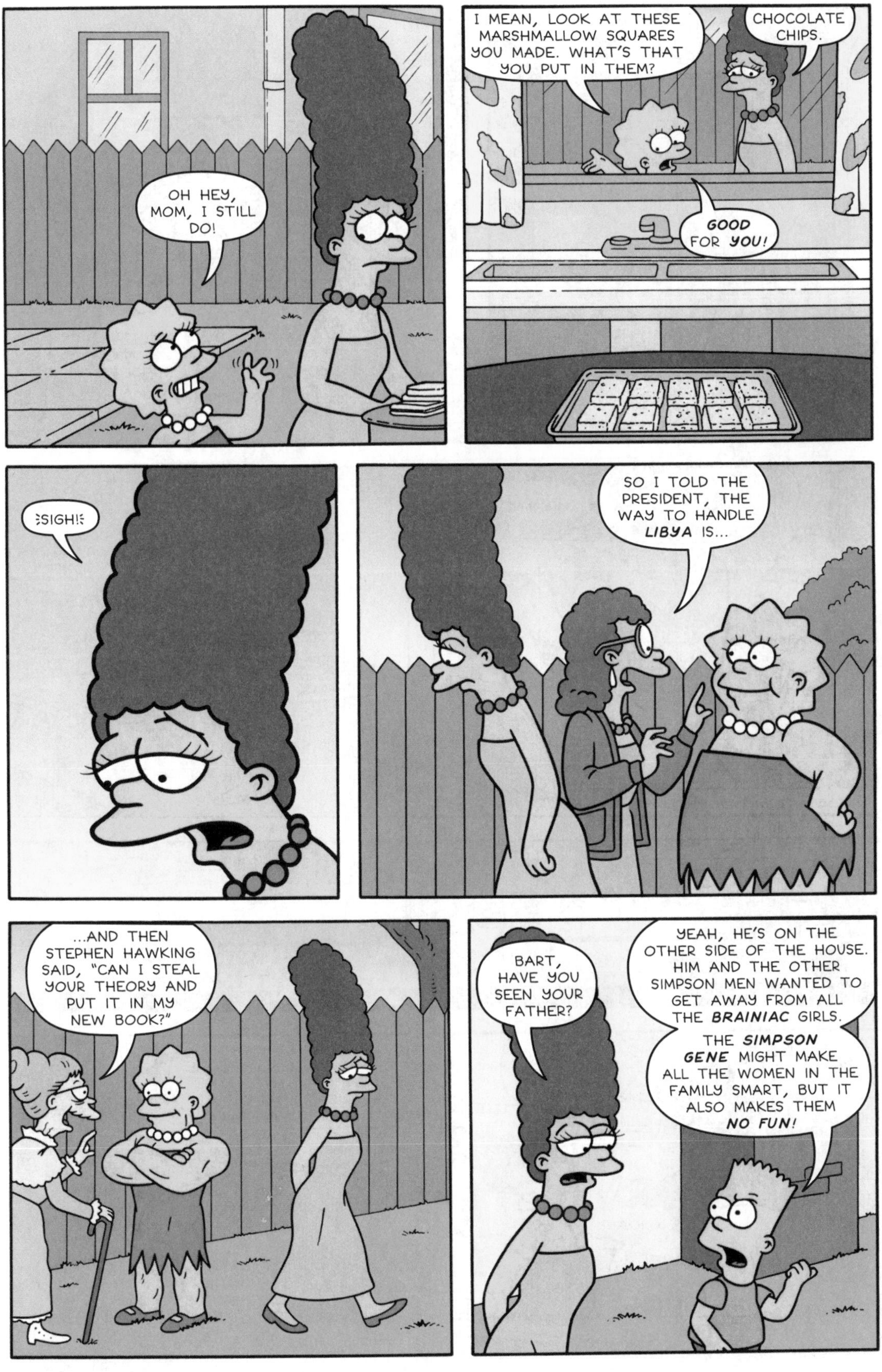

OH HEY, MOM, I STILL DO!
I MEAN, LOOK AT THESE MARSHMALLOW SQUARES YOU MADE. WHAT'S THAT YOU PUT IN THEM?
CHOCOLATE CHIPS.
GOOD FOR YOU!
SIGH!
SO I TOLD THE PRESIDENT, THE WAY TO HANDLE LIBYA IS...
...AND THEN STEPHEN HAWKING SAID, "CAN I STEAL YOUR THEORY AND PUT IT IN MY NEW BOOK?"
BART, HAVE YOU SEEN YOUR FATHER?
YEAH, HE'S ON THE OTHER SIDE OF THE HOUSE. HIM AND THE OTHER SIMPSON MEN WANTED TO GET AWAY FROM ALL THE BRAINIAC GIRLS.
THE SIMPSON GENE MIGHT MAKE ALL THE WOMEN IN THE FAMILY SMART, BUT IT ALSO MAKES THEM NO FUN!

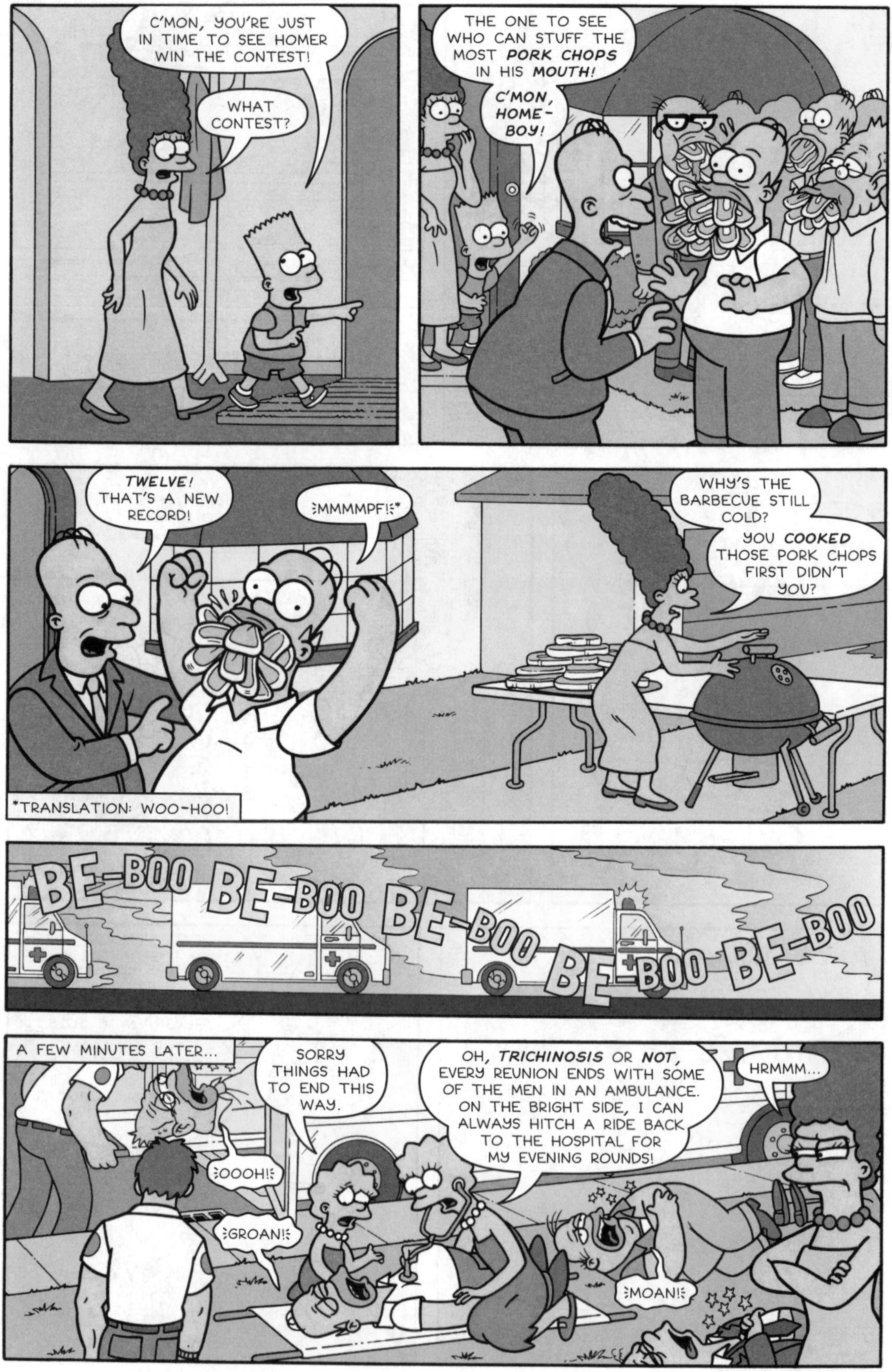
C'MON, YOU'RE JUST IN TIME TO SEE HOMER WIN THE CONTEST!
WHAT CONTEST?
THE ONE TO SEE WHO CAN STUFF THE MOST **PORK CHOPS** IN HIS **MOUTH!**
C'MON, HOME-BOY!
TWELVE! THAT'S A NEW RECORD!
MMMMPF!*
WHY'S THE BARBECUE STILL COLD?
YOU **COOKED** THOSE PORK CHOPS FIRST DIDN'T YOU?
*TRANSLATION: WOO-HOO!
BE-BOO BE-BOO BE-BOO BE-BOO BE-BOO
A FEW MINUTES LATER...
SORRY THINGS HAD TO END THIS WAY.
OH, ***TRICHINOSIS*** OR ***NOT,*** EVERY REUNION ENDS WITH SOME OF THE MEN IN AN AMBULANCE. ON THE BRIGHT SIDE, I CAN ALWAYS HITCH A RIDE BACK TO THE HOSPITAL FOR MY EVENING ROUNDS!
HRMMM...
OOOH!
GROAN!
MOAN!

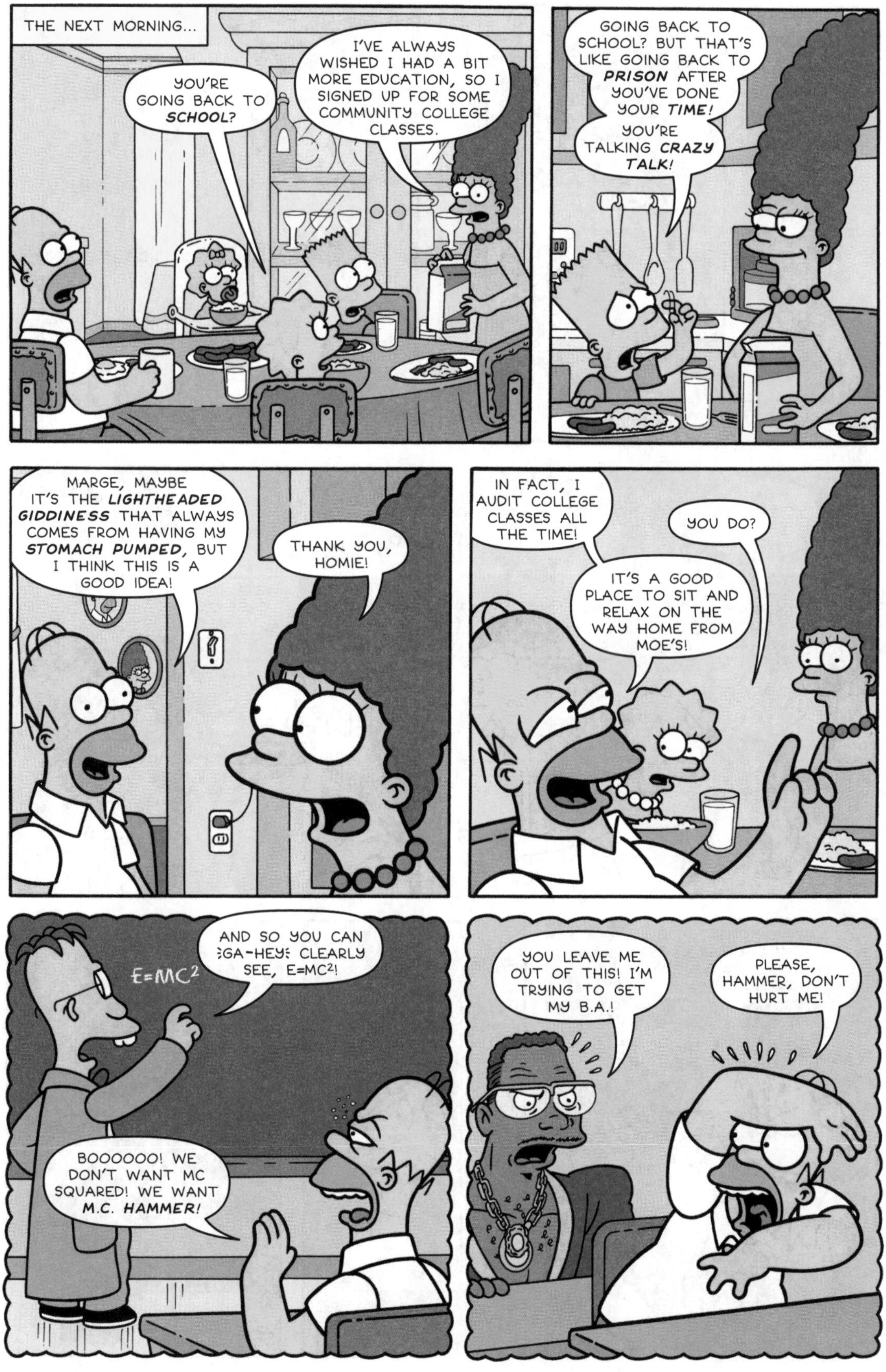
THE NEXT MORNING...
YOU'RE GOING BACK TO **SCHOOL**?
I'VE ALWAYS WISHED I HAD A BIT MORE EDUCATION, SO I SIGNED UP FOR SOME COMMUNITY COLLEGE CLASSES.
GOING BACK TO SCHOOL? BUT THAT'S LIKE GOING BACK TO **PRISON** AFTER YOU'VE DONE YOUR **TIME!**
YOU'RE TALKING **CRAZY TALK!**
MARGE, MAYBE IT'S THE **LIGHTHEADED GIDDINESS** THAT ALWAYS COMES FROM HAVING MY **STOMACH PUMPED,** BUT I THINK THIS IS A GOOD IDEA!
THANK YOU, HOMIE!
IN FACT, I AUDIT COLLEGE CLASSES ALL THE TIME!
YOU DO?
IT'S A GOOD PLACE TO SIT AND RELAX ON THE WAY HOME FROM MOE'S!
E=MC²
AND SO YOU CAN :GA-HEY: CLEARLY SEE, E=MC²!
BOOOOOOO! WE DON'T WANT MC SQUARED! WE WANT **M.C. HAMMER!**
YOU LEAVE ME OUT OF THIS! I'M TRYING TO GET MY B.A.!
PLEASE, HAMMER, DON'T HURT ME!

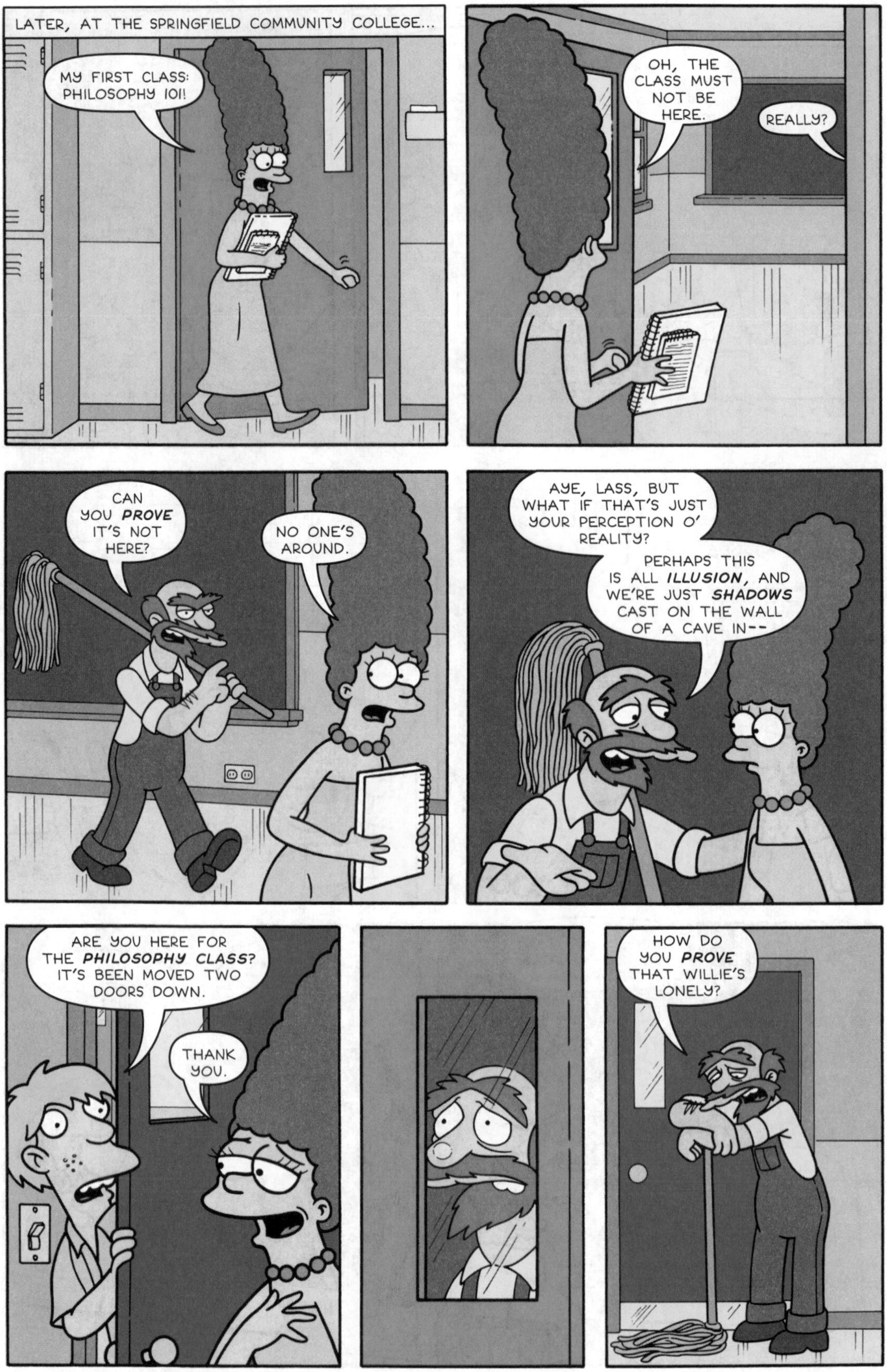
LATER, AT THE SPRINGFIELD COMMUNITY COLLEGE...
MY FIRST CLASS: PHILOSOPHY 101!
OH, THE CLASS MUST NOT BE HERE.
REALLY?
CAN YOU PROVE IT'S NOT HERE?
NO ONE'S AROUND.
AYE, LASS, BUT WHAT IF THAT'S JUST YOUR PERCEPTION O' REALITY?
PERHAPS THIS IS ALL ILLUSION, AND WE'RE JUST SHADOWS CAST ON THE WALL OF A CAVE IN--
ARE YOU HERE FOR THE PHILOSOPHY CLASS? IT'S BEEN MOVED TWO DOORS DOWN.
THANK YOU.
HOW DO YOU PROVE THAT WILLIE'S LONELY?

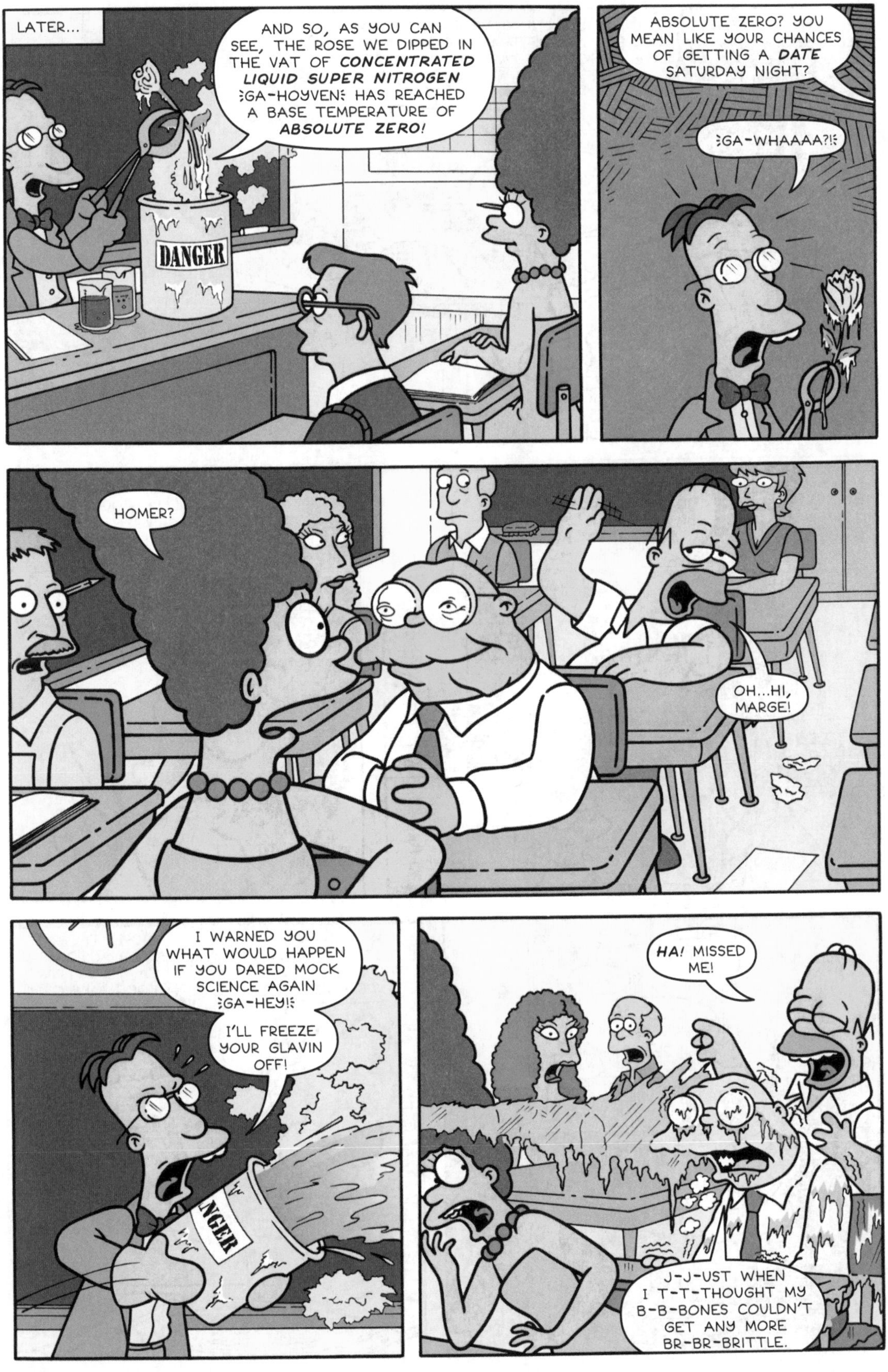
LATER...
AND SO, AS YOU CAN SEE, THE ROSE WE DIPPED IN THE VAT OF **CONCENTRATED LIQUID SUPER NITROGEN** ⁝GA-HOYVEN⁝ HAS REACHED A BASE TEMPERATURE OF ***ABSOLUTE ZERO!***
DANGER
ABSOLUTE ZERO? YOU MEAN LIKE YOUR CHANCES OF GETTING A ***DATE*** SATURDAY NIGHT?
⁝GA-WHAAAA?!⁝
HOMER?
OH...HI, MARGE!
I WARNED YOU WHAT WOULD HAPPEN IF YOU DARED MOCK SCIENCE AGAIN ⁝GA-HEY!⁝
I'LL FREEZE YOUR GLAVIN OFF!
NGER
HA! MISSED ME!
J-J-UST WHEN I T-T-THOUGHT MY B-B-BONES COULDN'T GET ANY MORE BR-BR-BRITTLE.

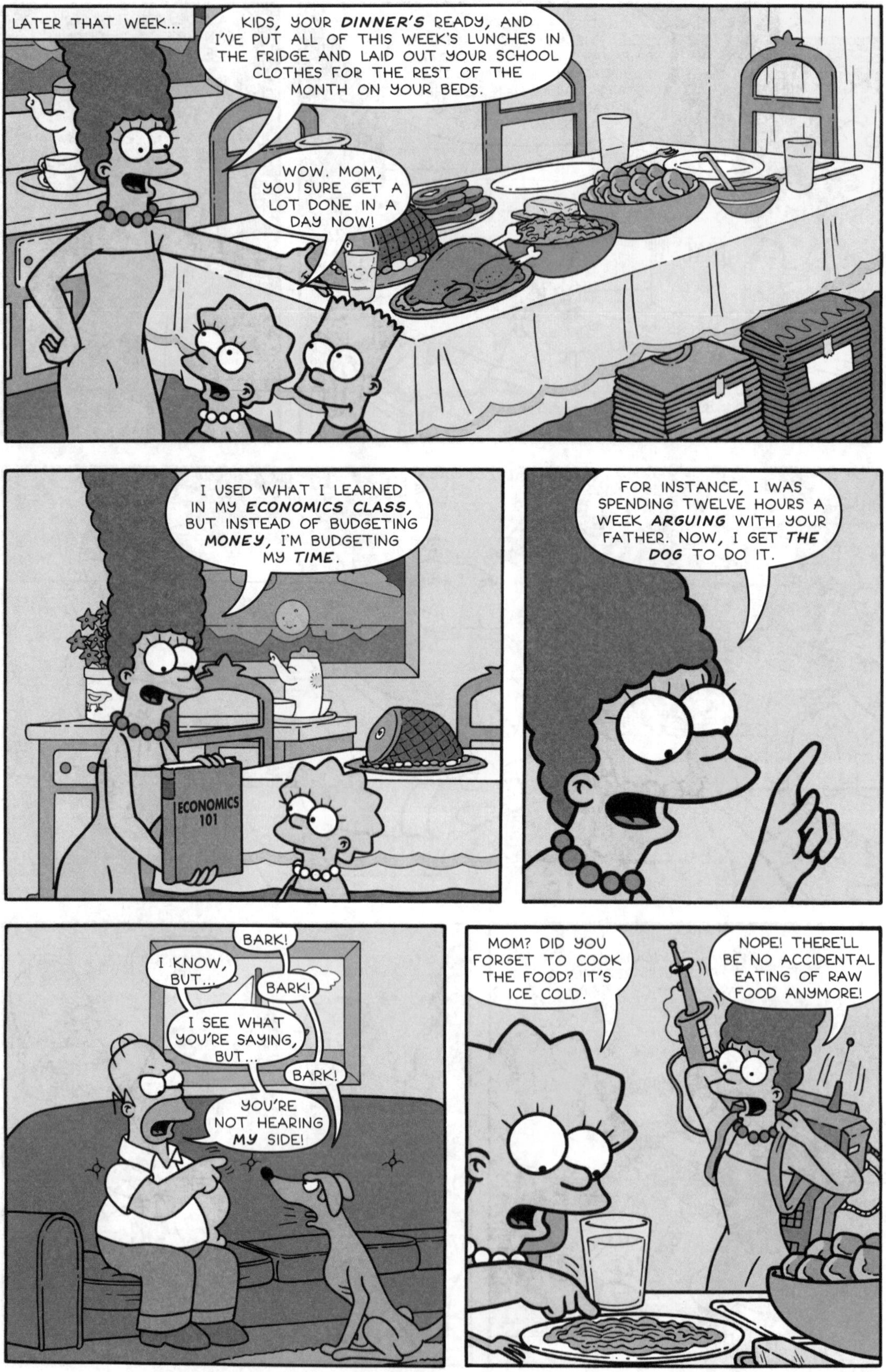

LATER THAT WEEK...
KIDS, YOUR DINNER'S READY, AND I'VE PUT ALL OF THIS WEEK'S LUNCHES IN THE FRIDGE AND LAID OUT YOUR SCHOOL CLOTHES FOR THE REST OF THE MONTH ON YOUR BEDS.
WOW. MOM, YOU SURE GET A LOT DONE IN A DAY NOW!
I USED WHAT I LEARNED IN MY ECONOMICS CLASS, BUT INSTEAD OF BUDGETING MONEY, I'M BUDGETING MY TIME.
ECONOMICS 101
FOR INSTANCE, I WAS SPENDING TWELVE HOURS A WEEK ARGUING WITH YOUR FATHER. NOW, I GET THE DOG TO DO IT.
BARK!
I KNOW, BUT...
BARK!
I SEE WHAT YOU'RE SAYING, BUT...
BARK!
YOU'RE NOT HEARING MY SIDE!
MOM? DID YOU FORGET TO COOK THE FOOD? IT'S ICE COLD.
NOPE! THERE'LL BE NO ACCIDENTAL EATING OF RAW FOOD ANYMORE!

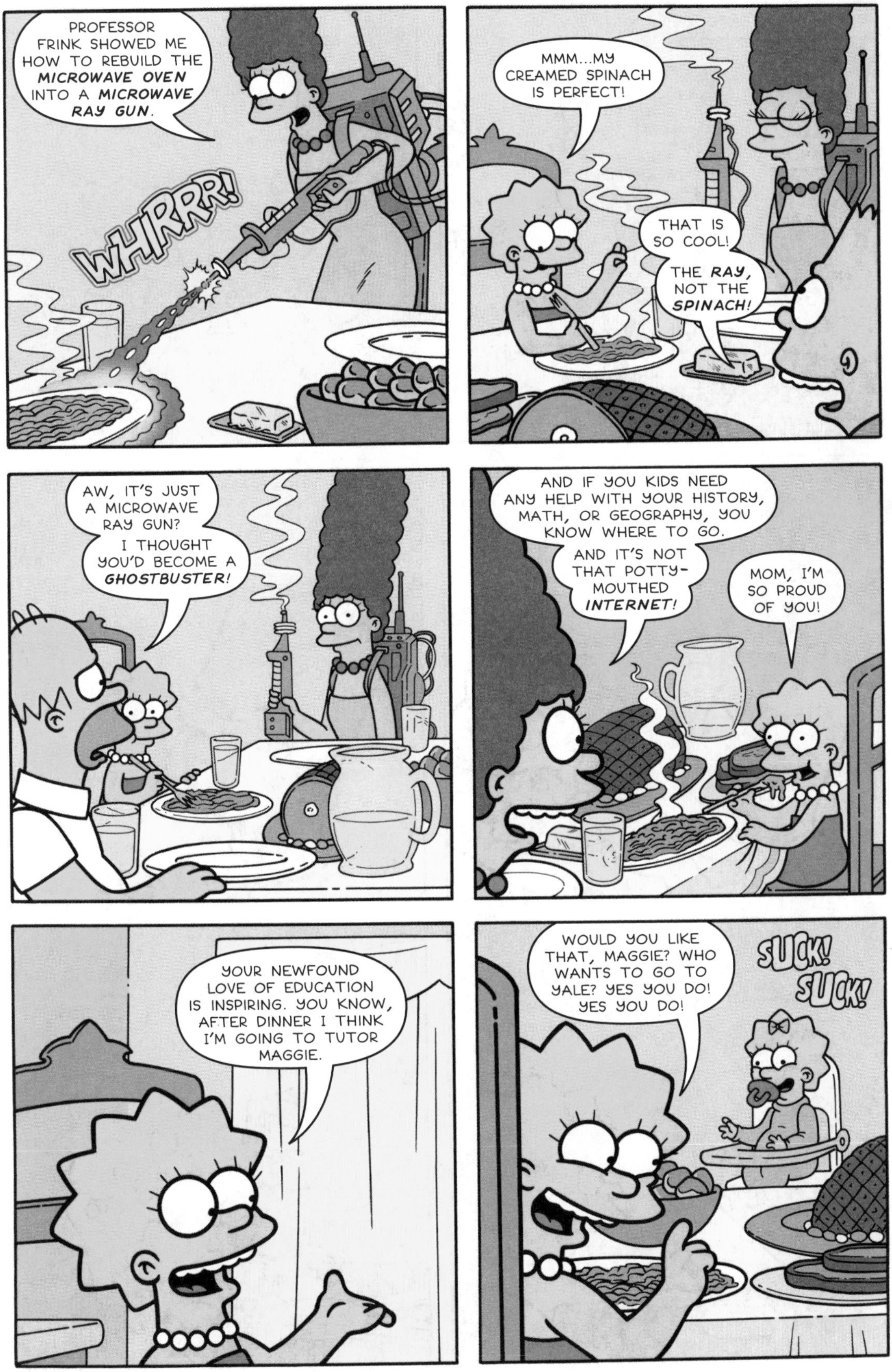
PROFESSOR FRINK SHOWED ME HOW TO REBUILD THE **MICROWAVE OVEN** INTO A **MICROWAVE RAY GUN**.
WHRRR!
MMM...MY CREAMED SPINACH IS PERFECT!
THAT IS SO COOL!
THE **RAY**, NOT THE **SPINACH**!
AW, IT'S JUST A MICROWAVE RAY GUN?
I THOUGHT YOU'D BECOME A **GHOSTBUSTER**!
AND IF YOU KIDS NEED ANY HELP WITH YOUR HISTORY, MATH, OR GEOGRAPHY, YOU KNOW WHERE TO GO.
AND IT'S NOT THAT POTTY-MOUTHED **INTERNET**!
MOM, I'M SO PROUD OF YOU!
YOUR NEWFOUND LOVE OF EDUCATION IS INSPIRING. YOU KNOW, AFTER DINNER I THINK I'M GOING TO TUTOR MAGGIE.
WOULD YOU LIKE THAT, MAGGIE? WHO WANTS TO GO TO YALE? YES YOU DO! YES YOU DO!
SUCK! SUCK!

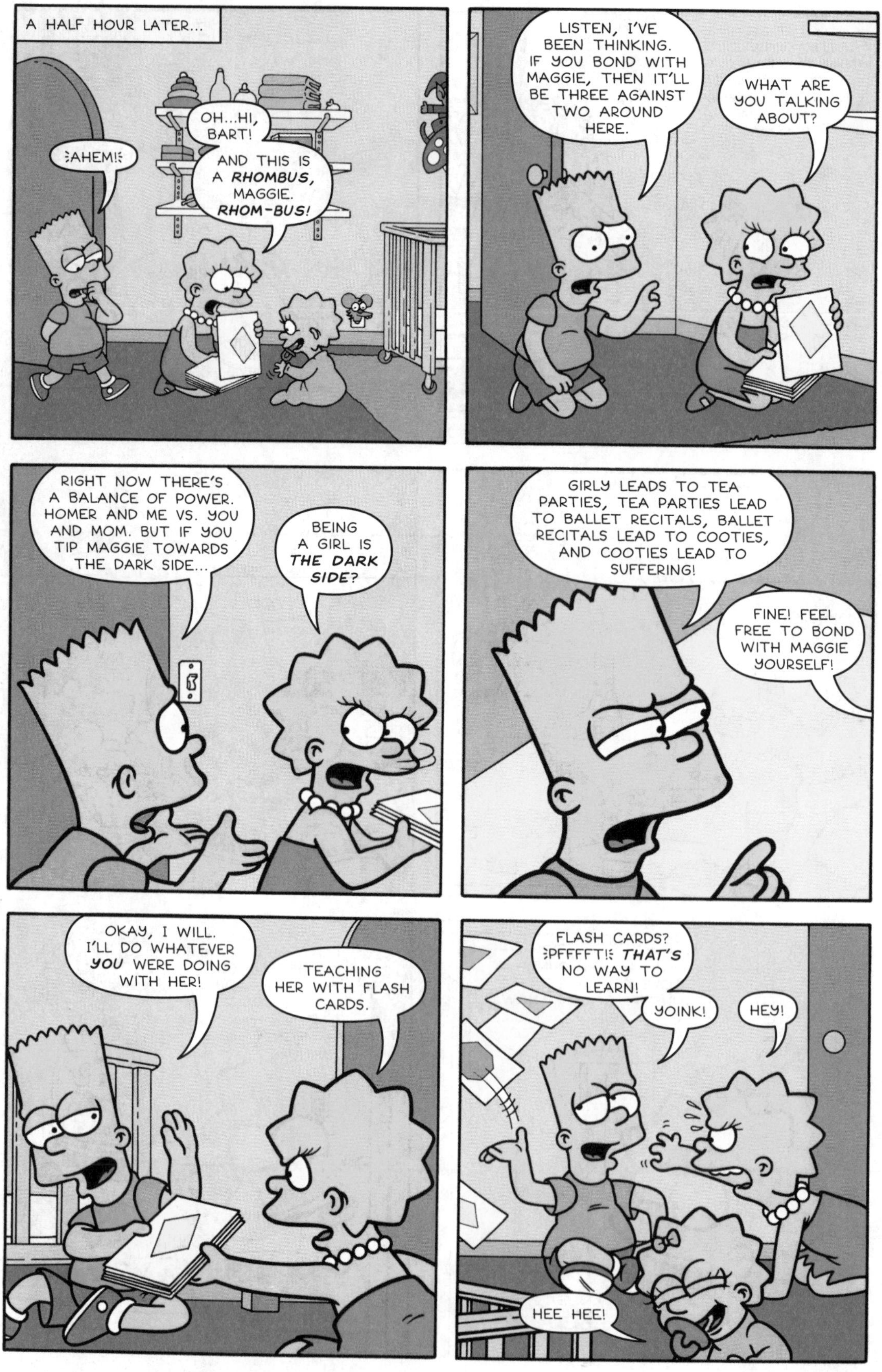

A HALF HOUR LATER...
AHEM!
OH...HI, BART!
AND THIS IS A RHOMBUS, MAGGIE. RHOM-BUS!
LISTEN, I'VE BEEN THINKING. IF YOU BOND WITH MAGGIE, THEN IT'LL BE THREE AGAINST TWO AROUND HERE.
WHAT ARE YOU TALKING ABOUT?
RIGHT NOW THERE'S A BALANCE OF POWER. HOMER AND ME VS. YOU AND MOM. BUT IF YOU TIP MAGGIE TOWARDS THE DARK SIDE...
BEING A GIRL IS THE DARK SIDE?
GIRLY LEADS TO TEA PARTIES, TEA PARTIES LEAD TO BALLET RECITALS, BALLET RECITALS LEAD TO COOTIES, AND COOTIES LEAD TO SUFFERING!
FINE! FEEL FREE TO BOND WITH MAGGIE YOURSELF!
OKAY, I WILL. I'LL DO WHATEVER YOU WERE DOING WITH HER!
TEACHING HER WITH FLASH CARDS.
FLASH CARDS? PFFFFT! THAT'S NO WAY TO LEARN!
YOINK!
HEY!
HEE HEE!

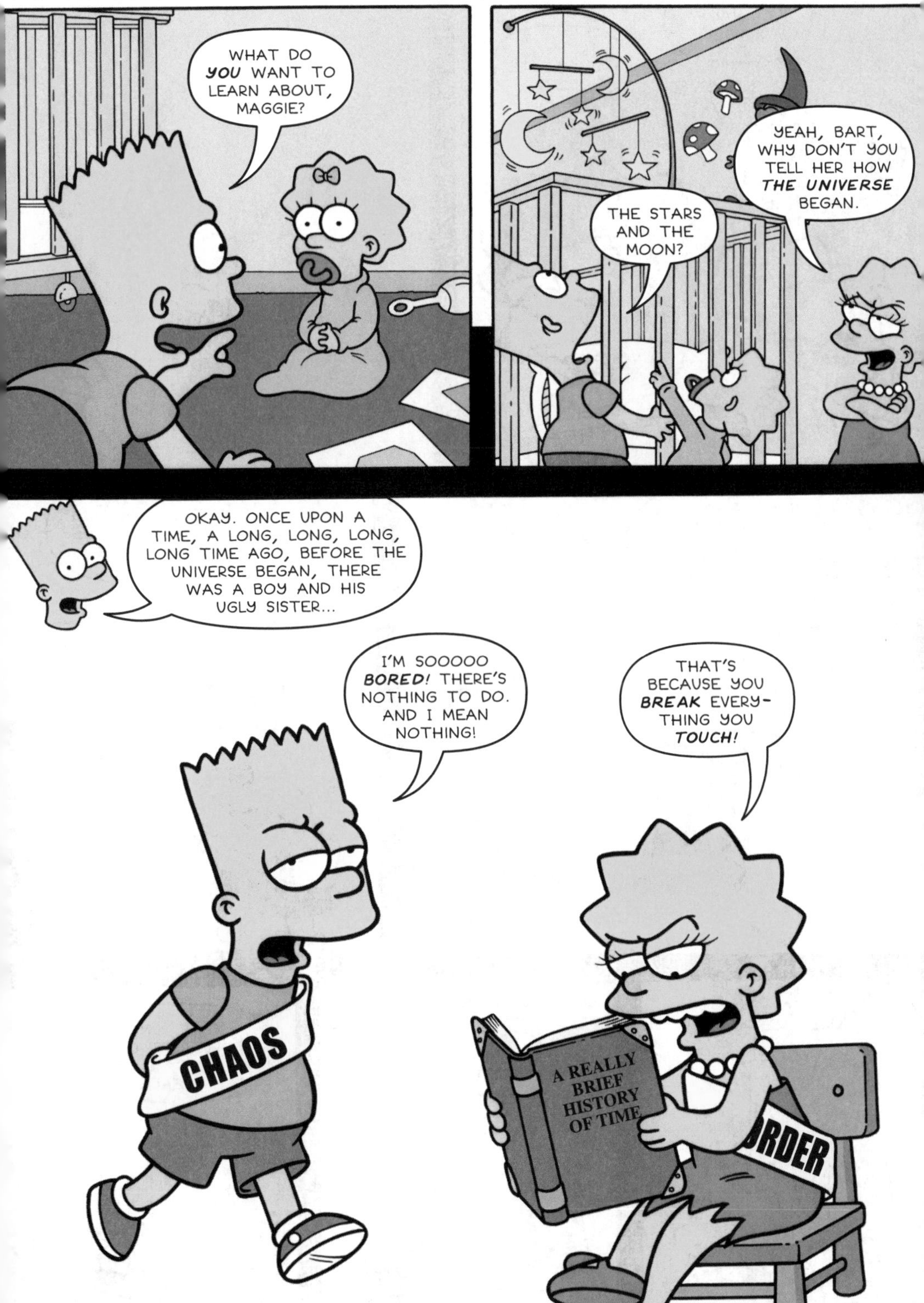
WHAT DO *YOU* WANT TO LEARN ABOUT, MAGGIE?
THE STARS AND THE MOON?
YEAH, BART, WHY DON'T YOU TELL HER HOW *THE UNIVERSE* BEGAN.
OKAY. ONCE UPON A TIME, A LONG, LONG, LONG, LONG TIME AGO, BEFORE THE UNIVERSE BEGAN, THERE WAS A BOY AND HIS UGLY SISTER...
I'M SOOOOO *BORED!* THERE'S NOTHING TO DO. AND I MEAN NOTHING!
THAT'S BECAUSE YOU *BREAK* EVERY-THING YOU *TOUCH!*
CHAOS
A REALLY BRIEF HISTORY OF TIME
ORDER

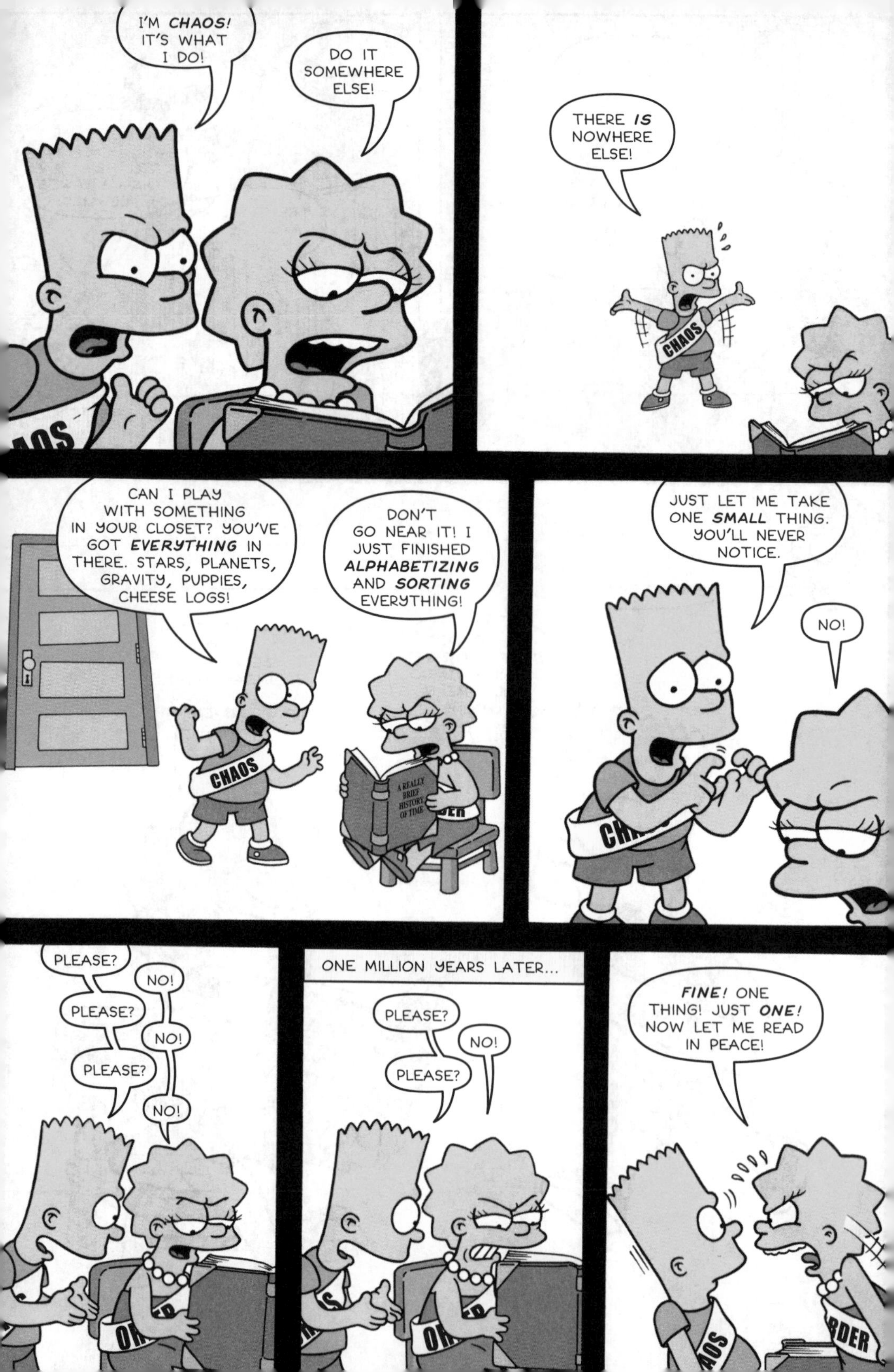
I'M CHAOS! IT'S WHAT I DO!
DO IT SOMEWHERE ELSE!
THERE IS NOWHERE ELSE!
CHAOS
CAN I PLAY WITH SOMETHING IN YOUR CLOSET? YOU'VE GOT EVERYTHING IN THERE. STARS, PLANETS, GRAVITY, PUPPIES, CHEESE LOGS!
DON'T GO NEAR IT! I JUST FINISHED ALPHABETIZING AND SORTING EVERYTHING!
CHAOS
A REALLY BRIEF HISTORY OF TIME
JUST LET ME TAKE ONE SMALL THING. YOU'LL NEVER NOTICE.
NO!
PLEASE?
NO!
PLEASE?
NO!
PLEASE?
NO!
ONE MILLION YEARS LATER...
PLEASE?
NO!
PLEASE?
FINE! ONE THING! JUST ONE! NOW LET ME READ IN PEACE!

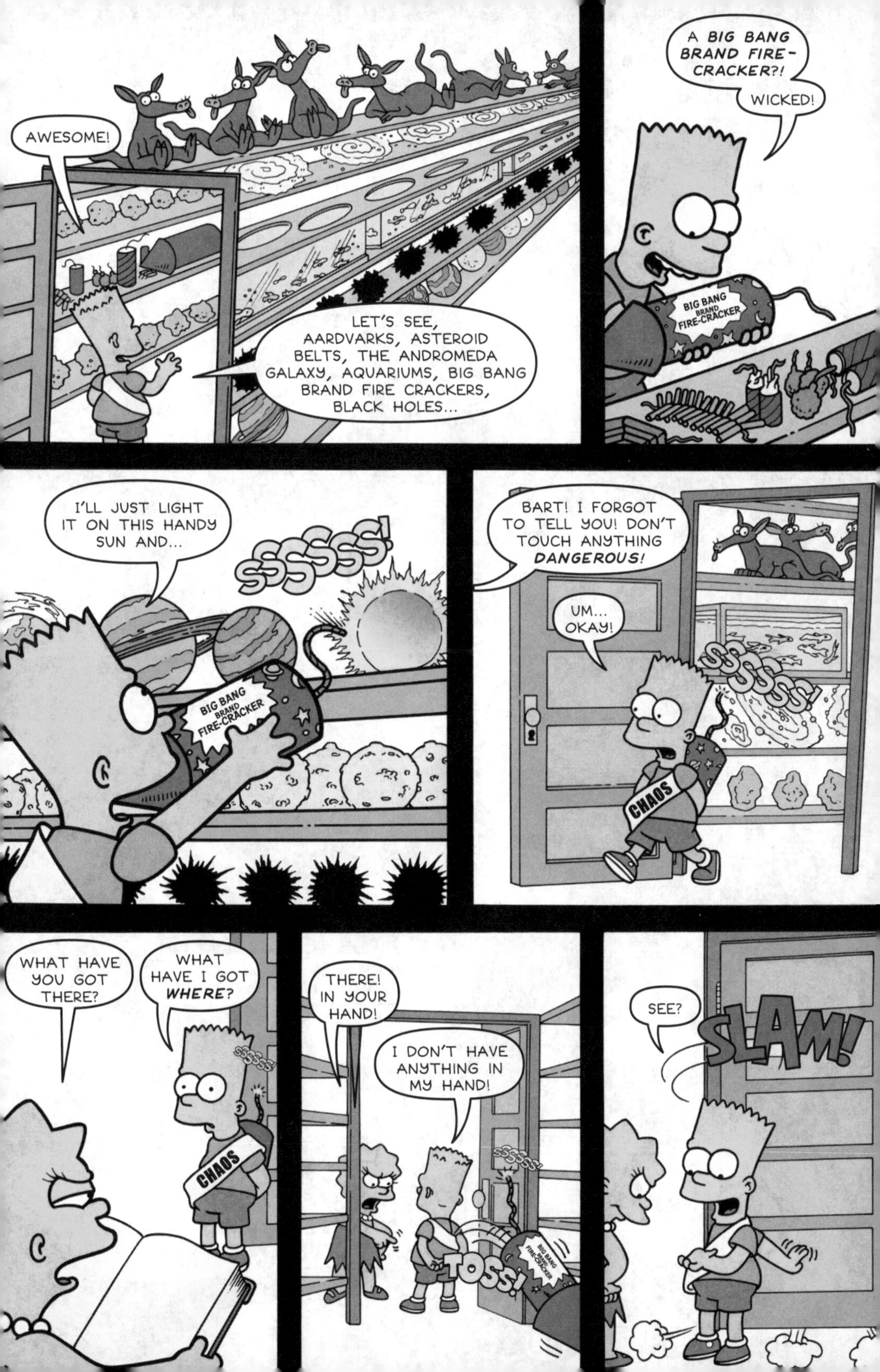

AWESOME!
LET'S SEE, AARDVARKS, ASTEROID BELTS, THE ANDROMEDA GALAXY, AQUARIUMS, BIG BANG BRAND FIRE CRACKERS, BLACK HOLES...
A BIG BANG BRAND FIRE-CRACKER?!
WICKED!
BIG BANG BRAND FIRE-CRACKER
I'LL JUST LIGHT IT ON THIS HANDY SUN AND...
SSSSSS!
BIG BANG BRAND FIRE-CRACKER
BART! I FORGOT TO TELL YOU! DON'T TOUCH ANYTHING DANGEROUS!
UM... OKAY!
SSSSSS!
CHAOS
WHAT HAVE YOU GOT THERE?
WHAT HAVE I GOT WHERE?
CHAOS
THERE! IN YOUR HAND!
I DON'T HAVE ANYTHING IN MY HAND!
TOSS!
BIG BANG BRAND FIRE-CRACKER
SEE?
SLAM!

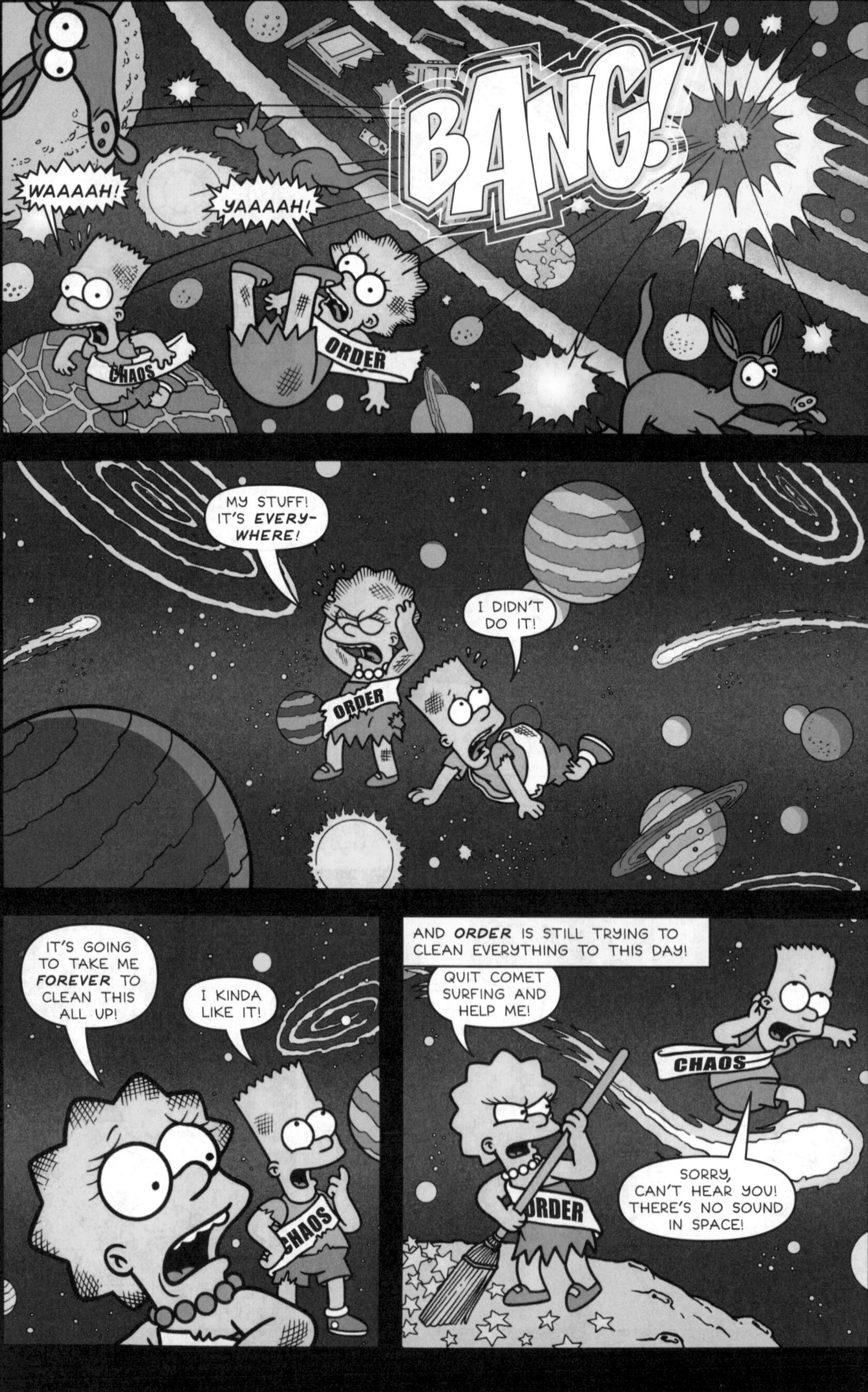
WAAAAH!
YAAAAH!
BANG!
CHAOS
ORDER
MY STUFF! IT'S *EVERY-WHERE*!
I DIDN'T DO IT!
ORDER
IT'S GOING TO TAKE ME *FOREVER* TO CLEAN THIS ALL UP!
I KINDA LIKE IT!
CHAOS
AND *ORDER* IS STILL TRYING TO CLEAN EVERYTHING TO THIS DAY!
QUIT COMET SURFING AND HELP ME!
CHAOS
SORRY, CAN'T HEAR YOU! THERE'S NO SOUND IN SPACE!
ORDER

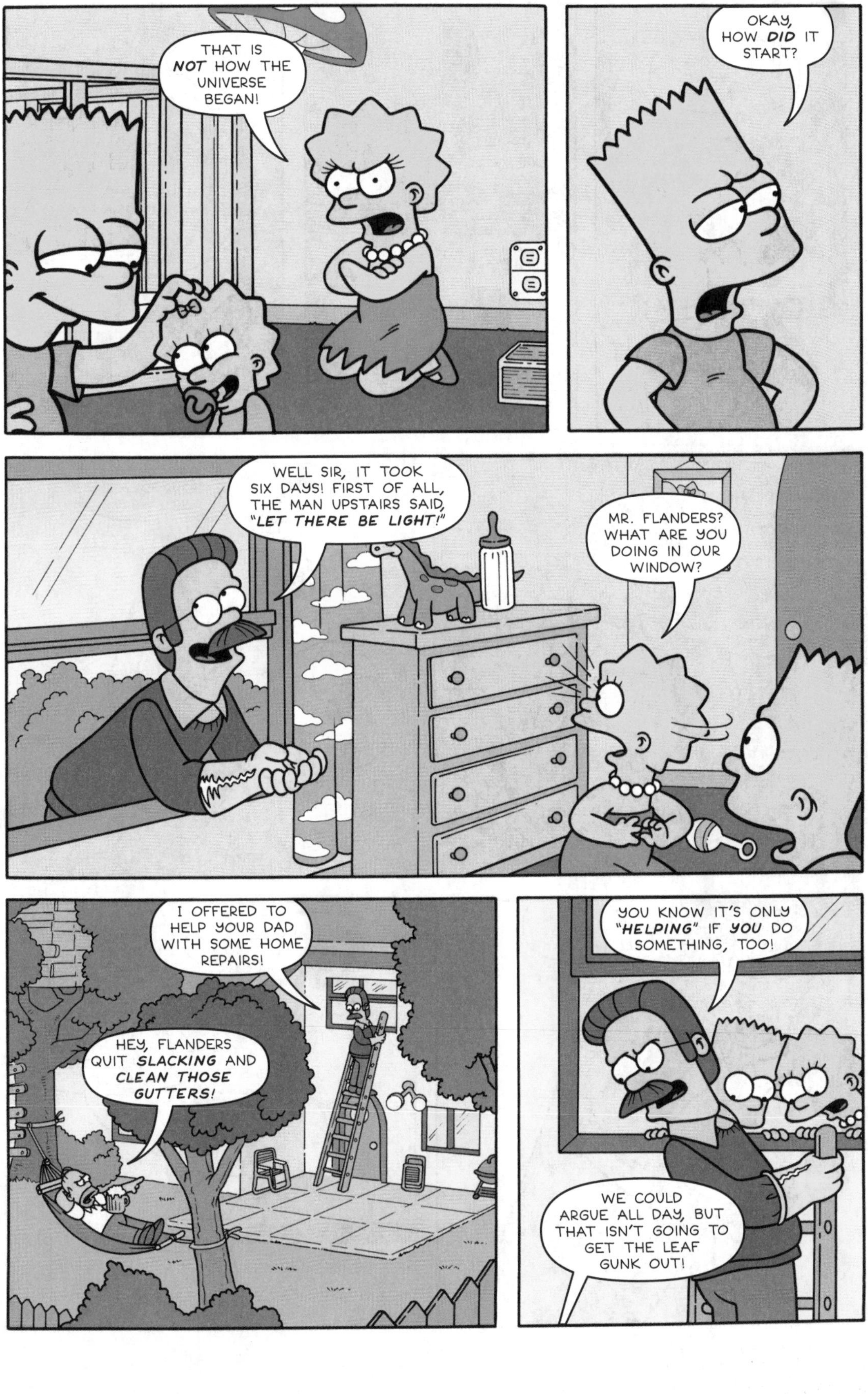
THAT IS *NOT* HOW THE UNIVERSE BEGAN!
OKAY, HOW *DID* IT START?
WELL SIR, IT TOOK SIX DAYS! FIRST OF ALL, THE MAN UPSTAIRS SAID, "*LET THERE BE LIGHT!*"
MR. FLANDERS? WHAT ARE YOU DOING IN OUR WINDOW?
I OFFERED TO HELP YOUR DAD WITH SOME HOME REPAIRS!
HEY, FLANDERS QUIT *SLACKING* AND *CLEAN THOSE GUTTERS!*
YOU KNOW IT'S ONLY "*HELPING*" IF *YOU* DO SOMETHING, TOO!
WE COULD ARGUE ALL DAY, BUT THAT ISN'T GOING TO GET THE LEAF GUNK OUT!

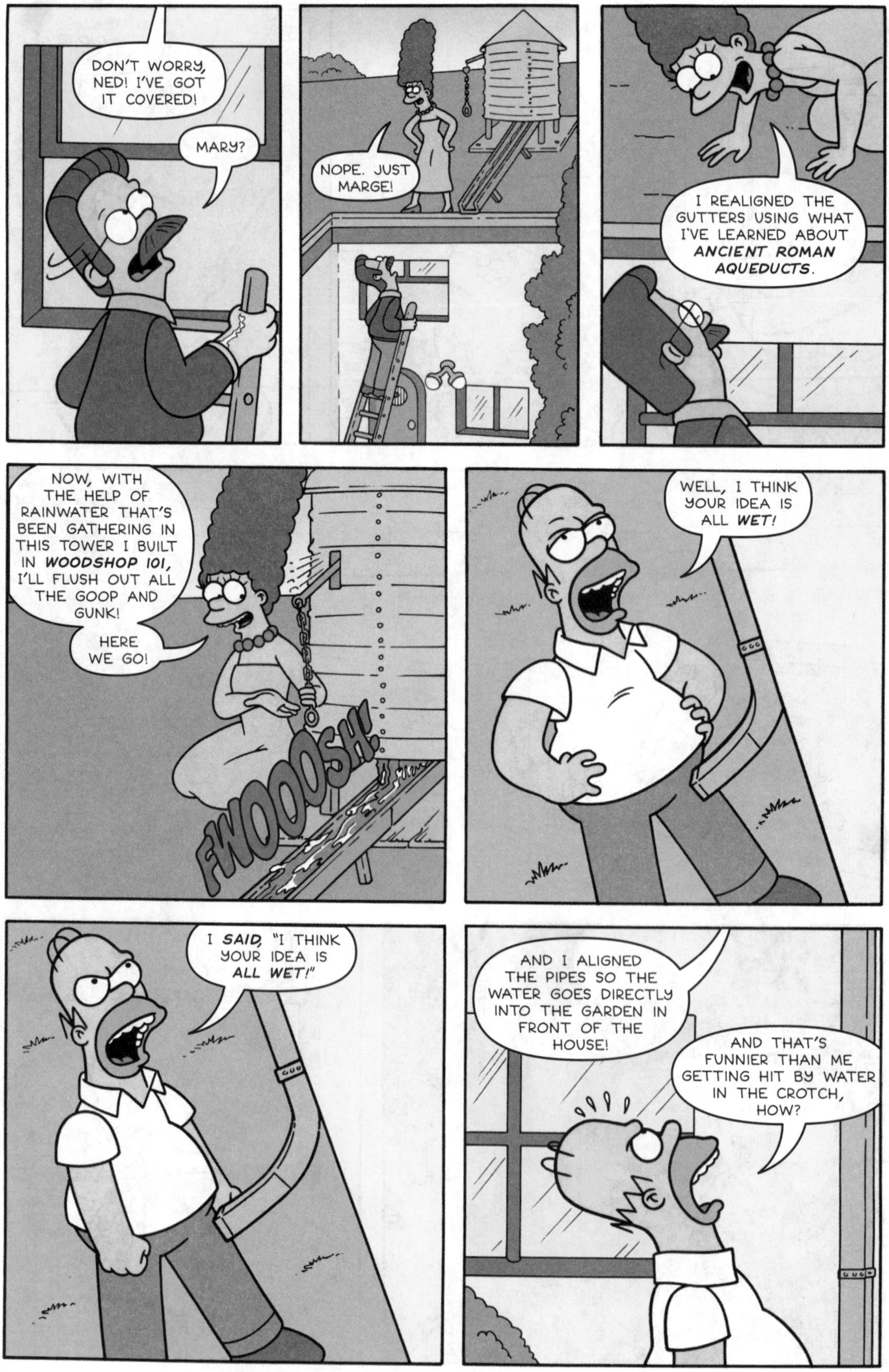
DON'T WORRY, NED! I'VE GOT IT COVERED!
MARY?
NOPE. JUST MARGE!
I REALIGNED THE GUTTERS USING WHAT I'VE LEARNED ABOUT ***ANCIENT ROMAN AQUEDUCTS***.
NOW, WITH THE HELP OF RAINWATER THAT'S BEEN GATHERING IN THIS TOWER I BUILT IN ***WOODSHOP 101,*** I'LL FLUSH OUT ALL THE GOOP AND GUNK!
HERE WE GO!
FWOOOSH!
WELL, I THINK YOUR IDEA IS ALL ***WET***!
I ***SAID,*** "I THINK YOUR IDEA IS ***ALL WET!***"
AND I ALIGNED THE PIPES SO THE WATER GOES DIRECTLY INTO THE GARDEN IN FRONT OF THE HOUSE!
AND THAT'S FUNNIER THAN ME GETTING HIT BY WATER IN THE CROTCH, HOW?

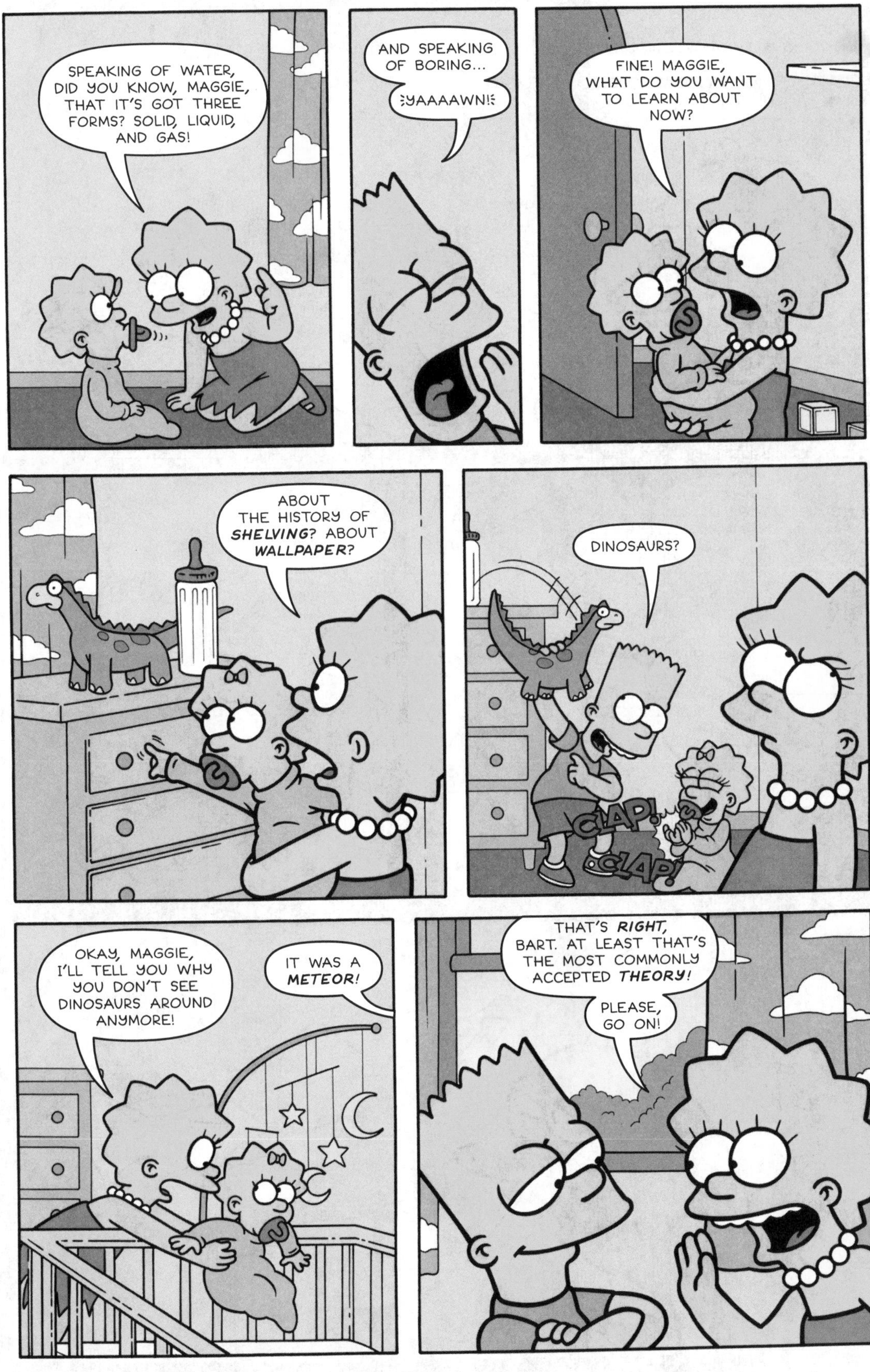
SPEAKING OF WATER, DID YOU KNOW, MAGGIE, THAT IT'S GOT THREE FORMS? SOLID, LIQUID, AND GAS!
AND SPEAKING OF BORING...
YAAAAWN!
FINE! MAGGIE, WHAT DO YOU WANT TO LEARN ABOUT NOW?
ABOUT THE HISTORY OF *SHELVING*? ABOUT *WALLPAPER*?
DINOSAURS?
CLAP!
CLAP!
OKAY, MAGGIE, I'LL TELL YOU WHY YOU DON'T SEE DINOSAURS AROUND ANYMORE!
IT WAS A *METEOR*!
THAT'S *RIGHT*, BART. AT LEAST THAT'S THE MOST COMMONLY ACCEPTED *THEORY*!
PLEASE, GO ON!

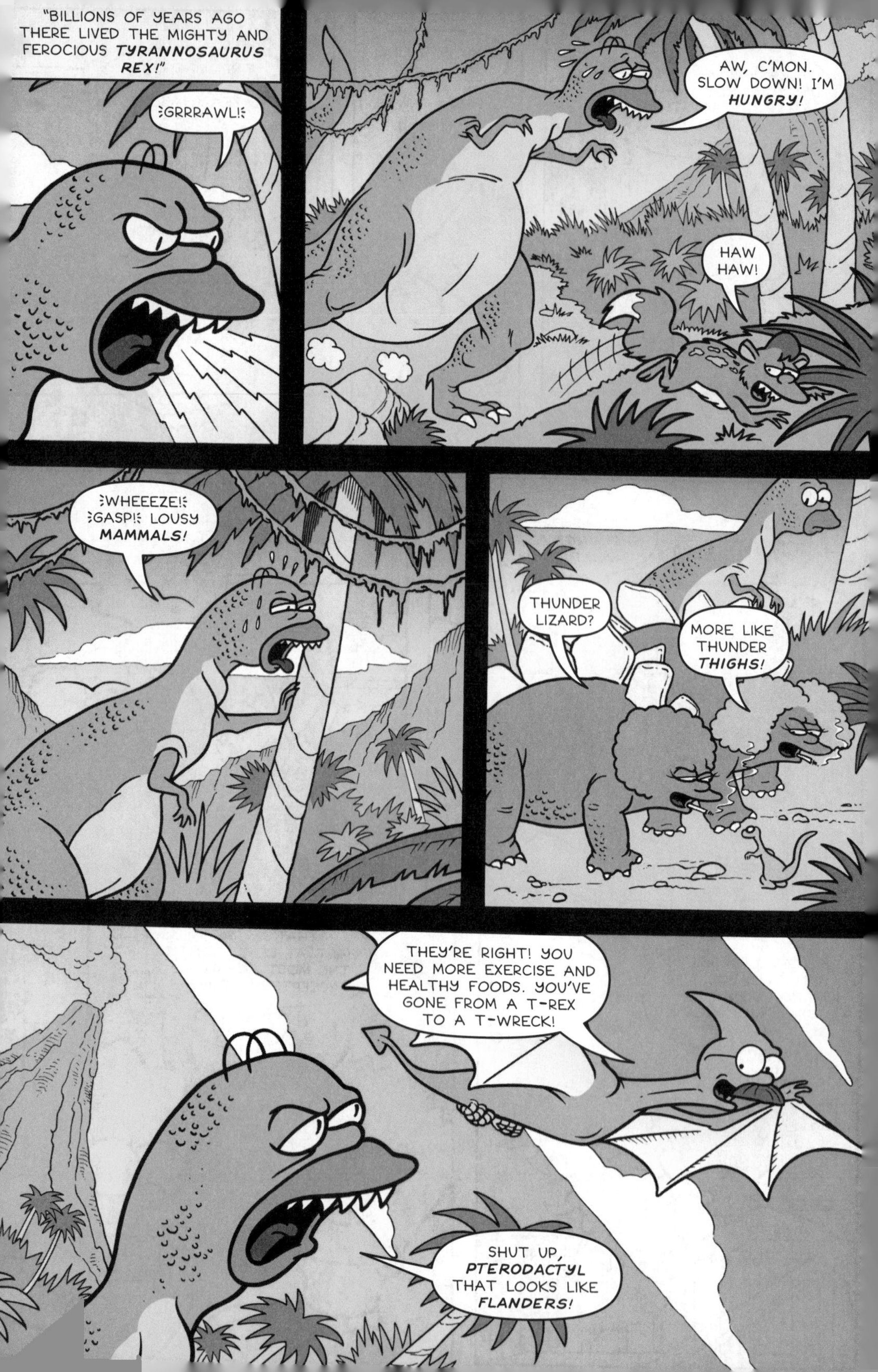
"BILLIONS OF YEARS AGO THERE LIVED THE MIGHTY AND FEROCIOUS TYRANNOSAURUS REX!"
GRRRAWL!
AW, C'MON. SLOW DOWN! I'M HUNGRY!
HAW HAW!
WHEEEZE! GASP! LOUSY MAMMALS!
THUNDER LIZARD?
MORE LIKE THUNDER THIGHS!
THEY'RE RIGHT! YOU NEED MORE EXERCISE AND HEALTHY FOODS. YOU'VE GONE FROM A T-REX TO A T-WRECK!
SHUT UP, PTERODACTYL THAT LOOKS LIKE FLANDERS!

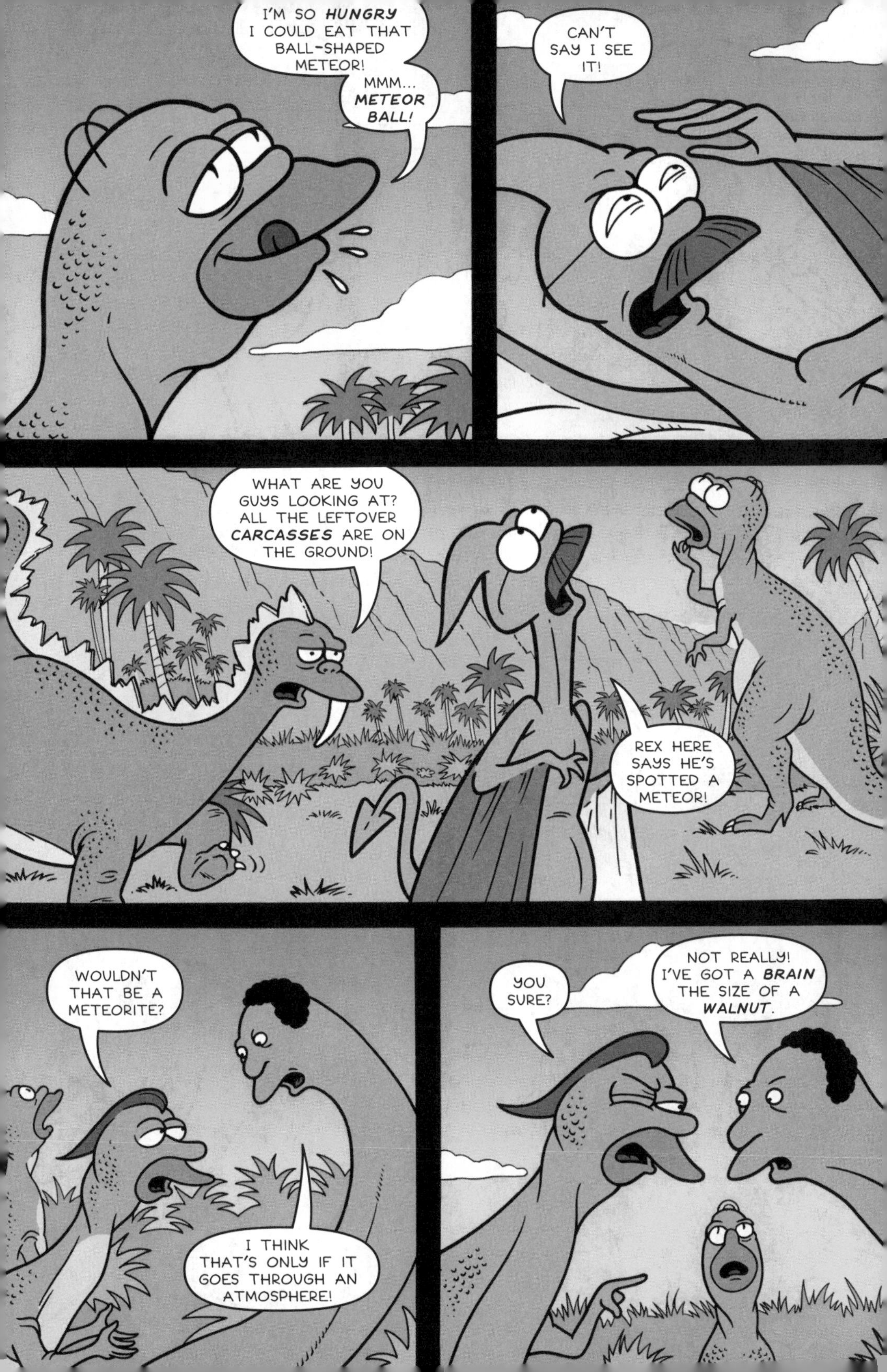
I'M SO **HUNGRY** I COULD EAT THAT BALL-SHAPED METEOR!
MMM... **METEOR BALL!**
CAN'T SAY I SEE IT!
WHAT ARE YOU GUYS LOOKING AT? ALL THE LEFTOVER **CARCASSES** ARE ON THE GROUND!
REX HERE SAYS HE'S SPOTTED A METEOR!
WOULDN'T THAT BE A METEORITE?
I THINK THAT'S ONLY IF IT GOES THROUGH AN ATMOSPHERE!
YOU SURE?
NOT REALLY! I'VE GOT A **BRAIN** THE SIZE OF A **WALNUT**.

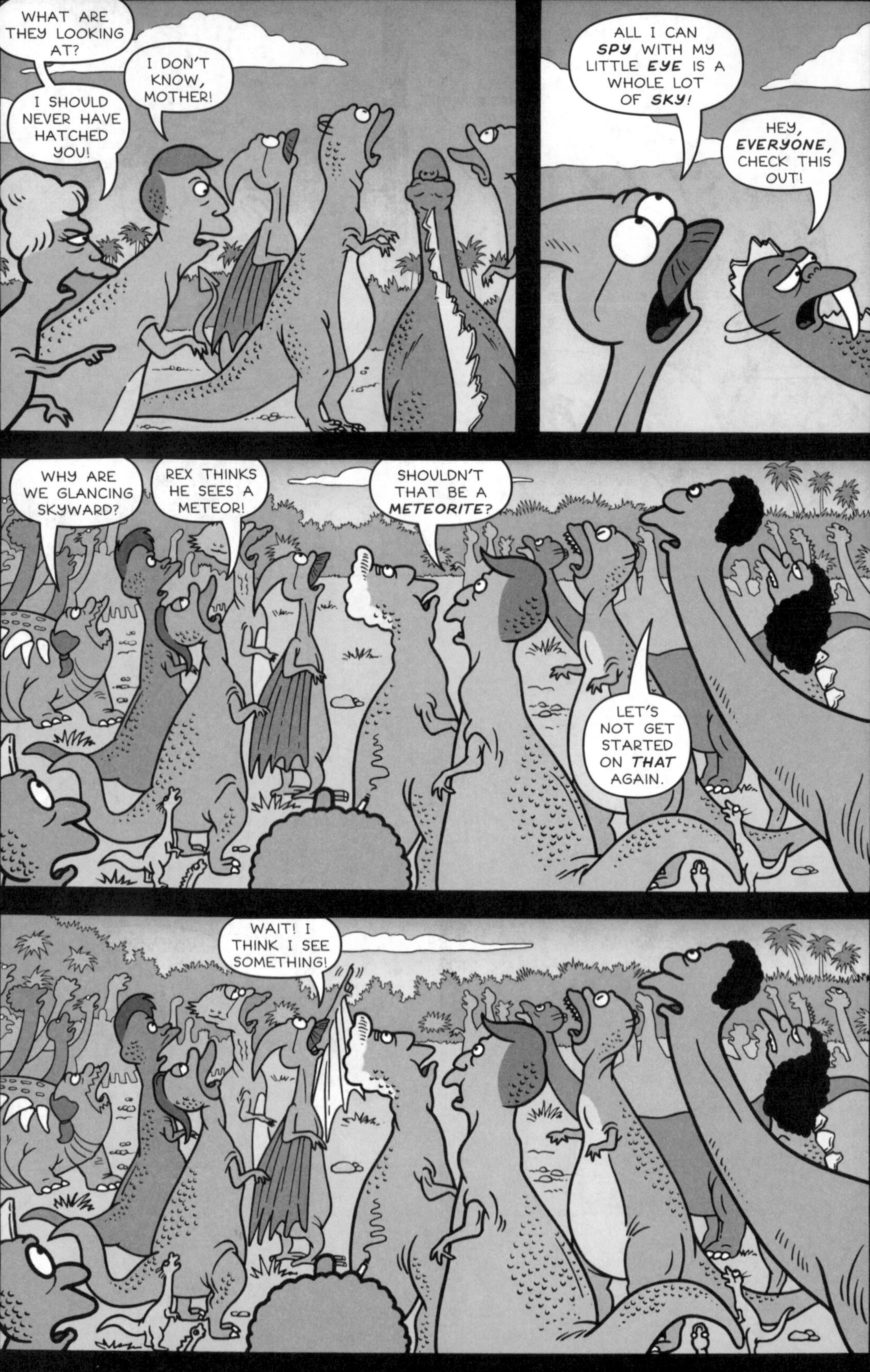
WHAT ARE THEY LOOKING AT?
I SHOULD NEVER HAVE HATCHED YOU!
I DON'T KNOW, MOTHER!
ALL I CAN SPY WITH MY LITTLE EYE IS A WHOLE LOT OF SKY!
HEY, EVERYONE, CHECK THIS OUT!
WHY ARE WE GLANCING SKYWARD?
REX THINKS HE SEES A METEOR!
SHOULDN'T THAT BE A METEORITE?
LET'S NOT GET STARTED ON THAT AGAIN.
WAIT! I THINK I SEE SOMETHING!

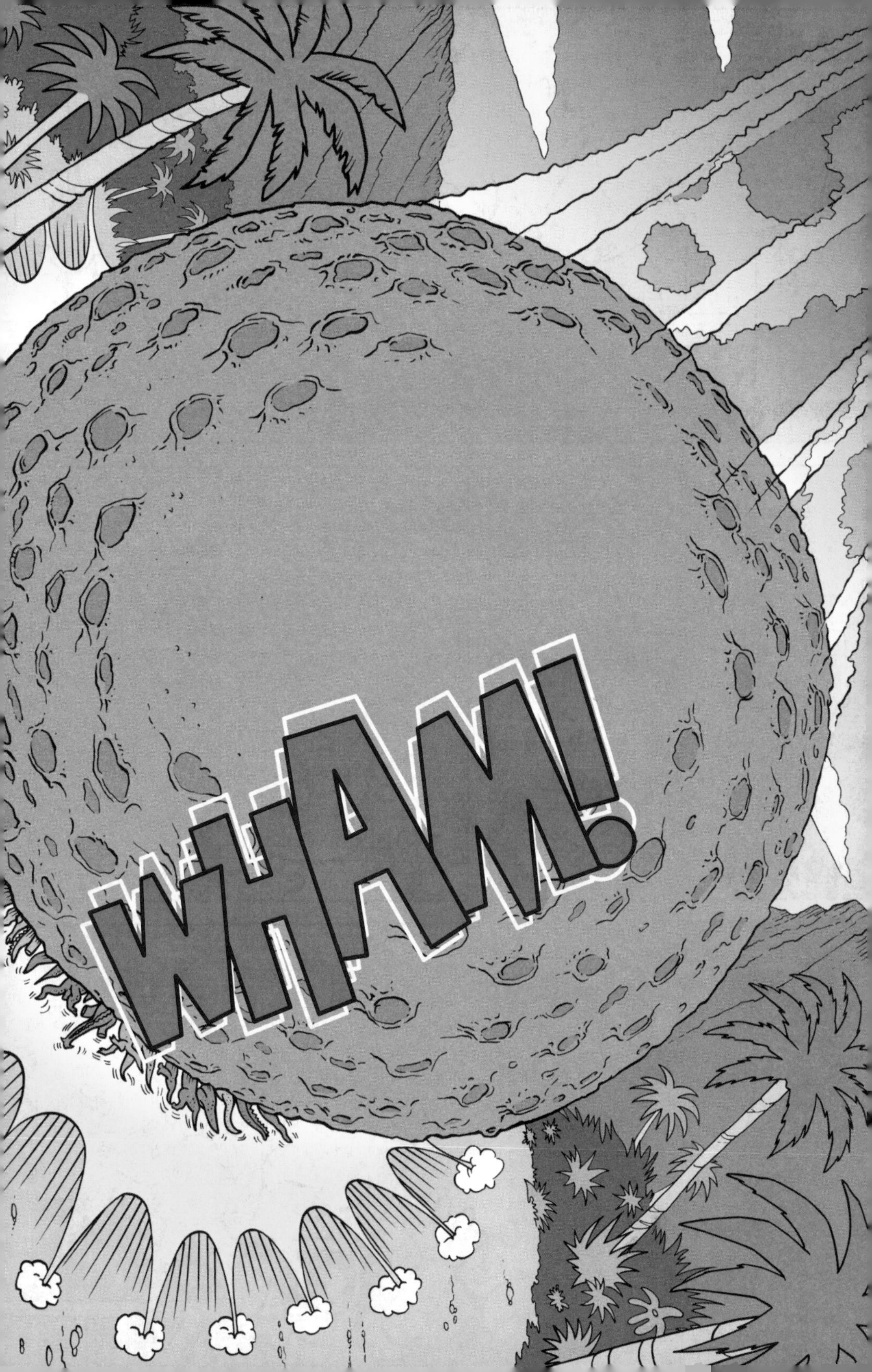
WHAM!

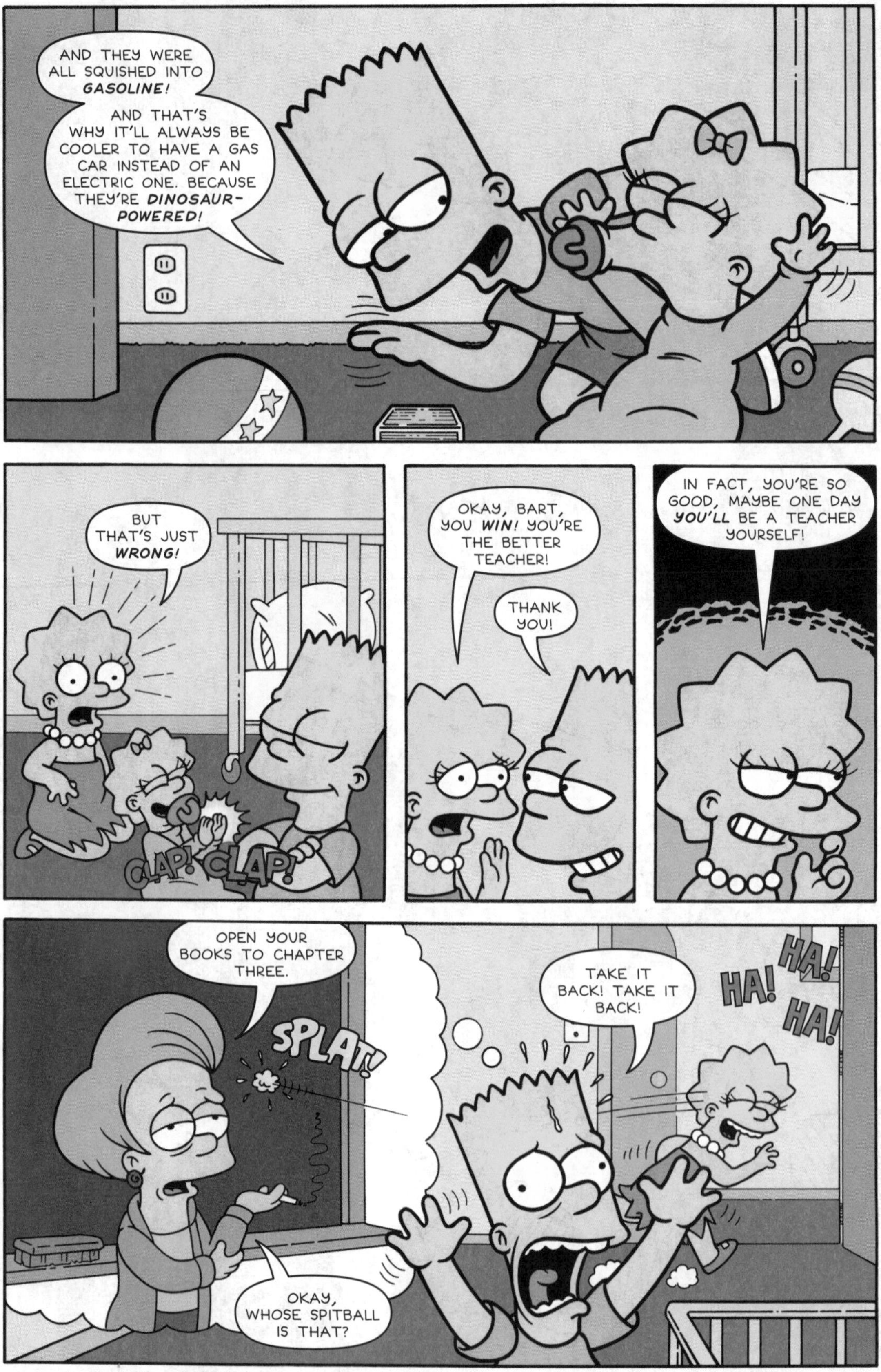
AND THEY WERE ALL SQUISHED INTO GASOLINE!
AND THAT'S WHY IT'LL ALWAYS BE COOLER TO HAVE A GAS CAR INSTEAD OF AN ELECTRIC ONE. BECAUSE THEY'RE DINOSAUR-POWERED!
BUT THAT'S JUST WRONG!
CLAP! CLAP!
OKAY, BART, YOU WIN! YOU'RE THE BETTER TEACHER!
THANK YOU!
IN FACT, YOU'RE SO GOOD, MAYBE ONE DAY YOU'LL BE A TEACHER YOURSELF!
OPEN YOUR BOOKS TO CHAPTER THREE.
SPLAT!
OKAY, WHOSE SPITBALL IS THAT?
TAKE IT BACK! TAKE IT BACK!
HA! HA! HA!

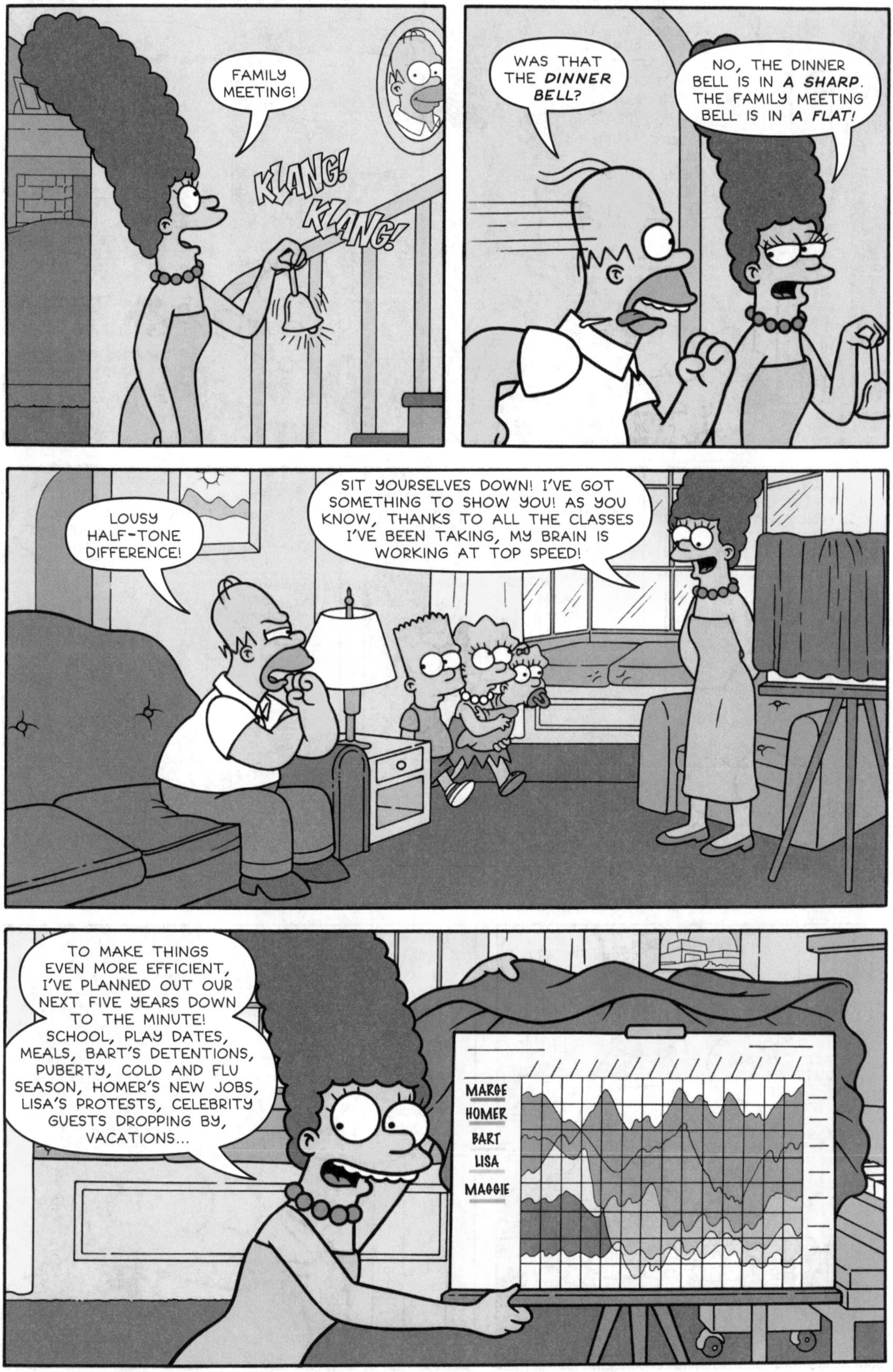
FAMILY MEETING!
KLANG!
KLANG!
WAS THAT THE **DINNER BELL**?
NO, THE DINNER BELL IS IN **A SHARP**. THE FAMILY MEETING BELL IS IN **A FLAT!**
LOUSY HALF-TONE DIFFERENCE!
SIT YOURSELVES DOWN! I'VE GOT SOMETHING TO SHOW YOU! AS YOU KNOW, THANKS TO ALL THE CLASSES I'VE BEEN TAKING, MY BRAIN IS WORKING AT TOP SPEED!
TO MAKE THINGS EVEN MORE EFFICIENT, I'VE PLANNED OUT OUR NEXT FIVE YEARS DOWN TO THE MINUTE! SCHOOL, PLAY DATES, MEALS, BART'S DETENTIONS, PUBERTY, COLD AND FLU SEASON, HOMER'S NEW JOBS, LISA'S PROTESTS, CELEBRITY GUESTS DROPPING BY, VACATIONS...
MARGE
HOMER
BART
LISA
MAGGIE

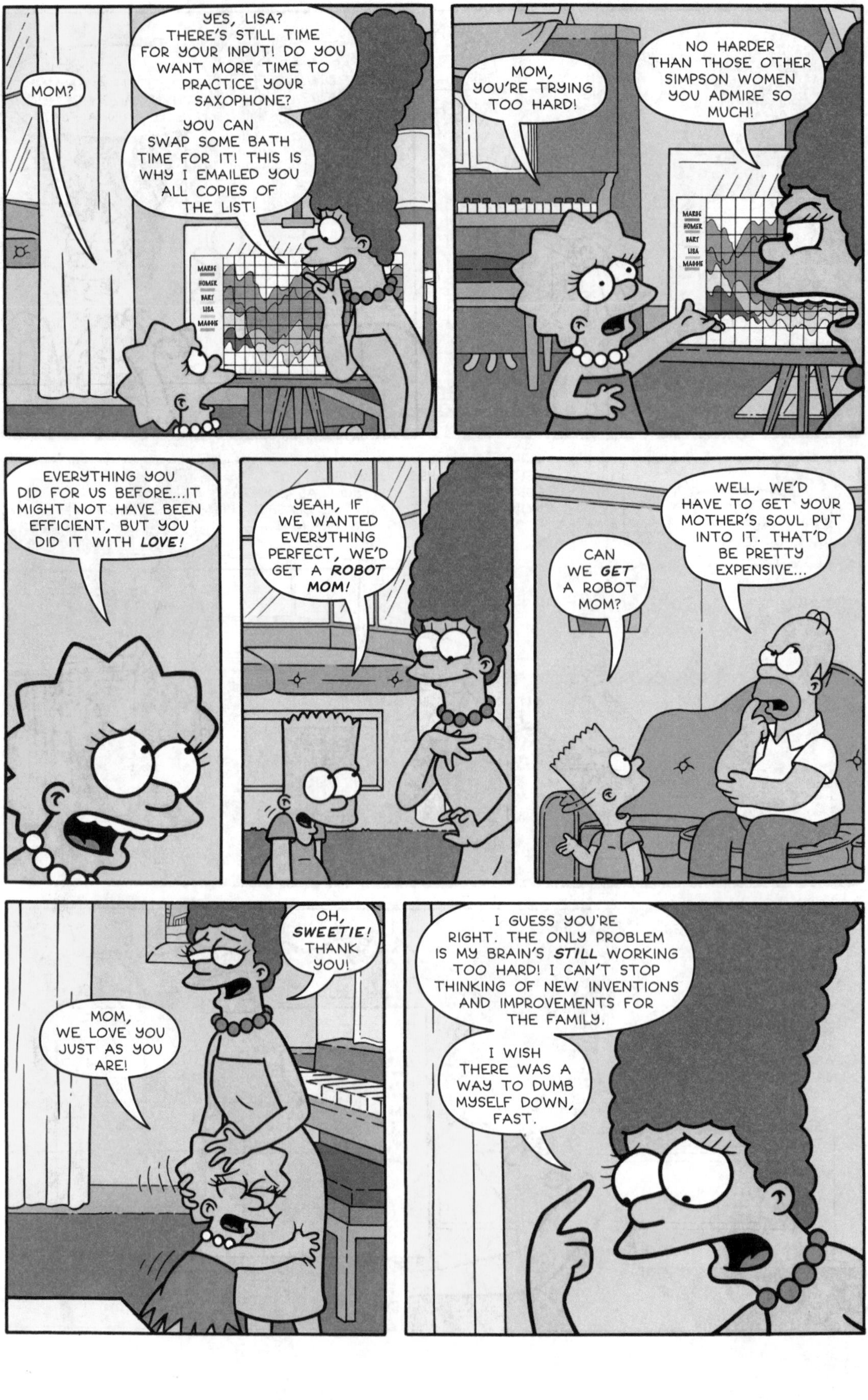

MOM?
YES, LISA? THERE'S STILL TIME FOR YOUR INPUT! DO YOU WANT MORE TIME TO PRACTICE YOUR SAXOPHONE?
YOU CAN SWAP SOME BATH TIME FOR IT! THIS IS WHY I EMAILED YOU ALL COPIES OF THE LIST!
MOM, YOU'RE TRYING TOO HARD!
NO HARDER THAN THOSE OTHER SIMPSON WOMEN YOU ADMIRE SO MUCH!
EVERYTHING YOU DID FOR US BEFORE...IT MIGHT NOT HAVE BEEN EFFICIENT, BUT YOU DID IT WITH LOVE!
YEAH, IF WE WANTED EVERYTHING PERFECT, WE'D GET A ROBOT MOM!
CAN WE GET A ROBOT MOM?
WELL, WE'D HAVE TO GET YOUR MOTHER'S SOUL PUT INTO IT. THAT'D BE PRETTY EXPENSIVE...
MOM, WE LOVE YOU JUST AS YOU ARE!
OH, SWEETIE! THANK YOU!
I GUESS YOU'RE RIGHT. THE ONLY PROBLEM IS MY BRAIN'S STILL WORKING TOO HARD! I CAN'T STOP THINKING OF NEW INVENTIONS AND IMPROVEMENTS FOR THE FAMILY.
I WISH THERE WAS A WAY TO DUMB MYSELF DOWN, FAST.

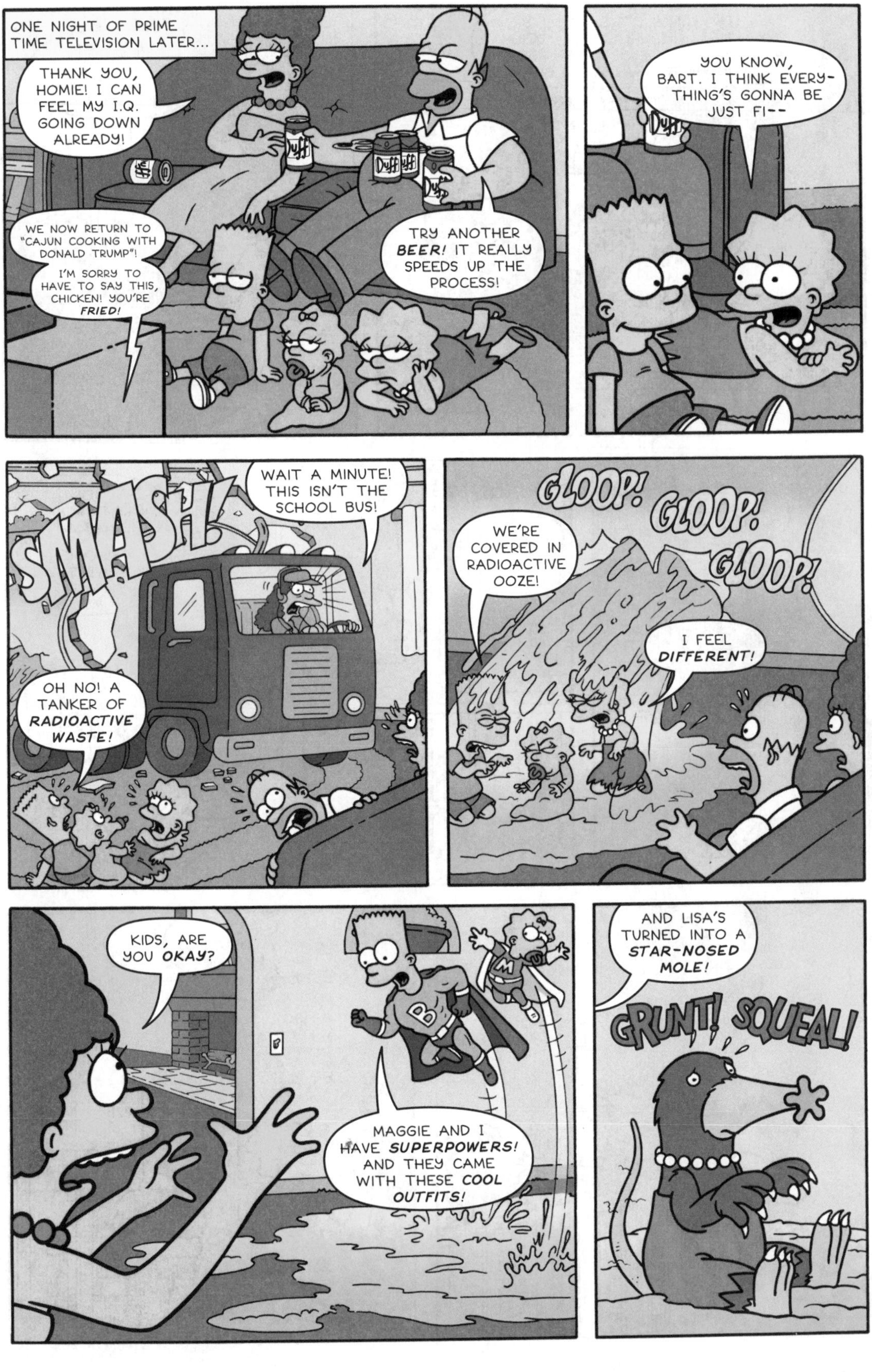
ONE NIGHT OF PRIME TIME TELEVISION LATER...
THANK YOU, HOMIE! I CAN FEEL MY I.Q. GOING DOWN ALREADY!
TRY ANOTHER BEER! IT REALLY SPEEDS UP THE PROCESS!
WE NOW RETURN TO "CAJUN COOKING WITH DONALD TRUMP"!
I'M SORRY TO HAVE TO SAY THIS, CHICKEN! YOU'RE FRIED!
YOU KNOW, BART. I THINK EVERYTHING'S GONNA BE JUST FI--
SMASH!
WAIT A MINUTE! THIS ISN'T THE SCHOOL BUS!
OH NO! A TANKER OF RADIOACTIVE WASTE!
GLOOP! GLOOP! GLOOP!
WE'RE COVERED IN RADIOACTIVE OOZE!
I FEEL DIFFERENT!
KIDS, ARE YOU OKAY?
MAGGIE AND I HAVE SUPERPOWERS! AND THEY CAME WITH THESE COOL OUTFITS!
AND LISA'S TURNED INTO A STAR-NOSED MOLE!
GRUNT! SQUEAL!

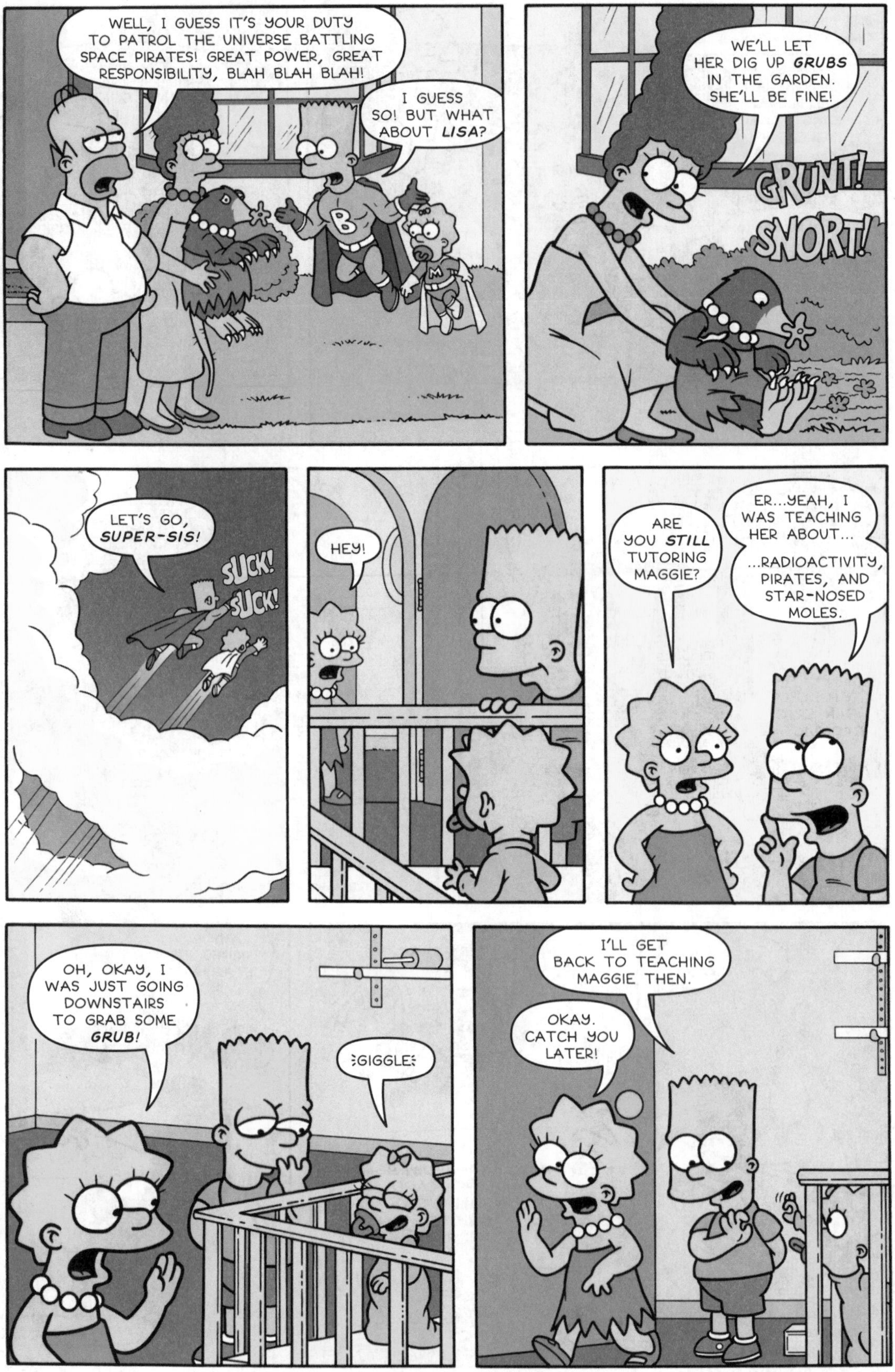

WELL, I GUESS IT'S YOUR DUTY TO PATROL THE UNIVERSE BATTLING SPACE PIRATES! GREAT POWER, GREAT RESPONSIBILITY, BLAH BLAH BLAH!
I GUESS SO! BUT WHAT ABOUT *LISA*?
WE'LL LET HER DIG UP ***GRUBS*** IN THE GARDEN. SHE'LL BE FINE!
GRUNT!
SNORT!
LET'S GO, ***SUPER-SIS***!
SUCK!
SUCK!
HEY!
ARE YOU ***STILL*** TUTORING MAGGIE?
ER...YEAH, I WAS TEACHING HER ABOUT...
...RADIOACTIVITY, PIRATES, AND STAR-NOSED MOLES.
OH, OKAY, I WAS JUST GOING DOWNSTAIRS TO GRAB SOME ***GRUB***!
GIGGLE
I'LL GET BACK TO TEACHING MAGGIE THEN.
OKAY. CATCH YOU LATER!

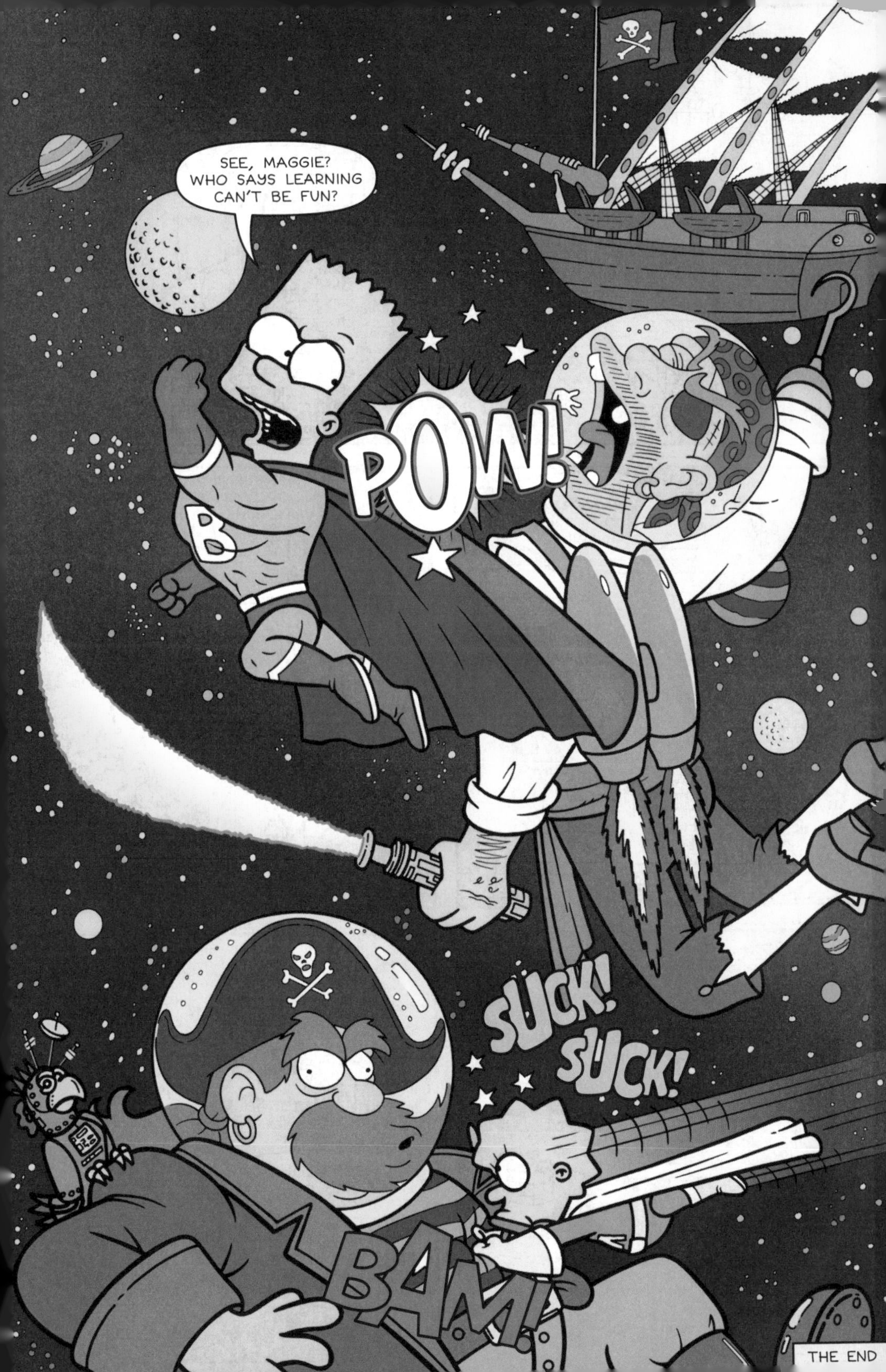
SEE, MAGGIE? WHO SAYS LEARNING CAN'T BE FUN?
POW!
SUCK!
SUCK!
BAM!
THE END

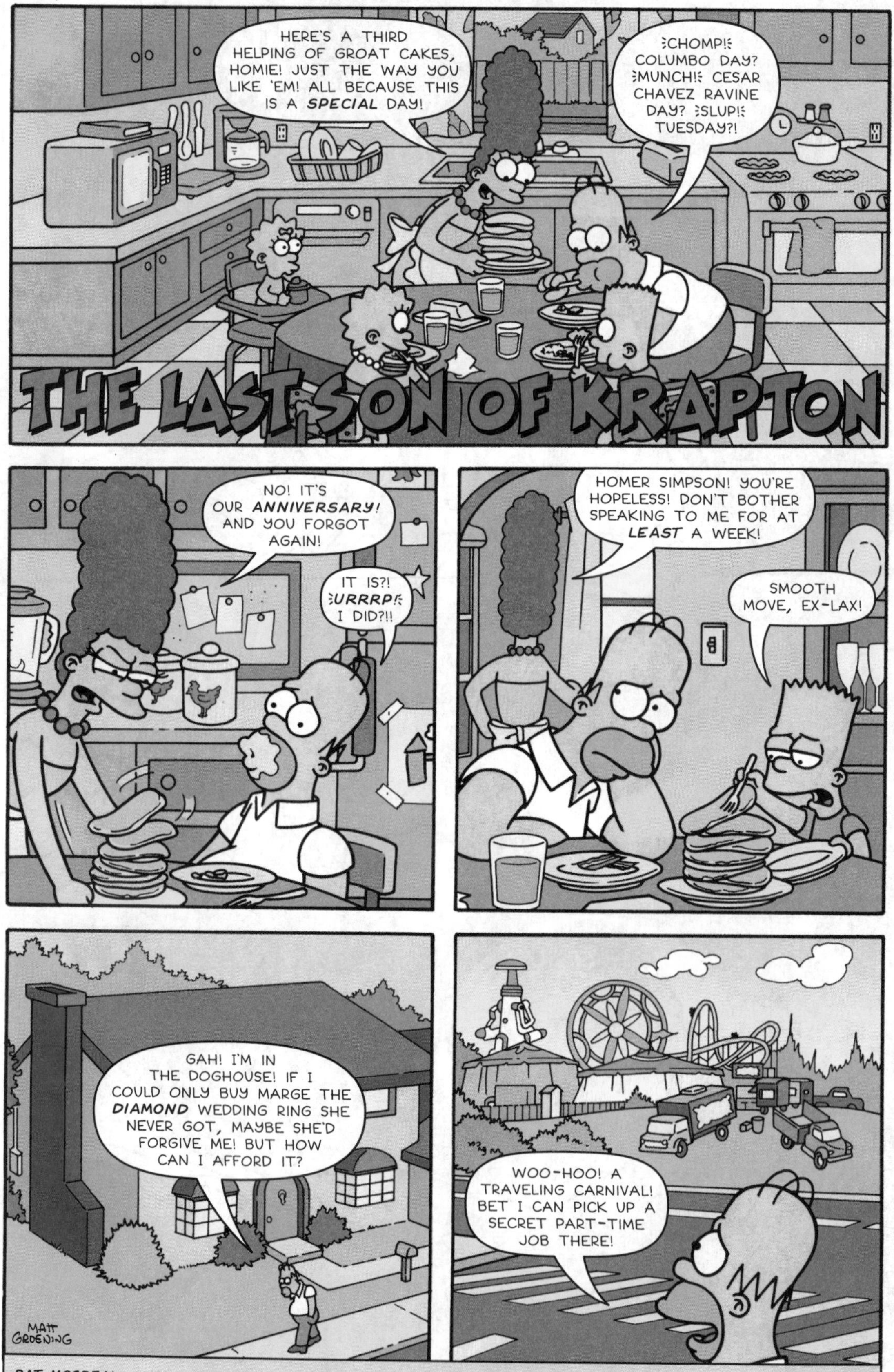

HERE'S A THIRD HELPING OF GROAT CAKES, HOMIE! JUST THE WAY YOU LIKE 'EM! ALL BECAUSE THIS IS A SPECIAL DAY!
CHOMP! COLUMBO DAY? MUNCH! CESAR CHAVEZ RAVINE DAY? SLUP! TUESDAY?!
THE LAST SON OF KRAPTON
NO! IT'S OUR ANNIVERSARY! AND YOU FORGOT AGAIN!
IT IS?! URRRP! I DID?!!
HOMER SIMPSON! YOU'RE HOPELESS! DON'T BOTHER SPEAKING TO ME FOR AT LEAST A WEEK!
SMOOTH MOVE, EX-LAX!
GAH! I'M IN THE DOGHOUSE! IF I COULD ONLY BUY MARGE THE DIAMOND WEDDING RING SHE NEVER GOT, MAYBE SHE'D FORGIVE ME! BUT HOW CAN I AFFORD IT?
WOO-HOO! A TRAVELING CARNIVAL! BET I CAN PICK UP A SECRET PART-TIME JOB THERE!
MATT GROENING

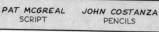

PAT MCGREAL SCRIPT | *JOHN COSTANZA* PENCILS | *PHYLLIS NOVIN* INKS | *ALAN HELLARD* COLORS | *KAREN BATES* LETTERS | *BILL MORRISON* EDITOR

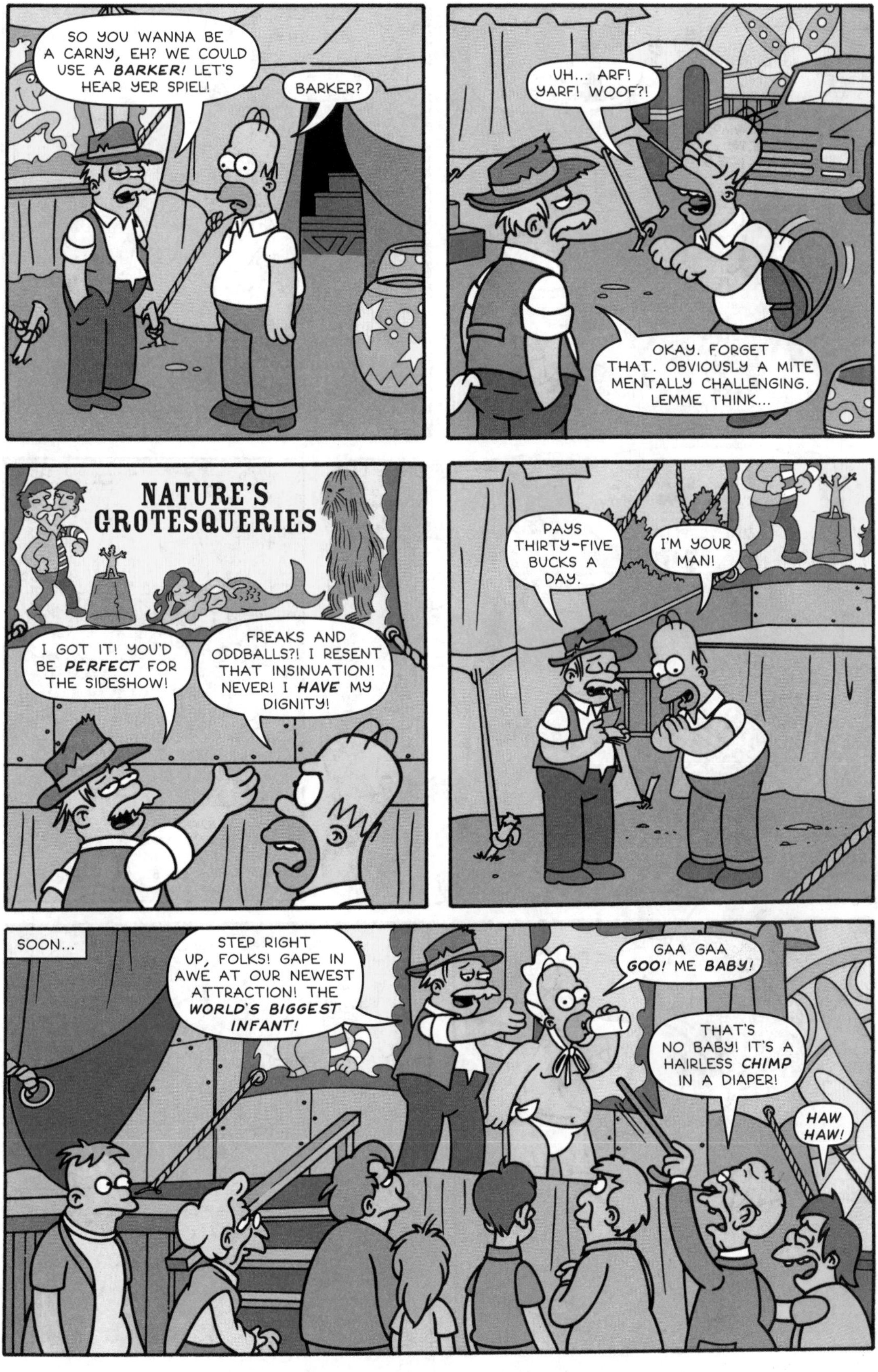

SO YOU WANNA BE A CARNY, EH? WE COULD USE A *BARKER!* LET'S HEAR YER SPIEL!
BARKER?
UH... ARF! YARF! WOOF?!
OKAY. FORGET THAT. OBVIOUSLY A MITE MENTALLY CHALLENGING. LEMME THINK...
NATURE'S GROTESQUERIES
I GOT IT! YOU'D BE *PERFECT* FOR THE SIDESHOW!
FREAKS AND ODDBALLS?! I RESENT THAT INSINUATION! NEVER! I *HAVE* MY DIGNITY!
PAYS THIRTY-FIVE BUCKS A DAY.
I'M YOUR MAN!
SOON...
STEP RIGHT UP, FOLKS! GAPE IN AWE AT OUR NEWEST ATTRACTION! THE *WORLD'S BIGGEST INFANT!*
GAA GAA *GOO!* ME *BABY!*
THAT'S NO BABY! IT'S A HAIRLESS *CHIMP* IN A DIAPER!
HAW HAW!

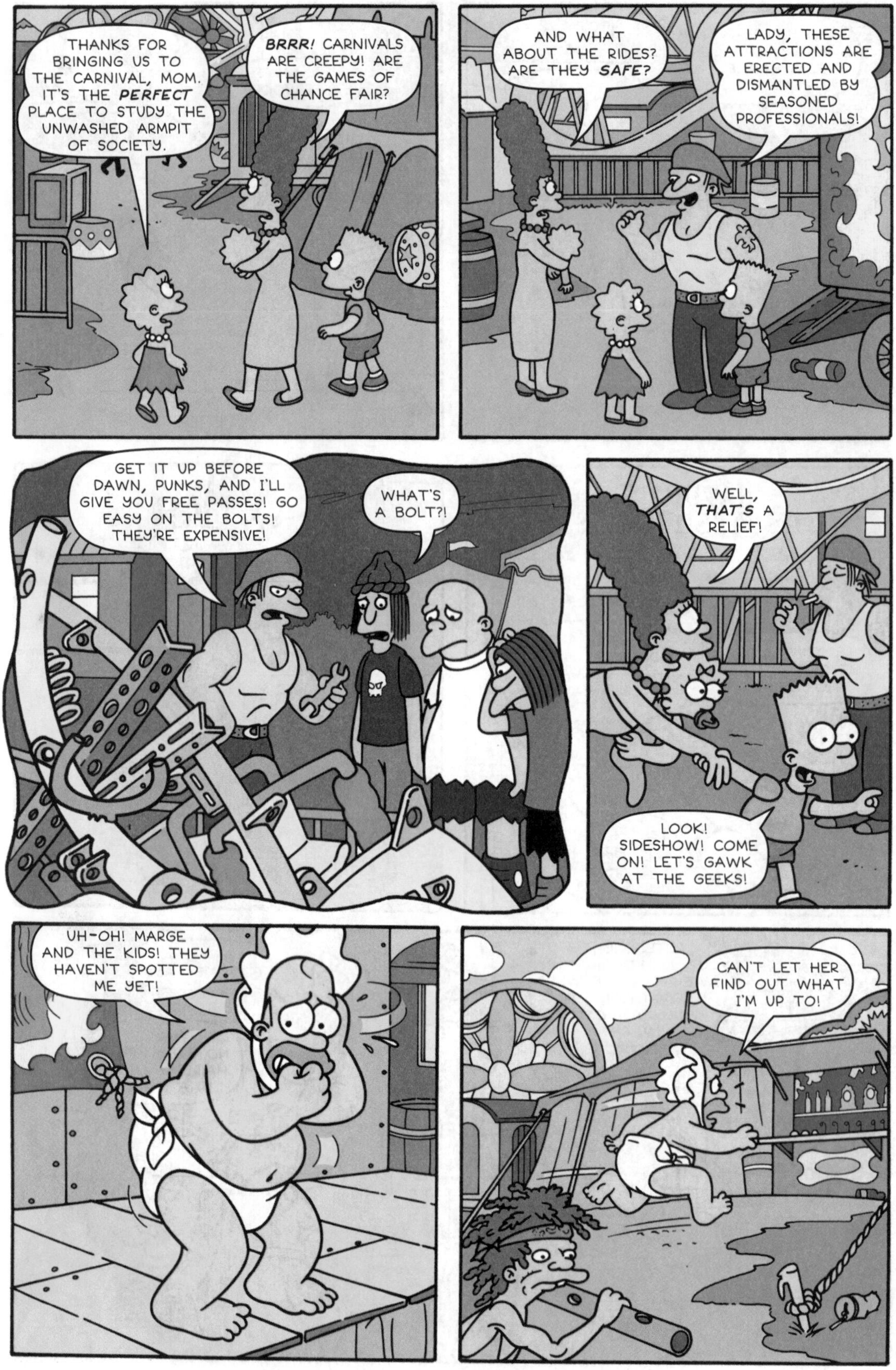
THANKS FOR BRINGING US TO THE CARNIVAL, MOM. IT'S THE **PERFECT** PLACE TO STUDY THE UNWASHED ARMPIT OF SOCIETY.
BRRR! CARNIVALS ARE CREEPY! ARE THE GAMES OF CHANCE FAIR?
AND WHAT ABOUT THE RIDES? ARE THEY **SAFE?**
LADY, THESE ATTRACTIONS ARE ERECTED AND DISMANTLED BY SEASONED PROFESSIONALS!
GET IT UP BEFORE DAWN, PUNKS, AND I'LL GIVE YOU FREE PASSES! GO EASY ON THE BOLTS! THEY'RE EXPENSIVE!
WHAT'S A BOLT?!
WELL, **THAT'S** A RELIEF!
LOOK! SIDESHOW! COME ON! LET'S GAWK AT THE GEEKS!
UH-OH! MARGE AND THE KIDS! THEY HAVEN'T SPOTTED ME YET!
CAN'T LET HER FIND OUT WHAT I'M UP TO!

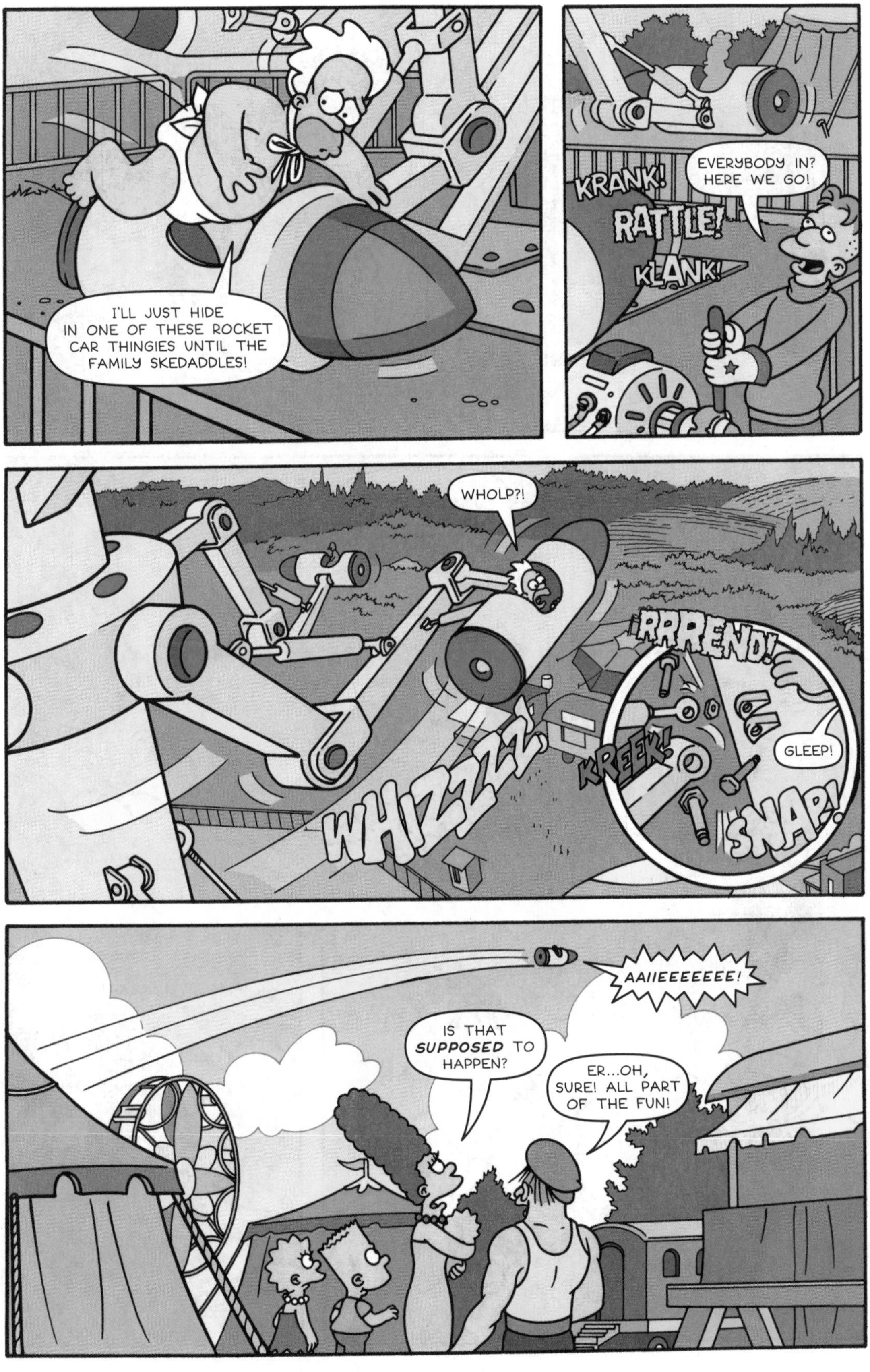
I'LL JUST HIDE IN ONE OF THESE ROCKET CAR THINGIES UNTIL THE FAMILY SKEDADDLES!
EVERYBODY IN? HERE WE GO!
KRANK!
RATTLE!
KLANK!
WHOLP?!
RRREND!
KREEK!
GLEEP!
SNAP!
WHIZZZZ
AAIIEEEEEEE!
IS THAT *SUPPOSED* TO HAPPEN?
ER...OH, SURE! ALL PART OF THE FUN!

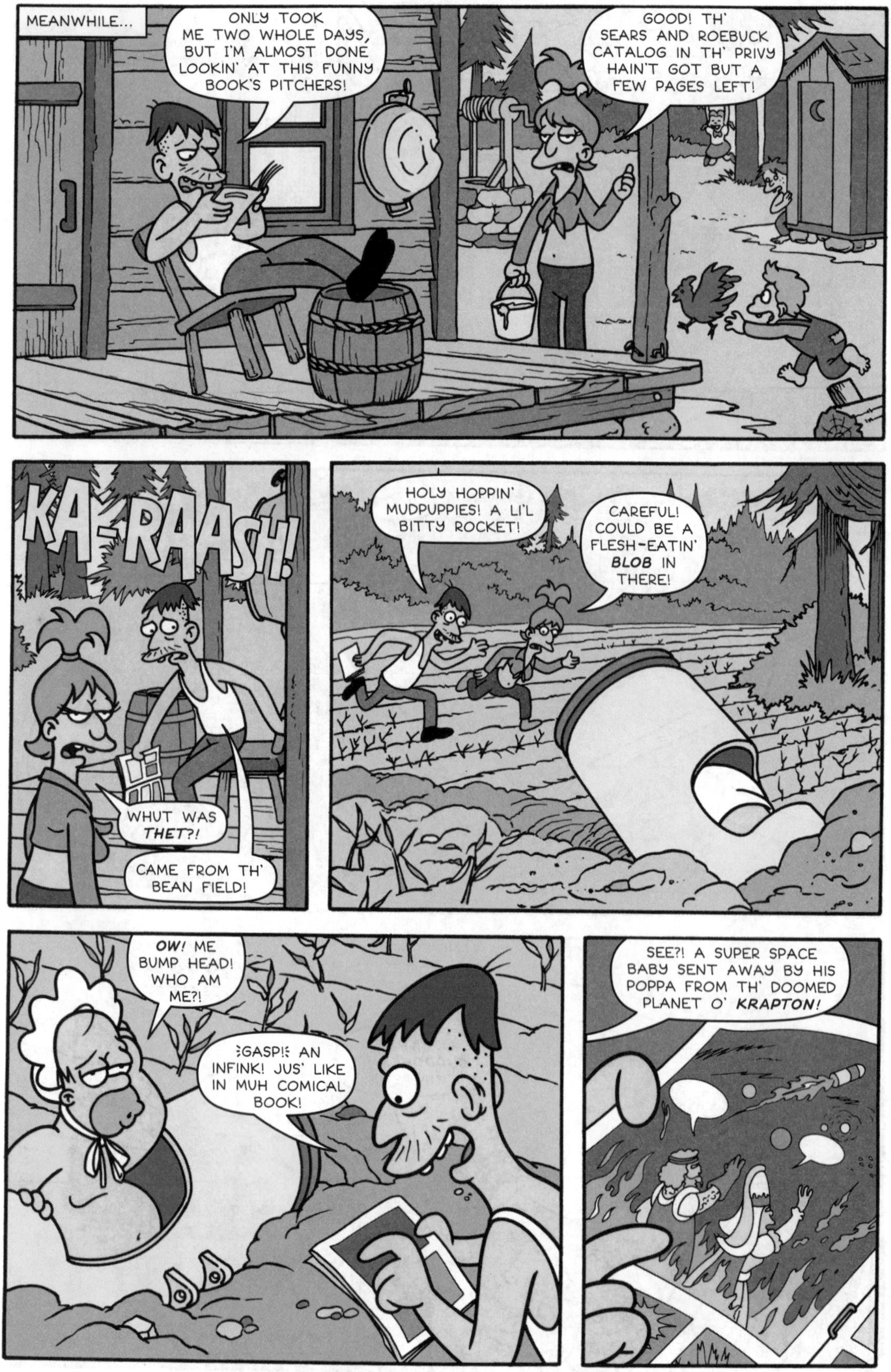
MEANWHILE...
ONLY TOOK ME TWO WHOLE DAYS, BUT I'M ALMOST DONE LOOKIN' AT THIS FUNNY BOOK'S PITCHERS!
GOOD! TH' SEARS AND ROEBUCK CATALOG IN TH' PRIVY HAIN'T GOT BUT A FEW PAGES LEFT!
KA-RAASH!
WHUT WAS THET?!
CAME FROM TH' BEAN FIELD!
HOLY HOPPIN' MUDPUPPIES! A LI'L BITTY ROCKET!
CAREFUL! COULD BE A FLESH-EATIN' BLOB IN THERE!
OW! ME BUMP HEAD! WHO AM ME?!
GASP! AN INFINK! JUS' LIKE IN MUH COMICAL BOOK!
SEE?! A SUPER SPACE BABY SENT AWAY BY HIS POPPA FROM TH' DOOMED PLANET O' KRAPTON!

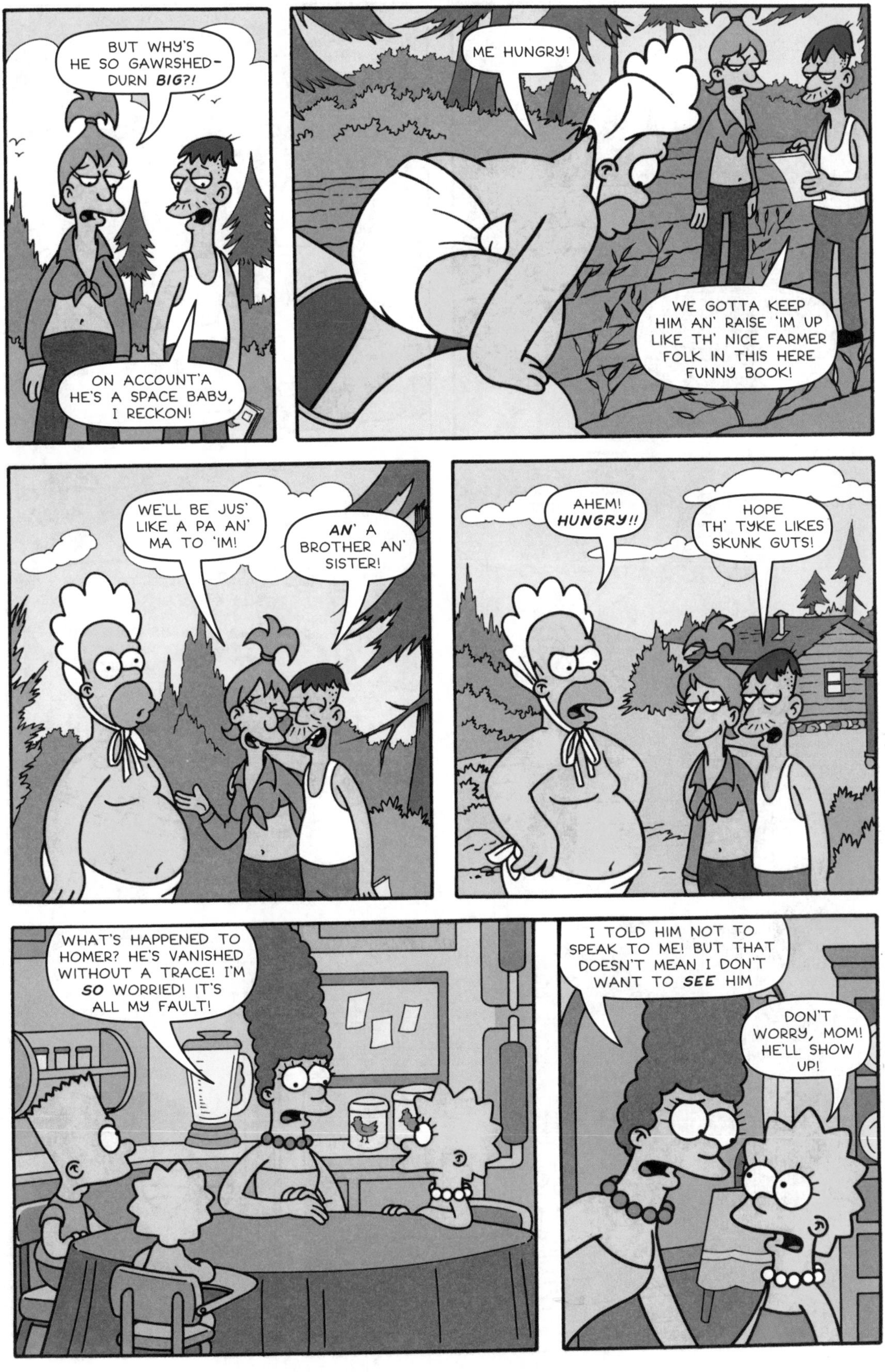
BUT WHY'S HE SO GAWRSHED-DURN **BIG**?!
ON ACCOUNT'A HE'S A SPACE BABY, I RECKON!
ME HUNGRY!
WE GOTTA KEEP HIM AN' RAISE 'IM UP LIKE TH' NICE FARMER FOLK IN THIS HERE FUNNY BOOK!
WE'LL BE JUS' LIKE A PA AN' MA TO 'IM!
AN' A BROTHER AN' SISTER!
AHEM! **HUNGRY!!**
HOPE TH' TYKE LIKES SKUNK GUTS!
WHAT'S HAPPENED TO HOMER? HE'S VANISHED WITHOUT A TRACE! I'M **SO** WORRIED! IT'S ALL MY FAULT!
I TOLD HIM NOT TO SPEAK TO ME! BUT THAT DOESN'T MEAN I DON'T WANT TO **SEE** HIM
DON'T WORRY, MOM! HE'LL SHOW UP!

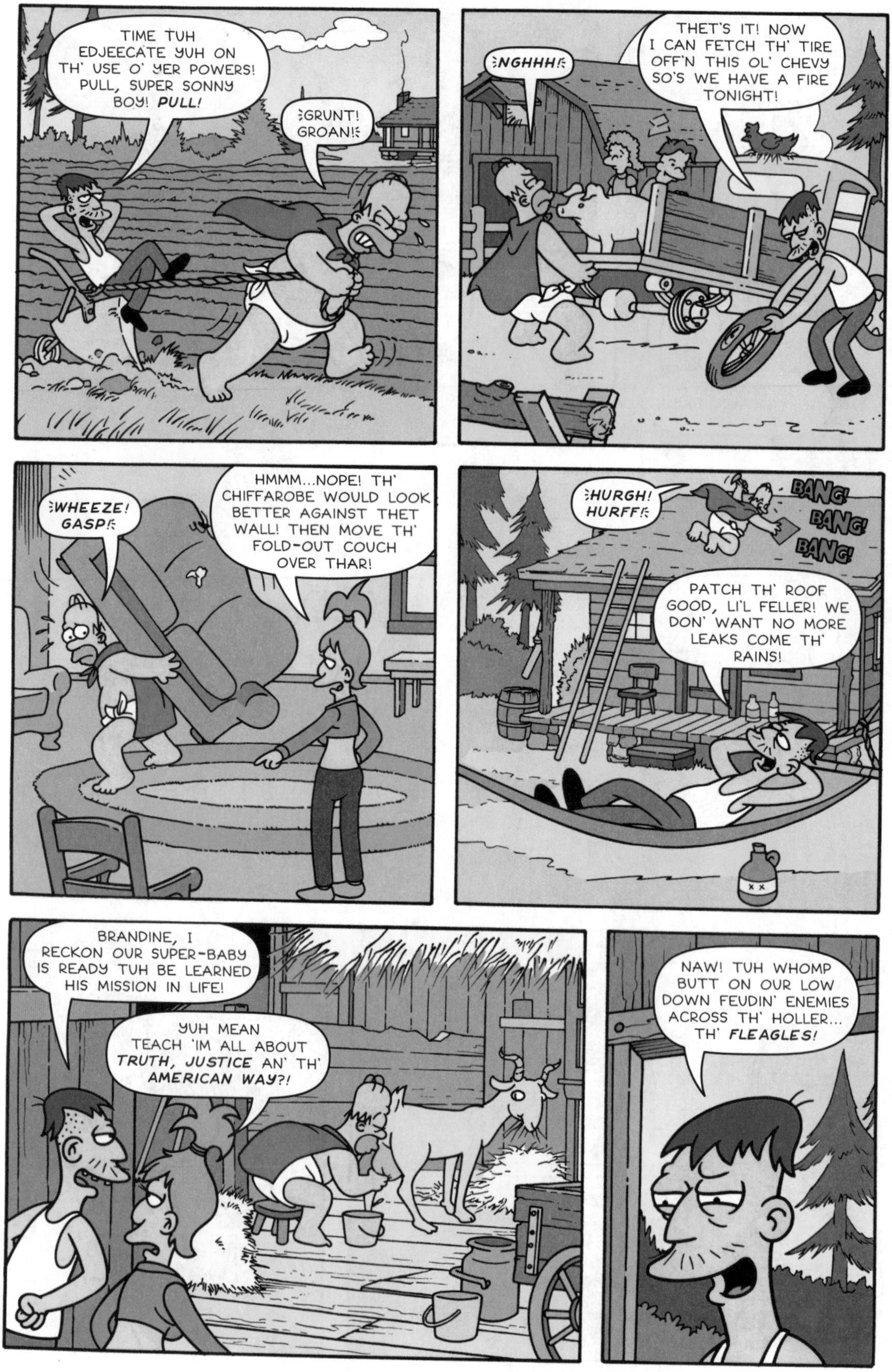
TIME TUH EDJEECATE YUH ON TH' USE O' YER POWERS! PULL, SUPER SONNY BOY! PULL!
GRUNT! GROAN!
NGHHH!
THET'S IT! NOW I CAN FETCH TH' TIRE OFF'N THIS OL' CHEVY SO'S WE HAVE A FIRE TONIGHT!
WHEEZE! GASP!
HMMM...NOPE! TH' CHIFFAROBE WOULD LOOK BETTER AGAINST THET WALL! THEN MOVE TH' FOLD-OUT COUCH OVER THAR!
HURGH! HURFF!
BANG! BANG! BANG!
PATCH TH' ROOF GOOD, LI'L FELLER! WE DON' WANT NO MORE LEAKS COME TH' RAINS!
BRANDINE, I RECKON OUR SUPER-BABY IS READY TUH BE LEARNED HIS MISSION IN LIFE!
YUH MEAN TEACH 'IM ALL ABOUT TRUTH, JUSTICE AN' TH' AMERICAN WAY?!
NAW! TUH WHOMP BUTT ON OUR LOW DOWN FEUDIN' ENEMIES ACROSS TH' HOLLER... TH' FLEAGLES!

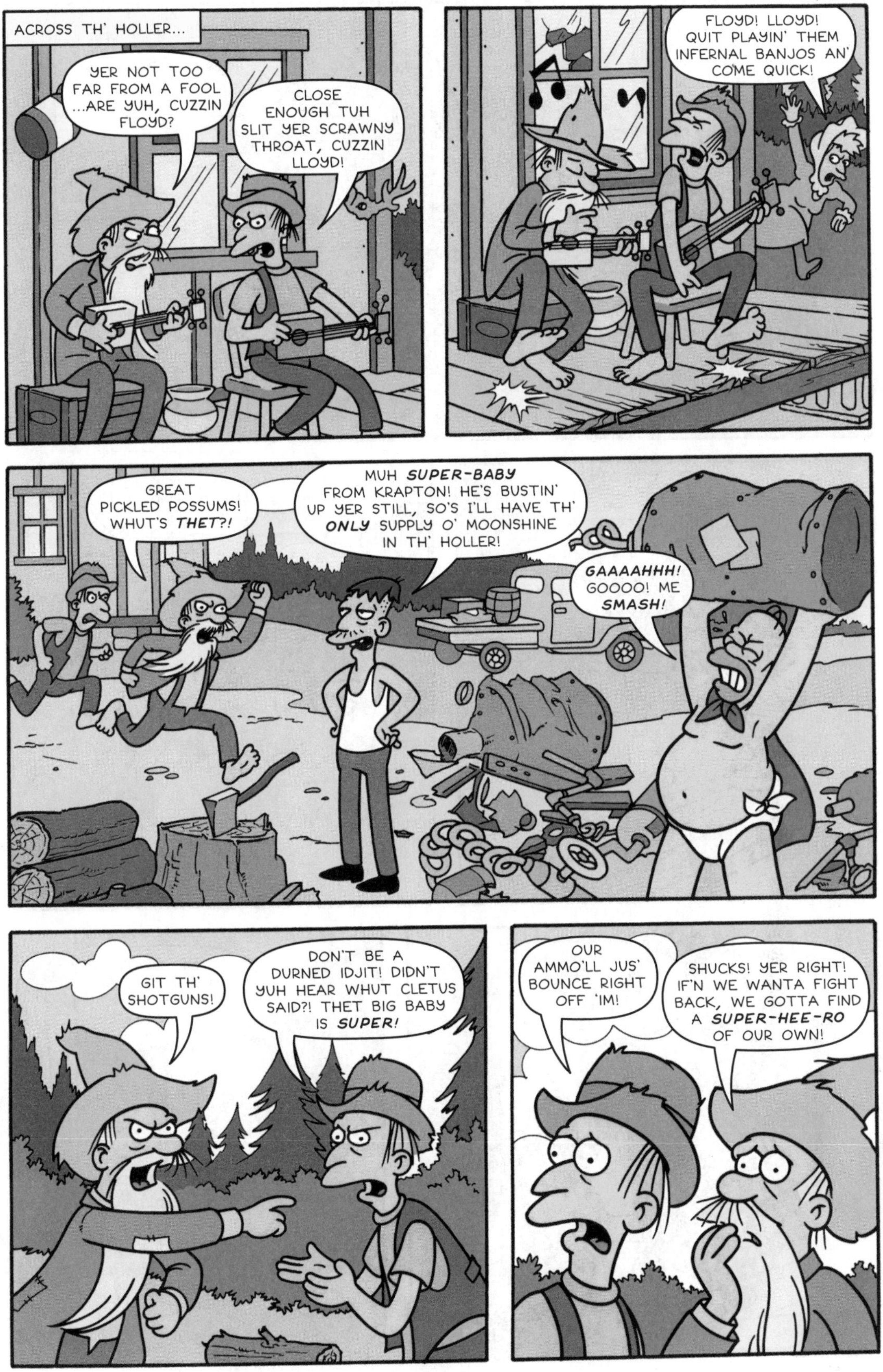

ACROSS TH' HOLLER...
YER NOT TOO FAR FROM A FOOL ...ARE YUH, CUZZIN FLOYD?
CLOSE ENOUGH TUH SLIT YER SCRAWNY THROAT, CUZZIN LLOYD!
FLOYD! LLOYD! QUIT PLAYIN' THEM INFERNAL BANJOS AN' COME QUICK!
GREAT PICKLED POSSUMS! WHUT'S THET?!
MUH SUPER-BABY FROM KRAPTON! HE'S BUSTIN' UP YER STILL, SO'S I'LL HAVE TH' ONLY SUPPLY O' MOONSHINE IN TH' HOLLER!
GAAAAHHH! GOOOO! ME SMASH!
GIT TH' SHOTGUNS!
DON'T BE A DURNED IDJIT! DIDN'T YUH HEAR WHUT CLETUS SAID?! THET BIG BABY IS SUPER!
OUR AMMO'LL JUS' BOUNCE RIGHT OFF 'IM!
SHUCKS! YER RIGHT! IF'N WE WANTA FIGHT BACK, WE GOTTA FIND A SUPER-HEE-RO OF OUR OWN!

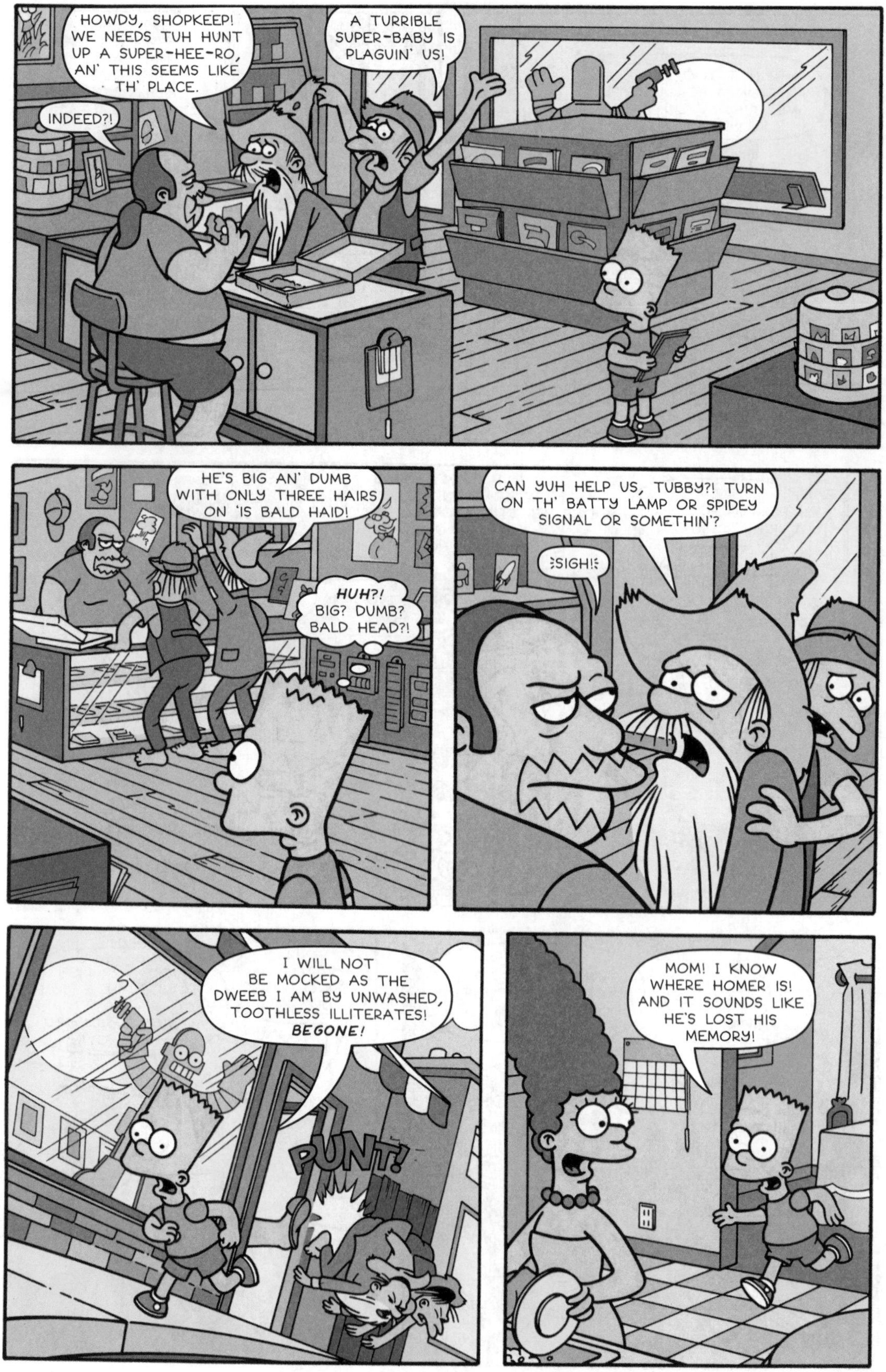
HOWDY, SHOPKEEP! WE NEEDS TUH HUNT UP A SUPER-HEE-RO, AN' THIS SEEMS LIKE TH' PLACE.
A TURRIBLE SUPER-BABY IS PLAGUIN' US!
INDEED?!
HE'S BIG AN' DUMB WITH ONLY THREE HAIRS ON 'IS BALD HAID!
HUH?! BIG? DUMB? BALD HEAD?!
CAN YUH HELP US, TUBBY?! TURN ON TH' BATTY LAMP OR SPIDEY SIGNAL OR SOMETHIN'?
SIGH!
I WILL NOT BE MOCKED AS THE DWEEB I AM BY UNWASHED, TOOTHLESS ILLITERATES! BEGONE!
PUNT!
MOM! I KNOW WHERE HOMER IS! AND IT SOUNDS LIKE HE'S LOST HIS MEMORY!

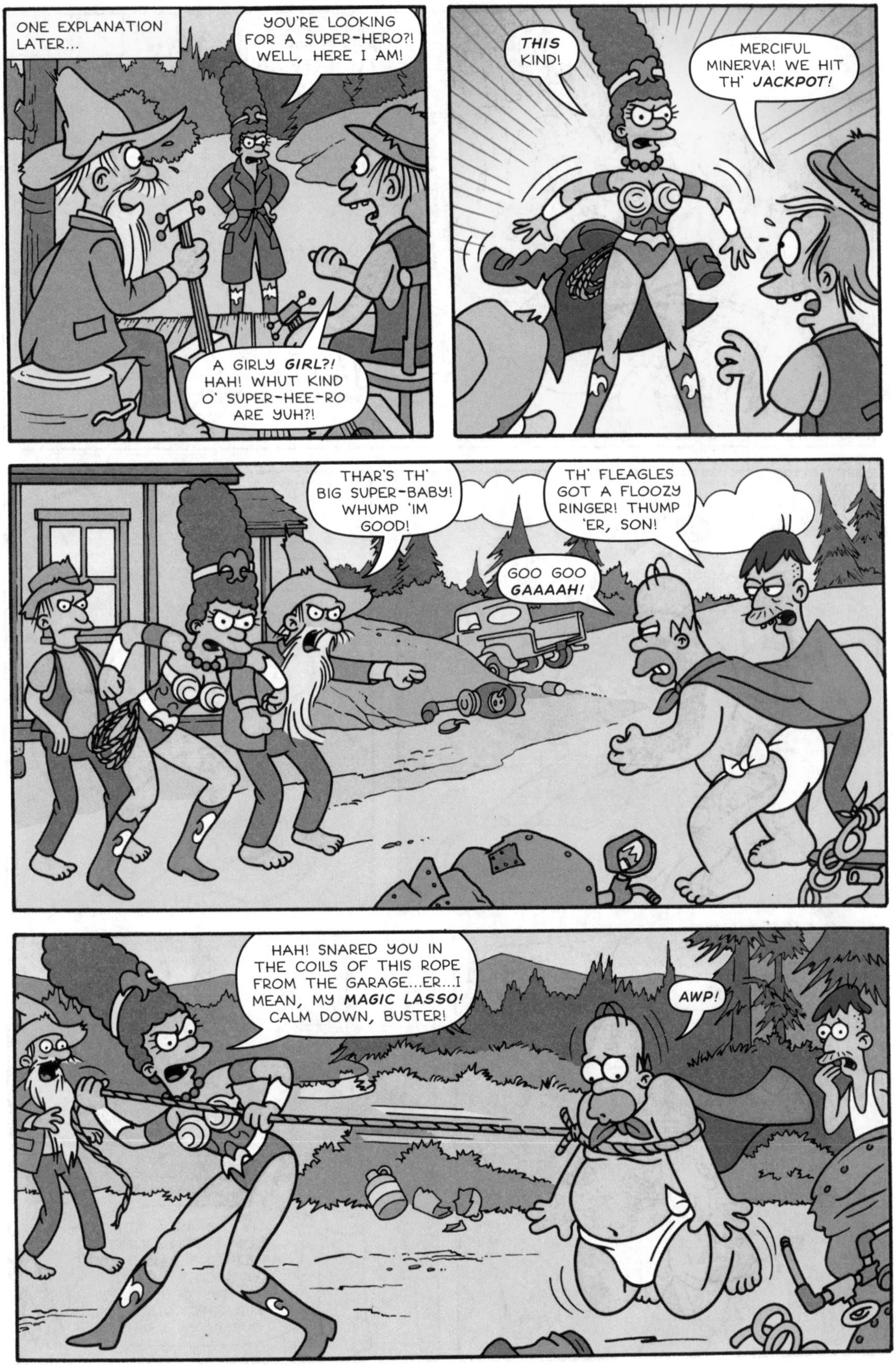
ONE EXPLANATION LATER...
YOU'RE LOOKING FOR A SUPER-HERO?! WELL, HERE I AM!
A GIRLY GIRL?! HAH! WHUT KIND O' SUPER-HEE-RO ARE YUH?!
THIS KIND!
MERCIFUL MINERVA! WE HIT TH' JACKPOT!
THAR'S TH' BIG SUPER-BABY! WHUMP 'IM GOOD!
TH' FLEAGLES GOT A FLOOZY RINGER! THUMP 'ER, SON!
GOO GOO GAAAAH!
HAH! SNARED YOU IN THE COILS OF THIS ROPE FROM THE GARAGE...ER...I MEAN, MY MAGIC LASSO! CALM DOWN, BUSTER!
AWP!

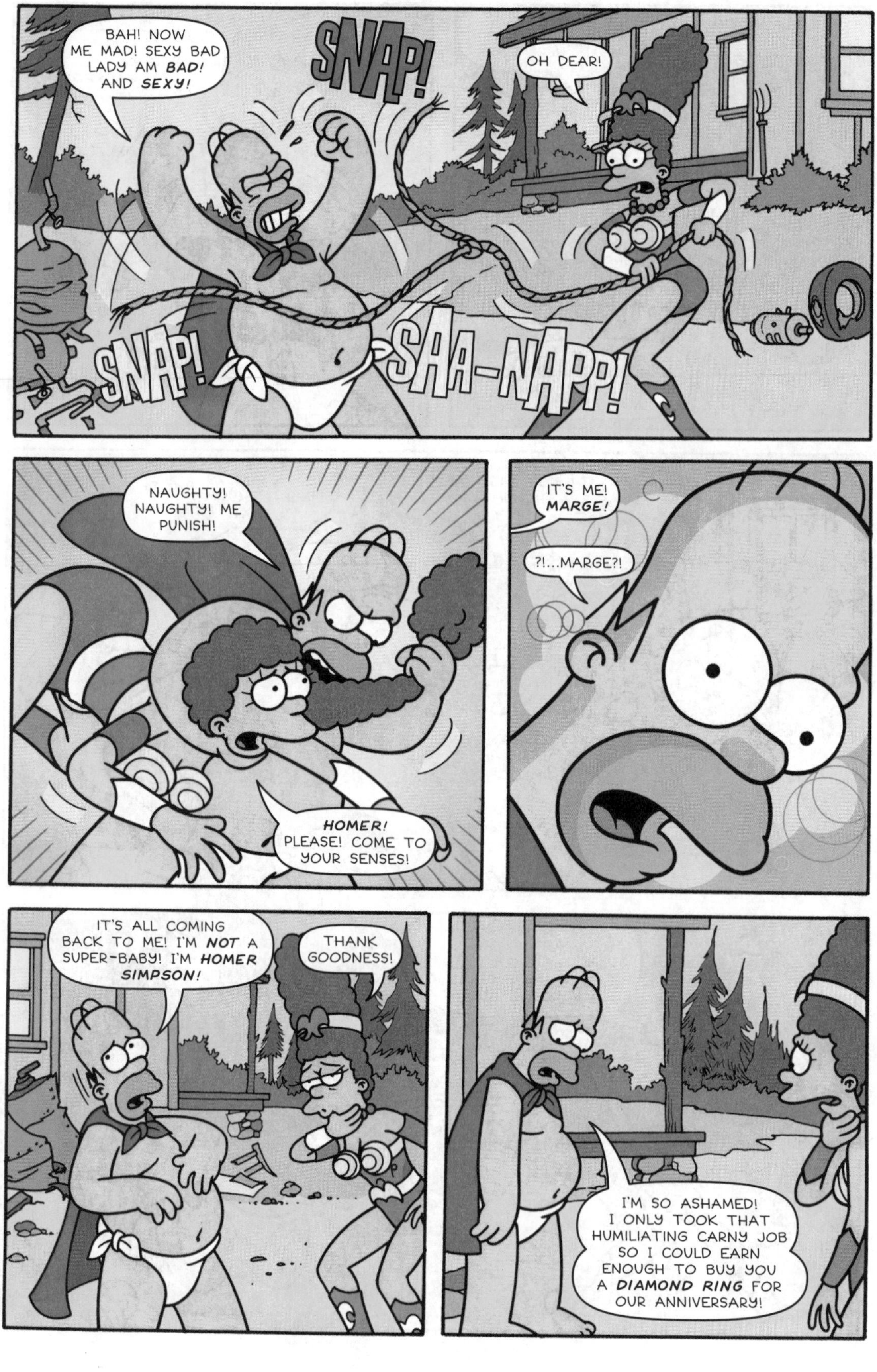
BAH! NOW ME MAD! SEXY BAD LADY AM BAD! AND SEXY!
SNAP!
OH DEAR!
SNAP!
SAA-NAPP!
NAUGHTY! NAUGHTY! ME PUNISH!
HOMER! PLEASE! COME TO YOUR SENSES!
IT'S ME! MARGE!
?!...MARGE?!
IT'S ALL COMING BACK TO ME! I'M NOT A SUPER-BABY! I'M HOMER SIMPSON!
THANK GOODNESS!
I'M SO ASHAMED! I ONLY TOOK THAT HUMILIATING CARNY JOB SO I COULD EARN ENOUGH TO BUY YOU A DIAMOND RING FOR OUR ANNIVERSARY!

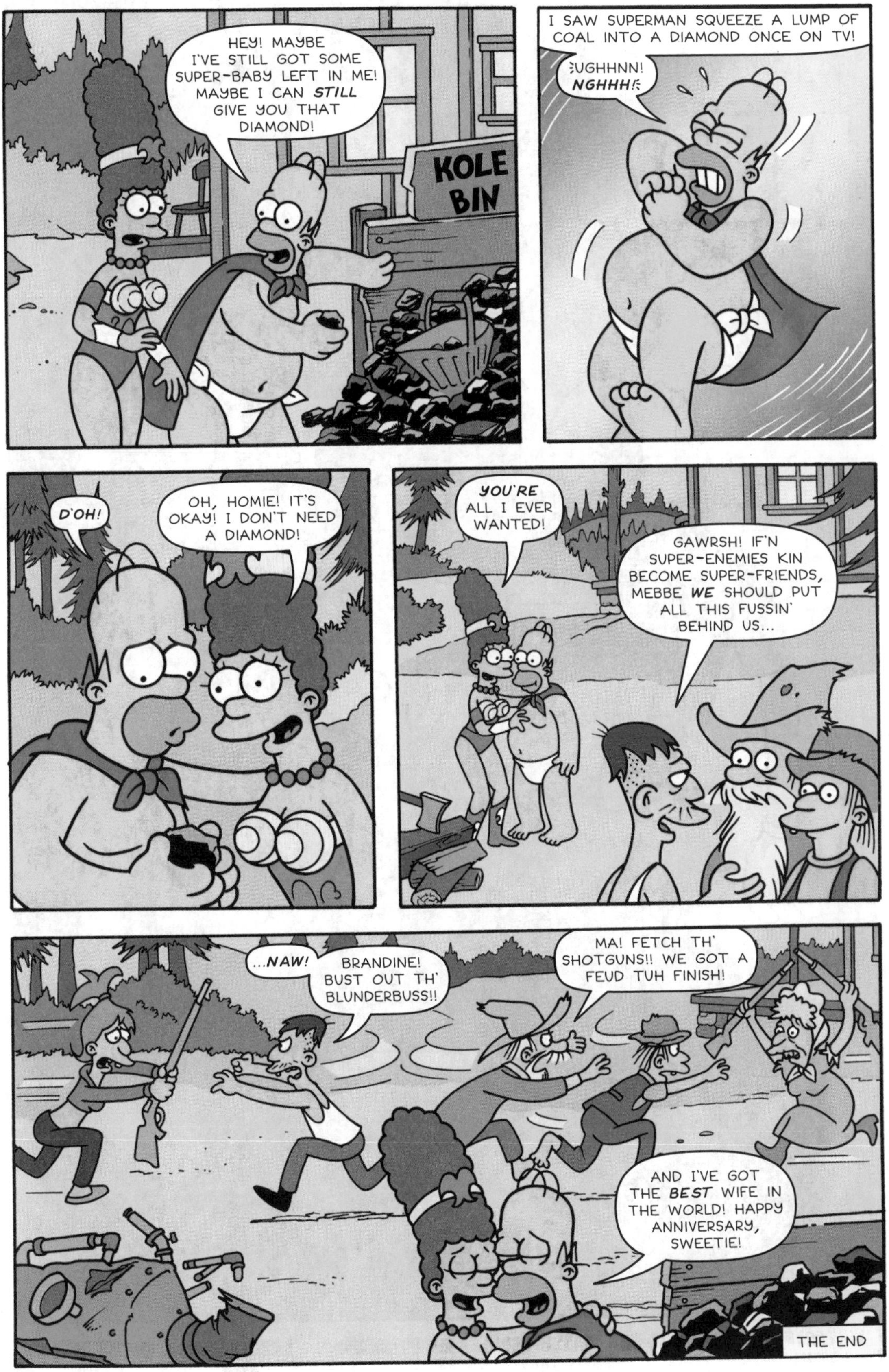
HEY! MAYBE I'VE STILL GOT SOME SUPER-BABY LEFT IN ME! MAYBE I CAN STILL GIVE YOU THAT DIAMOND!
KOLE BIN
I SAW SUPERMAN SQUEEZE A LUMP OF COAL INTO A DIAMOND ONCE ON TV!
UGHHNN! NGHHH!
D'OH!
OH, HOMIE! IT'S OKAY! I DON'T NEED A DIAMOND!
YOU'RE ALL I EVER WANTED!
GAWRSH! IF'N SUPER-ENEMIES KIN BECOME SUPER-FRIENDS, MEBBE WE SHOULD PUT ALL THIS FUSSIN' BEHIND US...
...NAW!
BRANDINE! BUST OUT TH' BLUNDERBUSS!!
MA! FETCH TH' SHOTGUNS!! WE GOT A FEUD TUH FINISH!
AND I'VE GOT THE BEST WIFE IN THE WORLD! HAPPY ANNIVERSARY, SWEETIE!
THE END

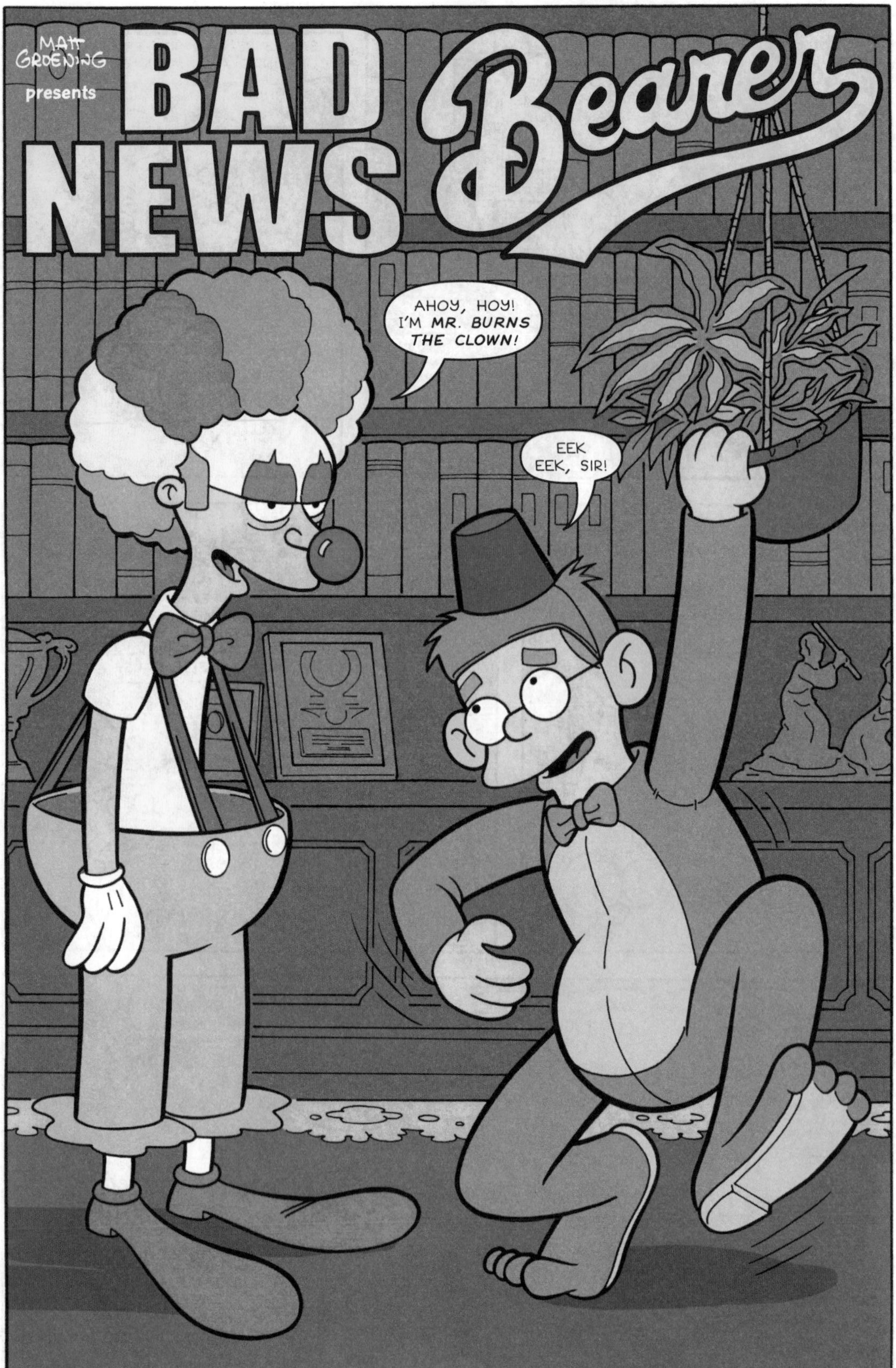
MATT GROENING presents
BAD NEWS Bearer
AHOY, HOY! I'M MR. BURNS THE CLOWN!
EEK EEK, SIR!

IAN BOOTHBY SCRIPT | JOHN COSTANZA PENCILS | MIKE DECARLO INKS | ART VILLANUEVA COLORS | KAREN BATES LETTERS | BILL MORRISON EDITOR

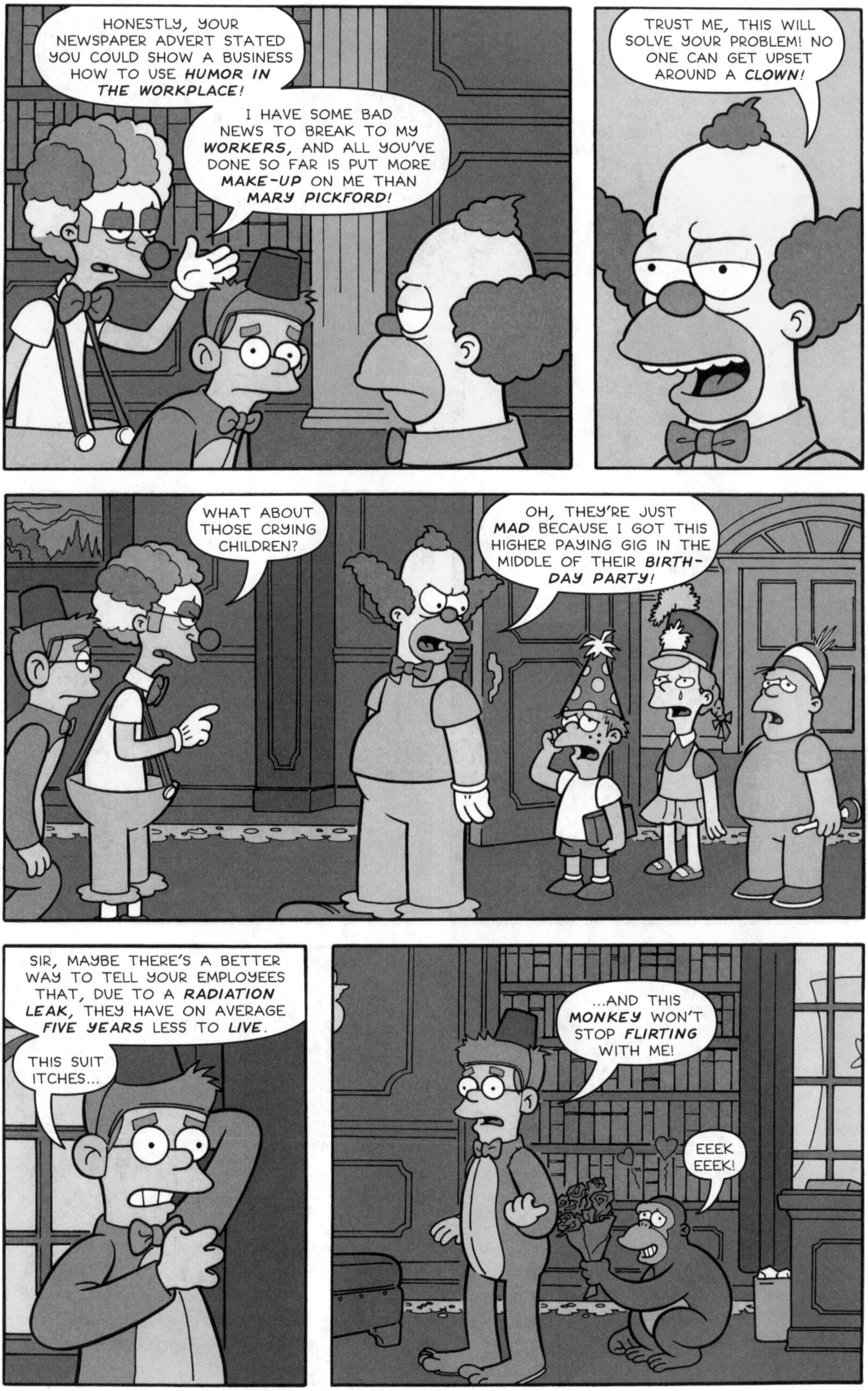
HONESTLY, YOUR NEWSPAPER ADVERT STATED YOU COULD SHOW A BUSINESS HOW TO USE HUMOR IN THE WORKPLACE!
I HAVE SOME BAD NEWS TO BREAK TO MY WORKERS, AND ALL YOU'VE DONE SO FAR IS PUT MORE MAKE-UP ON ME THAN MARY PICKFORD!
TRUST ME, THIS WILL SOLVE YOUR PROBLEM! NO ONE CAN GET UPSET AROUND A CLOWN!
WHAT ABOUT THOSE CRYING CHILDREN?
OH, THEY'RE JUST MAD BECAUSE I GOT THIS HIGHER PAYING GIG IN THE MIDDLE OF THEIR BIRTHDAY PARTY!
SIR, MAYBE THERE'S A BETTER WAY TO TELL YOUR EMPLOYEES THAT, DUE TO A RADIATION LEAK, THEY HAVE ON AVERAGE FIVE YEARS LESS TO LIVE.
THIS SUIT ITCHES...
...AND THIS MONKEY WON'T STOP FLIRTING WITH ME!
EEEK EEEK!

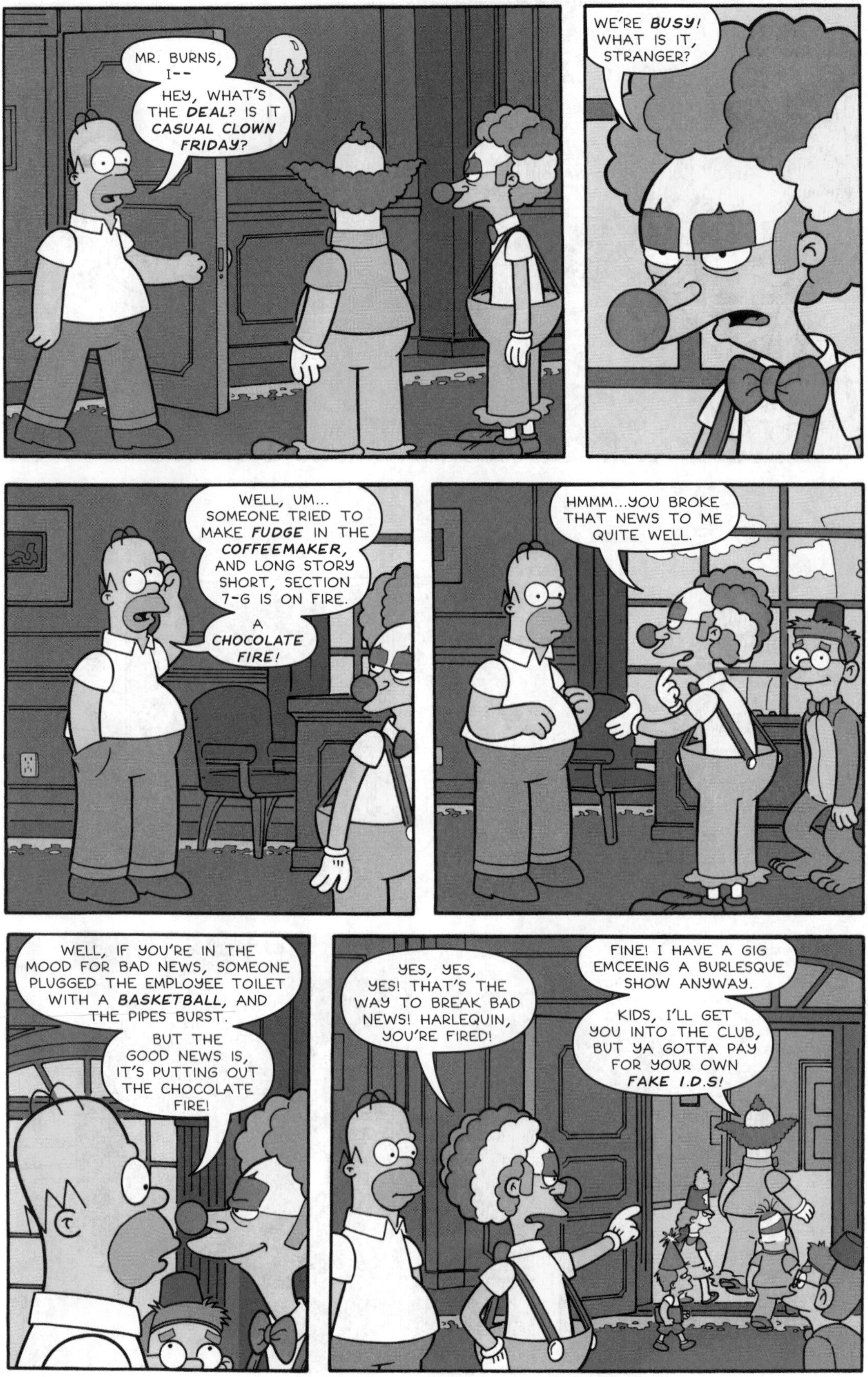

MR. BURNS, I--
HEY, WHAT'S THE DEAL? IS IT CASUAL CLOWN FRIDAY?
WE'RE BUSY! WHAT IS IT, STRANGER?
WELL, UM... SOMEONE TRIED TO MAKE FUDGE IN THE COFFEEMAKER, AND LONG STORY SHORT, SECTION 7-G IS ON FIRE.
A CHOCOLATE FIRE!
HMMM...YOU BROKE THAT NEWS TO ME QUITE WELL.
WELL, IF YOU'RE IN THE MOOD FOR BAD NEWS, SOMEONE PLUGGED THE EMPLOYEE TOILET WITH A BASKETBALL, AND THE PIPES BURST.
BUT THE GOOD NEWS IS, IT'S PUTTING OUT THE CHOCOLATE FIRE!
YES, YES, YES! THAT'S THE WAY TO BREAK BAD NEWS! HARLEQUIN, YOU'RE FIRED!
FINE! I HAVE A GIG EMCEEING A BURLESQUE SHOW ANYWAY.
KIDS, I'LL GET YOU INTO THE CLUB, BUT YA GOTTA PAY FOR YOUR OWN FAKE I.D.S!

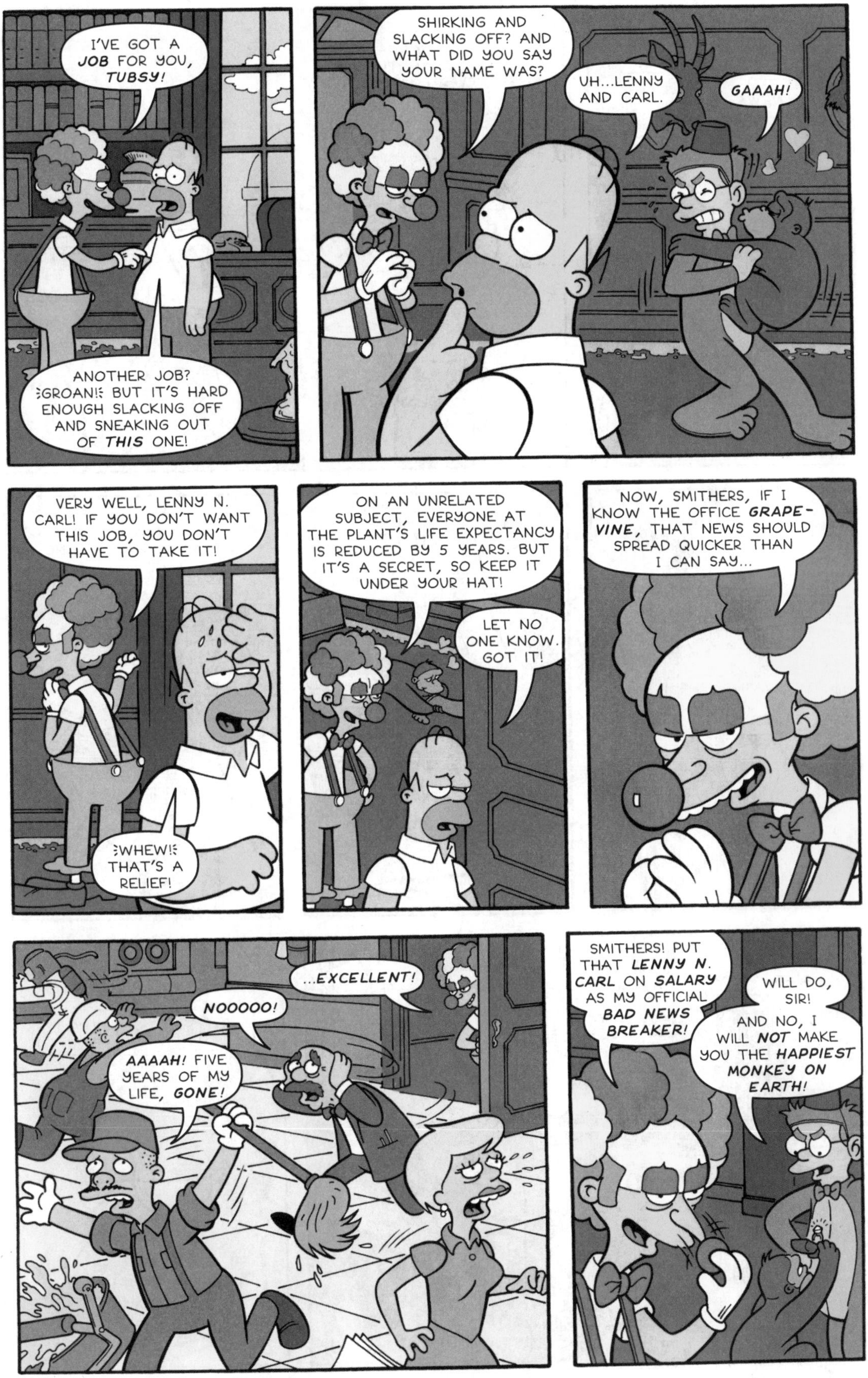

I'VE GOT A JOB FOR YOU, TUBSY!
ANOTHER JOB? GROAN! BUT IT'S HARD ENOUGH SLACKING OFF AND SNEAKING OUT OF THIS ONE!
SHIRKING AND SLACKING OFF? AND WHAT DID YOU SAY YOUR NAME WAS?
UH...LENNY AND CARL.
GAAAH!
VERY WELL, LENNY N. CARL! IF YOU DON'T WANT THIS JOB, YOU DON'T HAVE TO TAKE IT!
WHEW! THAT'S A RELIEF!
ON AN UNRELATED SUBJECT, EVERYONE AT THE PLANT'S LIFE EXPECTANCY IS REDUCED BY 5 YEARS. BUT IT'S A SECRET, SO KEEP IT UNDER YOUR HAT!
LET NO ONE KNOW. GOT IT!
NOW, SMITHERS, IF I KNOW THE OFFICE GRAPE-VINE, THAT NEWS SHOULD SPREAD QUICKER THAN I CAN SAY...
...EXCELLENT!
NOOOOO!
AAAAH! FIVE YEARS OF MY LIFE, GONE!
SMITHERS! PUT THAT LENNY N. CARL ON SALARY AS MY OFFICIAL BAD NEWS BREAKER!
WILL DO, SIR!
AND NO, I WILL NOT MAKE YOU THE HAPPIEST MONKEY ON EARTH!

SOON AFTER...

SO YOU SAY MY **MONTY** WANTED YOU TO TELL ME SOME **NEWS**?

RIGHT. NOW WHAT WAS IT?

IS IT ABOUT OUR **ENGAGEMENT**?

RIGHT! THAT'S IT! HE NEVER LOVED YOU, AND THE WEDDING IS OFF!

SPRINGFIELD GORGE

SNOOOON!

EOOOOH!E

OKAY, MAYBE THIS WASN'T THE **BEST** PLACE FOR THAT NEWS!

LANCE MURDOCK! WELL, I **NEVER**!

VROOOOM!

LUCKY FOR YOU I WAS PRACTICING JUMPING THE CANYON FOR MY UPCOMING SPECIAL! SO ARE YOU SINGLE, YOUNG LADY?

I AM **NOW**!

HOW **ROMANTIC**!

DID THEY MAKE IT TO THE OTHER SIDE WITH THAT EXTRA WEIGHT ON THE BIKE?

NO. EMUNCHE BIG CRASH. ECHEWE

THE LESS SAID THE BETTER!

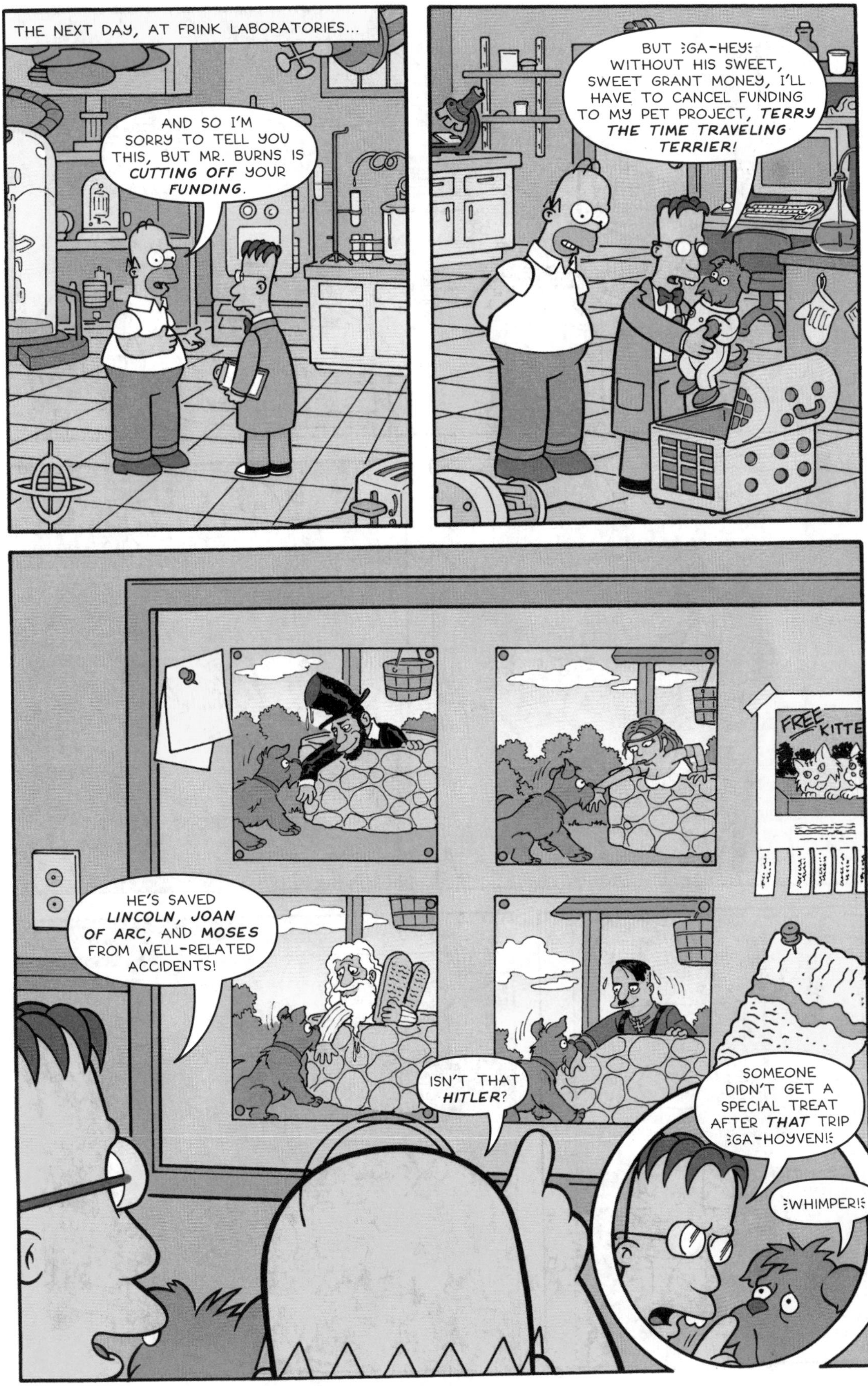
THE NEXT DAY, AT FRINK LABORATORIES...
AND SO I'M SORRY TO TELL YOU THIS, BUT MR. BURNS IS CUTTING OFF YOUR FUNDING.
BUT ~GA-HEY~ WITHOUT HIS SWEET, SWEET GRANT MONEY, I'LL HAVE TO CANCEL FUNDING TO MY PET PROJECT, TERRY THE TIME TRAVELING TERRIER!
FREE KITTE
HE'S SAVED LINCOLN, JOAN OF ARC, AND MOSES FROM WELL-RELATED ACCIDENTS!
ISN'T THAT HITLER?
SOMEONE DIDN'T GET A SPECIAL TREAT AFTER THAT TRIP ~GA-HOYVEN!~
~WHIMPER!~

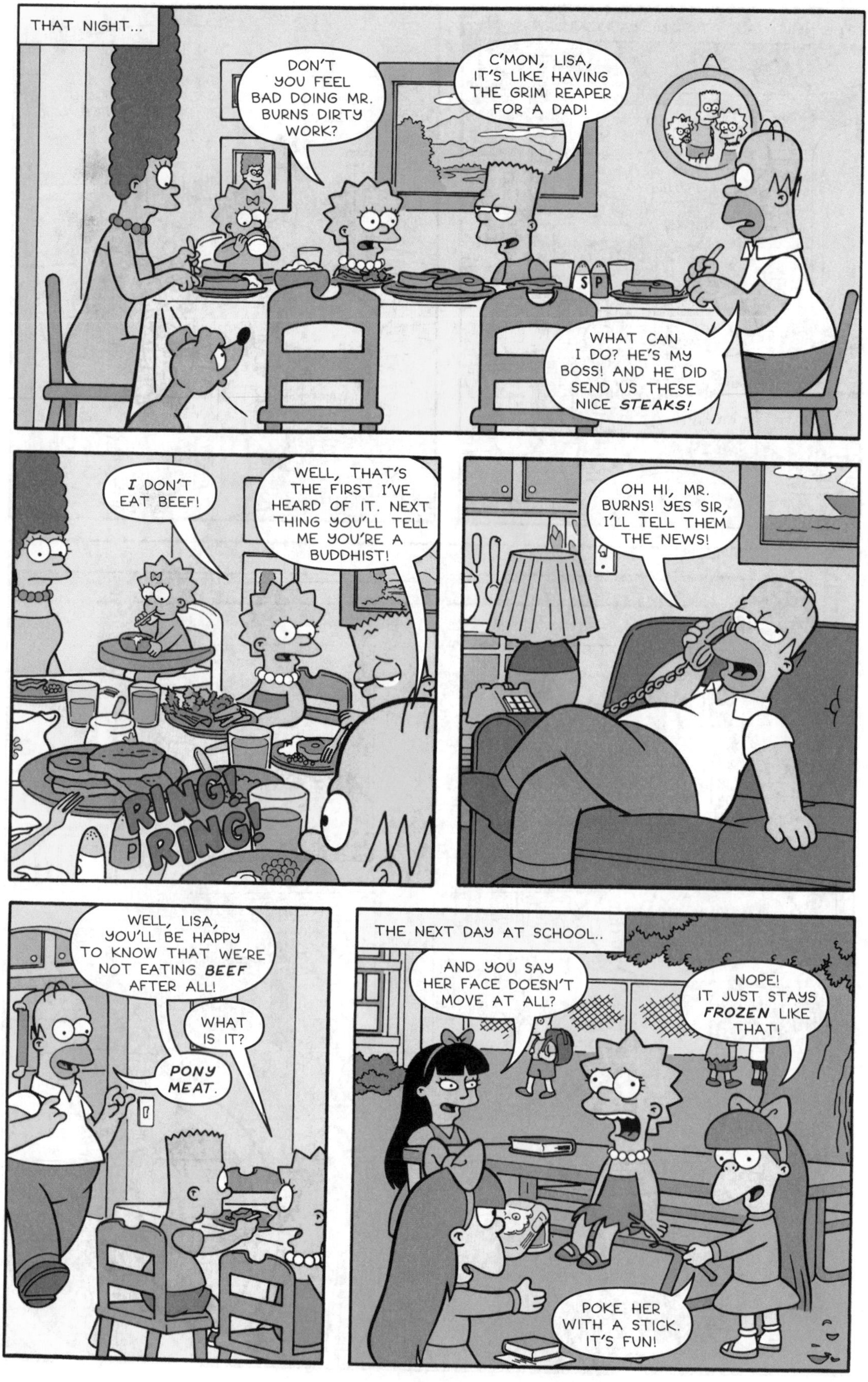
THAT NIGHT...
DON'T YOU FEEL BAD DOING MR. BURNS DIRTY WORK?
C'MON, LISA, IT'S LIKE HAVING THE GRIM REAPER FOR A DAD!
WHAT CAN I DO? HE'S MY BOSS! AND HE DID SEND US THESE NICE STEAKS!
I DON'T EAT BEEF!
WELL, THAT'S THE FIRST I'VE HEARD OF IT. NEXT THING YOU'LL TELL ME YOU'RE A BUDDHIST!
RING! RING!
OH HI, MR. BURNS! YES SIR, I'LL TELL THEM THE NEWS!
WELL, LISA, YOU'LL BE HAPPY TO KNOW THAT WE'RE NOT EATING BEEF AFTER ALL!
WHAT IS IT?
PONY MEAT.
THE NEXT DAY AT SCHOOL..
AND YOU SAY HER FACE DOESN'T MOVE AT ALL?
NOPE! IT JUST STAYS FROZEN LIKE THAT!
POKE HER WITH A STICK. IT'S FUN!

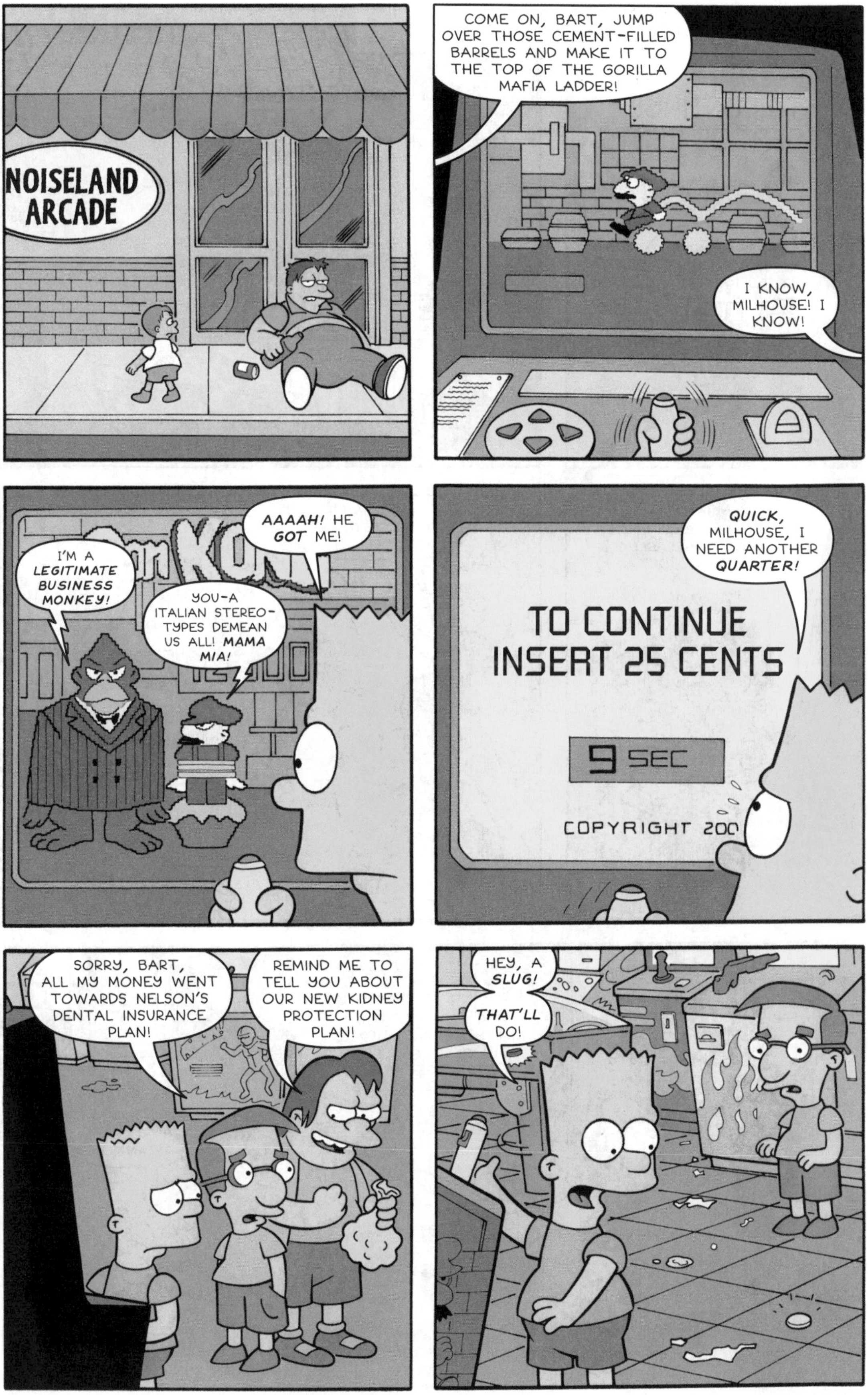
NOISELAND ARCADE
COME ON, BART, JUMP OVER THOSE CEMENT-FILLED BARRELS AND MAKE IT TO THE TOP OF THE GORILLA MAFIA LADDER!
I KNOW, MILHOUSE! I KNOW!
AAAAH! HE GOT ME!
I'M A LEGITIMATE BUSINESS MONKEY!
YOU-A ITALIAN STEREOTYPES DEMEAN US ALL! MAMA MIA!
QUICK, MILHOUSE, I NEED ANOTHER QUARTER!
TO CONTINUE INSERT 25 CENTS
9 SEC
COPYRIGHT 200
SORRY, BART, ALL MY MONEY WENT TOWARDS NELSON'S DENTAL INSURANCE PLAN!
REMIND ME TO TELL YOU ABOUT OUR NEW KIDNEY PROTECTION PLAN!
HEY, A SLUG!
THAT'LL DO!

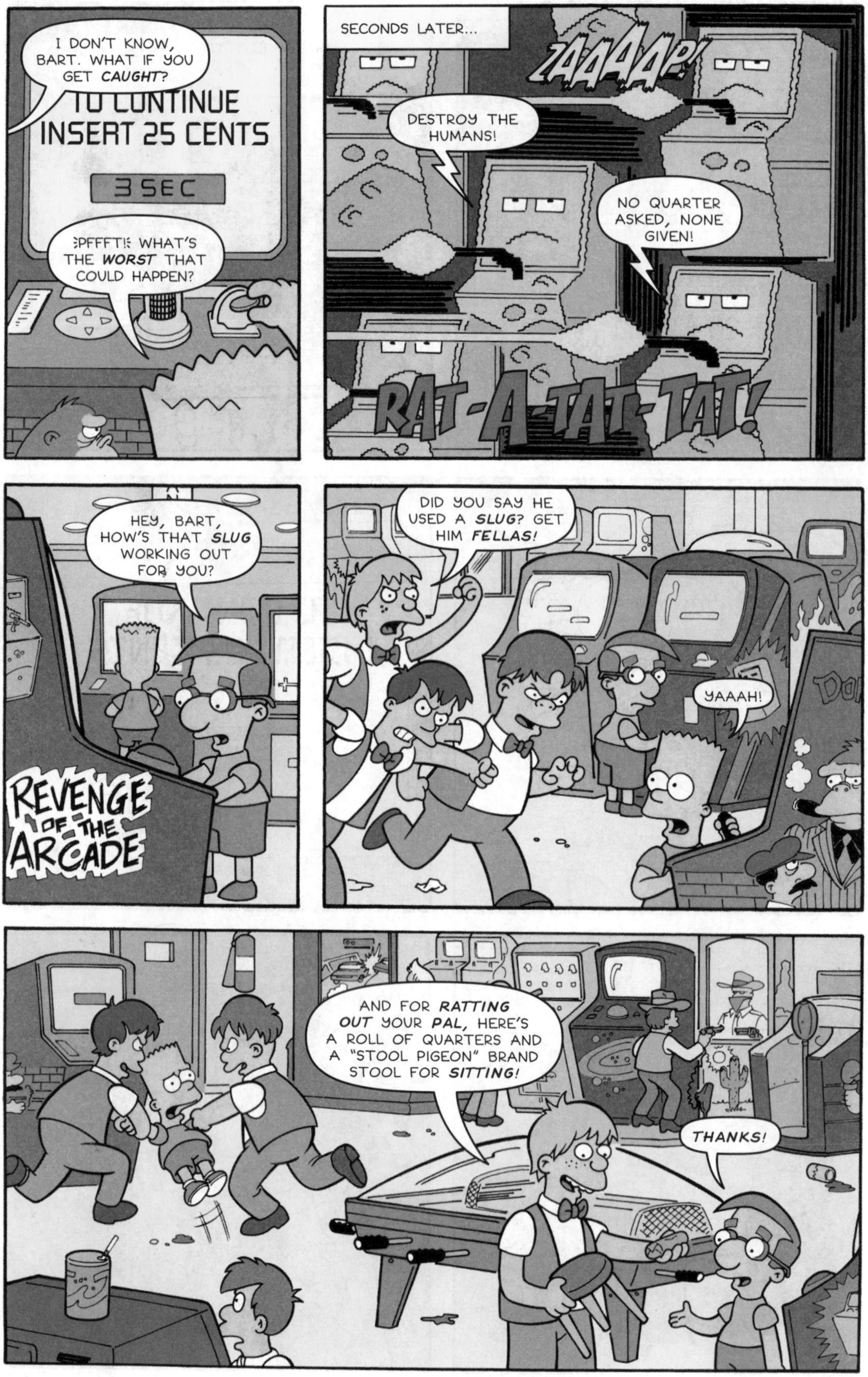

I DON'T KNOW, BART. WHAT IF YOU GET CAUGHT?
TO CONTINUE INSERT 25 CENTS
3 SEC
PFFFT! WHAT'S THE WORST THAT COULD HAPPEN?
SECONDS LATER...
ZAAAAP!
DESTROY THE HUMANS!
NO QUARTER ASKED, NONE GIVEN!
RAT-A-TAT-TAT!
HEY, BART, HOW'S THAT SLUG WORKING OUT FOR YOU?
REVENGE OF THE ARCADE
DID YOU SAY HE USED A SLUG? GET HIM FELLAS!
YAAAH!
AND FOR RATTING OUT YOUR PAL, HERE'S A ROLL OF QUARTERS AND A "STOOL PIGEON" BRAND STOOL FOR SITTING!
THANKS!

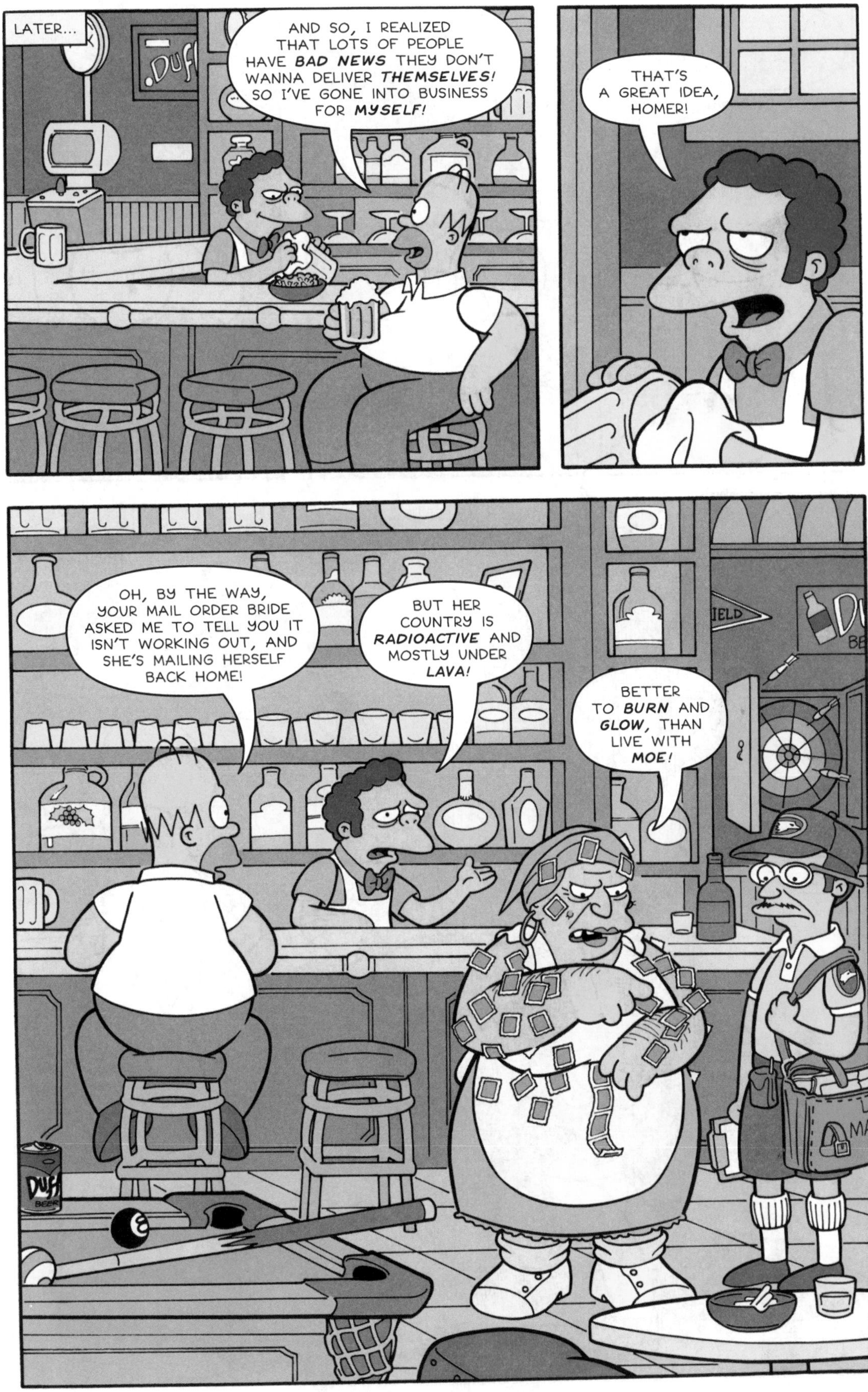
LATER...
AND SO, I REALIZED THAT LOTS OF PEOPLE HAVE **BAD NEWS** THEY DON'T WANNA DELIVER **THEMSELVES!** SO I'VE GONE INTO BUSINESS FOR **MYSELF!**
THAT'S A GREAT IDEA, HOMER!
OH, BY THE WAY, YOUR MAIL ORDER BRIDE ASKED ME TO TELL YOU IT ISN'T WORKING OUT, AND SHE'S MAILING HERSELF BACK HOME!
BUT HER COUNTRY IS **RADIOACTIVE** AND MOSTLY UNDER **LAVA!**
BETTER TO **BURN** AND **GLOW,** THAN LIVE WITH **MOE!**

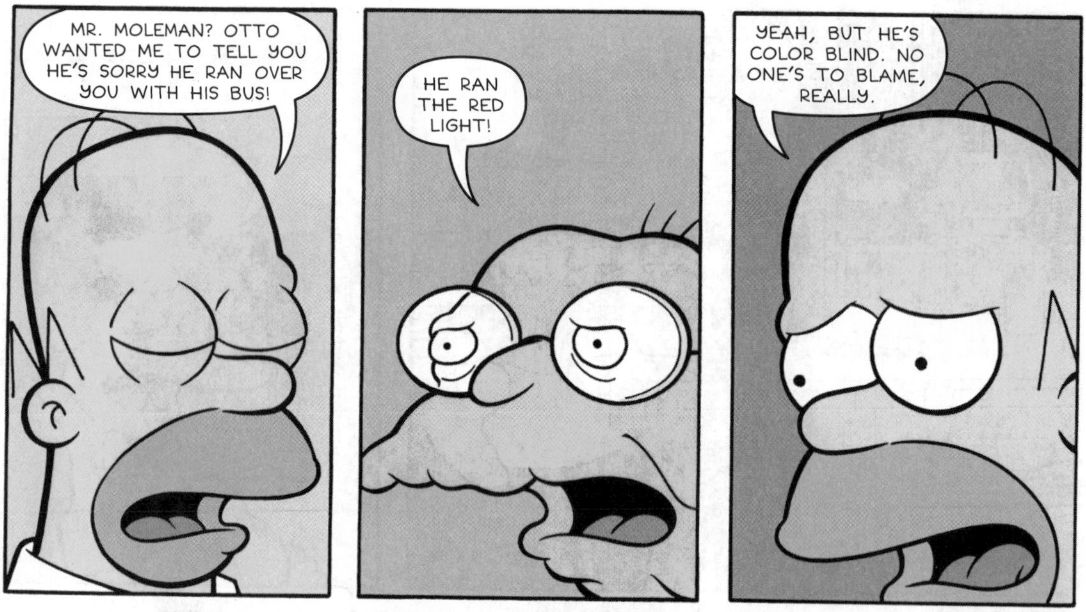

MR. MOLEMAN? OTTO WANTED ME TO TELL YOU HE'S SORRY HE RAN OVER YOU WITH HIS BUS!
HE RAN THE RED LIGHT!
YEAH, BUT HE'S COLOR BLIND. NO ONE'S TO BLAME, REALLY.

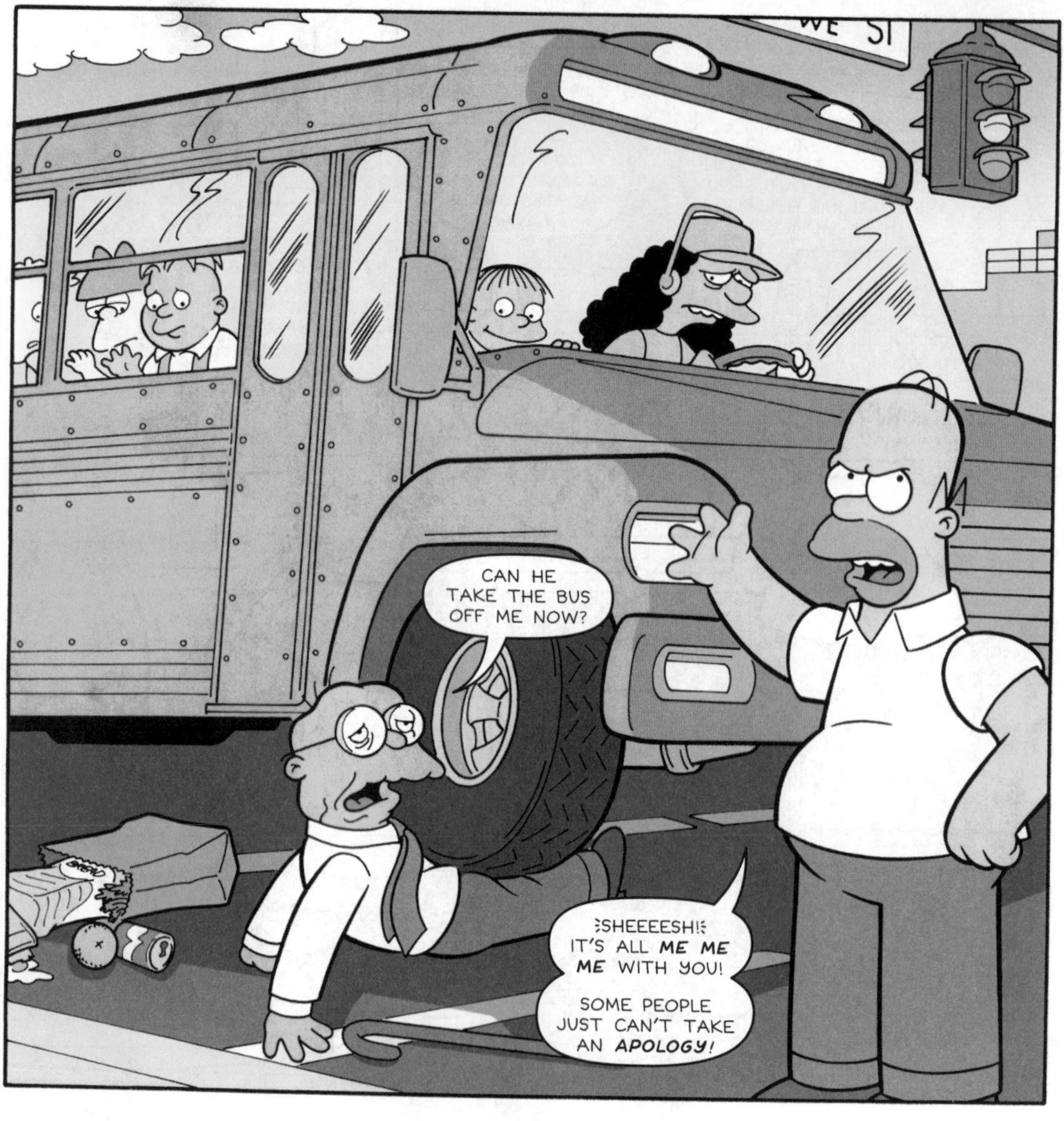

CAN HE TAKE THE BUS OFF ME NOW?
SHEEEESH!
IT'S ALL **ME ME ME** WITH YOU!
SOME PEOPLE JUST CAN'T TAKE AN ***APOLOGY!***

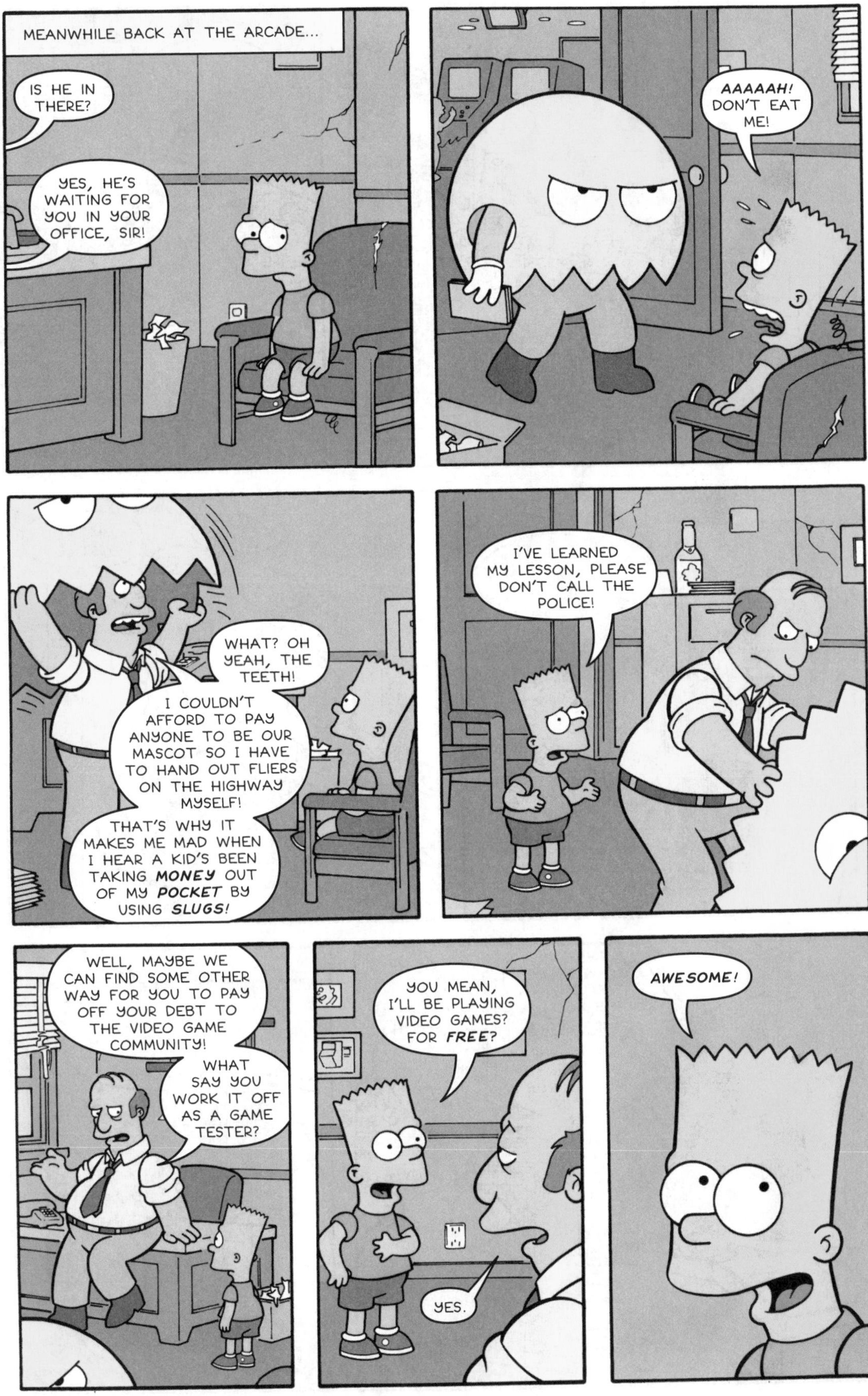

MEANWHILE BACK AT THE ARCADE...
IS HE IN THERE?
YES, HE'S WAITING FOR YOU IN YOUR OFFICE, SIR!
AAAAAH! DON'T EAT ME!
WHAT? OH YEAH, THE TEETH!
I COULDN'T AFFORD TO PAY ANYONE TO BE OUR MASCOT SO I HAVE TO HAND OUT FLIERS ON THE HIGHWAY MYSELF!
THAT'S WHY IT MAKES ME MAD WHEN I HEAR A KID'S BEEN TAKING MONEY OUT OF MY POCKET BY USING SLUGS!
I'VE LEARNED MY LESSON, PLEASE DON'T CALL THE POLICE!
WELL, MAYBE WE CAN FIND SOME OTHER WAY FOR YOU TO PAY OFF YOUR DEBT TO THE VIDEO GAME COMMUNITY!
WHAT SAY YOU WORK IT OFF AS A GAME TESTER?
YOU MEAN, I'LL BE PLAYING VIDEO GAMES? FOR FREE?
YES.
AWESOME!

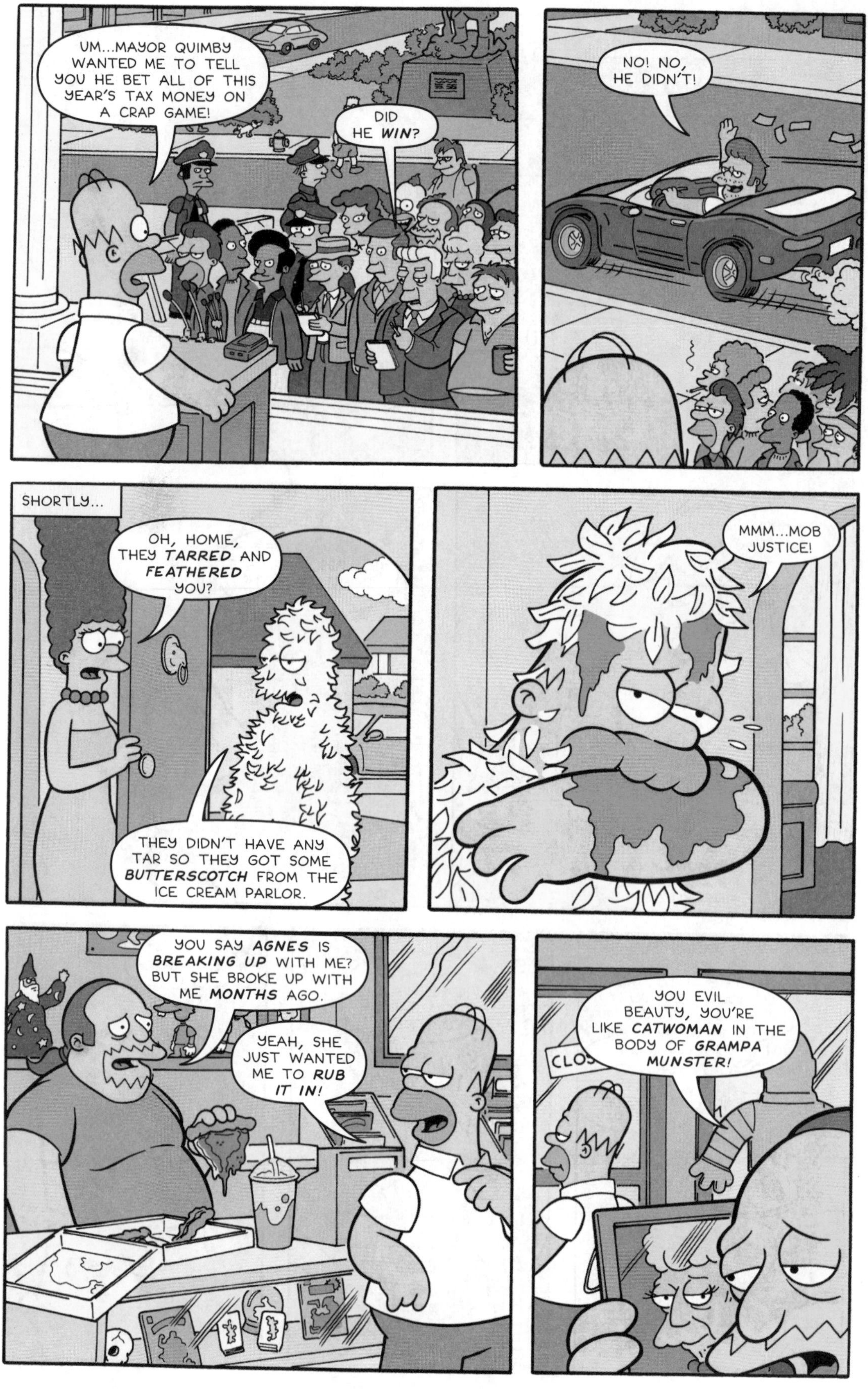
UM...MAYOR QUIMBY WANTED ME TO TELL YOU HE BET ALL OF THIS YEAR'S TAX MONEY ON A CRAP GAME!
DID HE *WIN*?
NO! NO, HE DIDN'T!
SHORTLY...
OH, HOMIE, THEY *TARRED* AND *FEATHERED* YOU?
THEY DIDN'T HAVE ANY TAR SO THEY GOT SOME *BUTTERSCOTCH* FROM THE ICE CREAM PARLOR.
MMM...MOB JUSTICE!
YOU SAY *AGNES* IS *BREAKING UP* WITH ME? BUT SHE BROKE UP WITH ME *MONTHS* AGO.
YEAH, SHE JUST WANTED ME TO *RUB IT IN*!
YOU EVIL BEAUTY, YOU'RE LIKE *CATWOMAN* IN THE BODY OF *GRAMPA MUNSTER*!

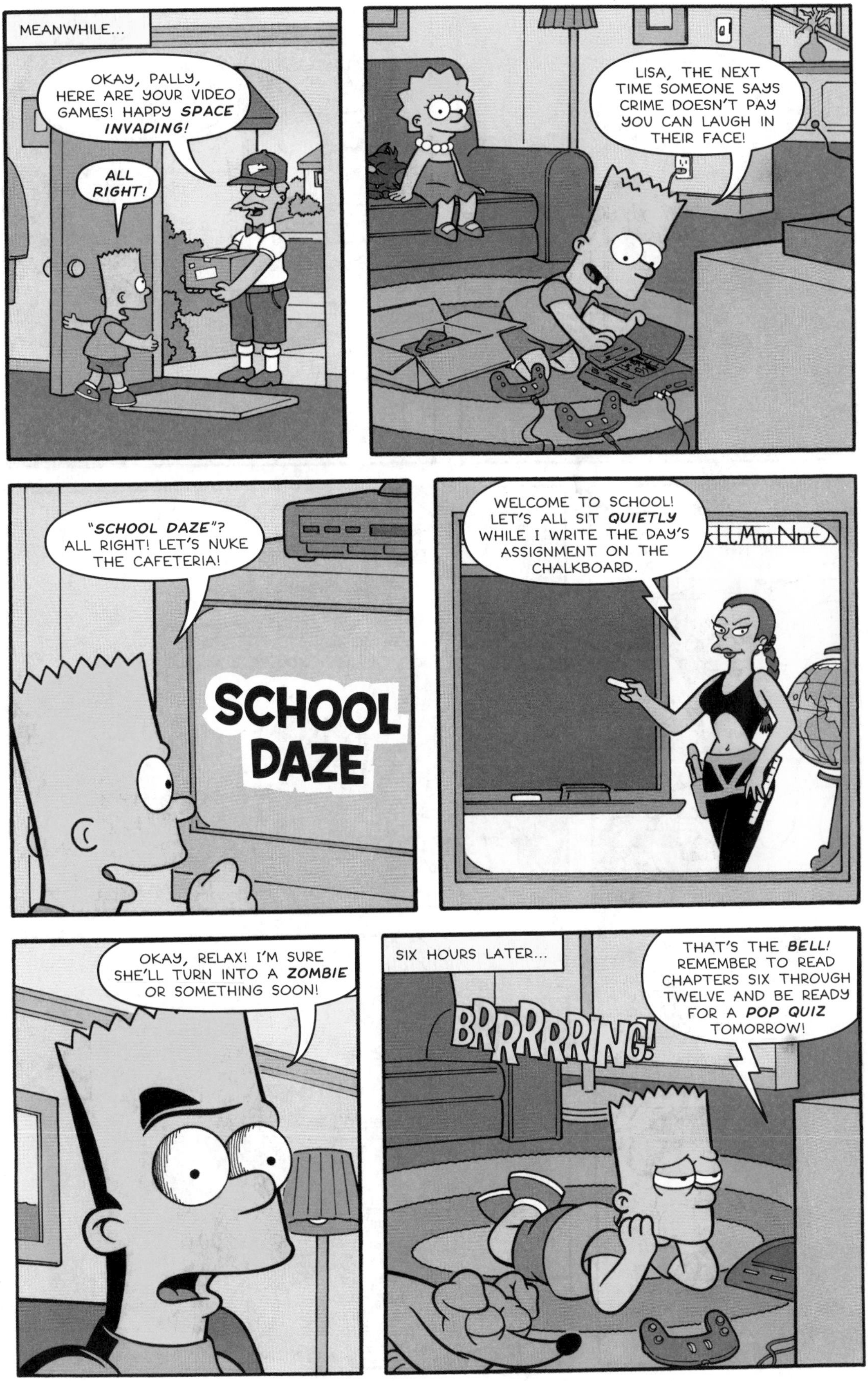

MEANWHILE...
OKAY, PALLY, HERE ARE YOUR VIDEO GAMES! HAPPY *SPACE INVADING!*
ALL RIGHT!
LISA, THE NEXT TIME SOMEONE SAYS CRIME DOESN'T PAY YOU CAN LAUGH IN THEIR FACE!
"*SCHOOL DAZE*"? ALL RIGHT! LET'S NUKE THE CAFETERIA!
SCHOOL DAZE
WELCOME TO SCHOOL! LET'S ALL SIT *QUIETLY* WHILE I WRITE THE DAY'S ASSIGNMENT ON THE CHALKBOARD.
OKAY, RELAX! I'M SURE SHE'LL TURN INTO A *ZOMBIE* OR SOMETHING SOON!
SIX HOURS LATER...
BRRRRRING!
THAT'S THE *BELL!* REMEMBER TO READ CHAPTERS SIX THROUGH TWELVE AND BE READY FOR A *POP QUIZ* TOMORROW!

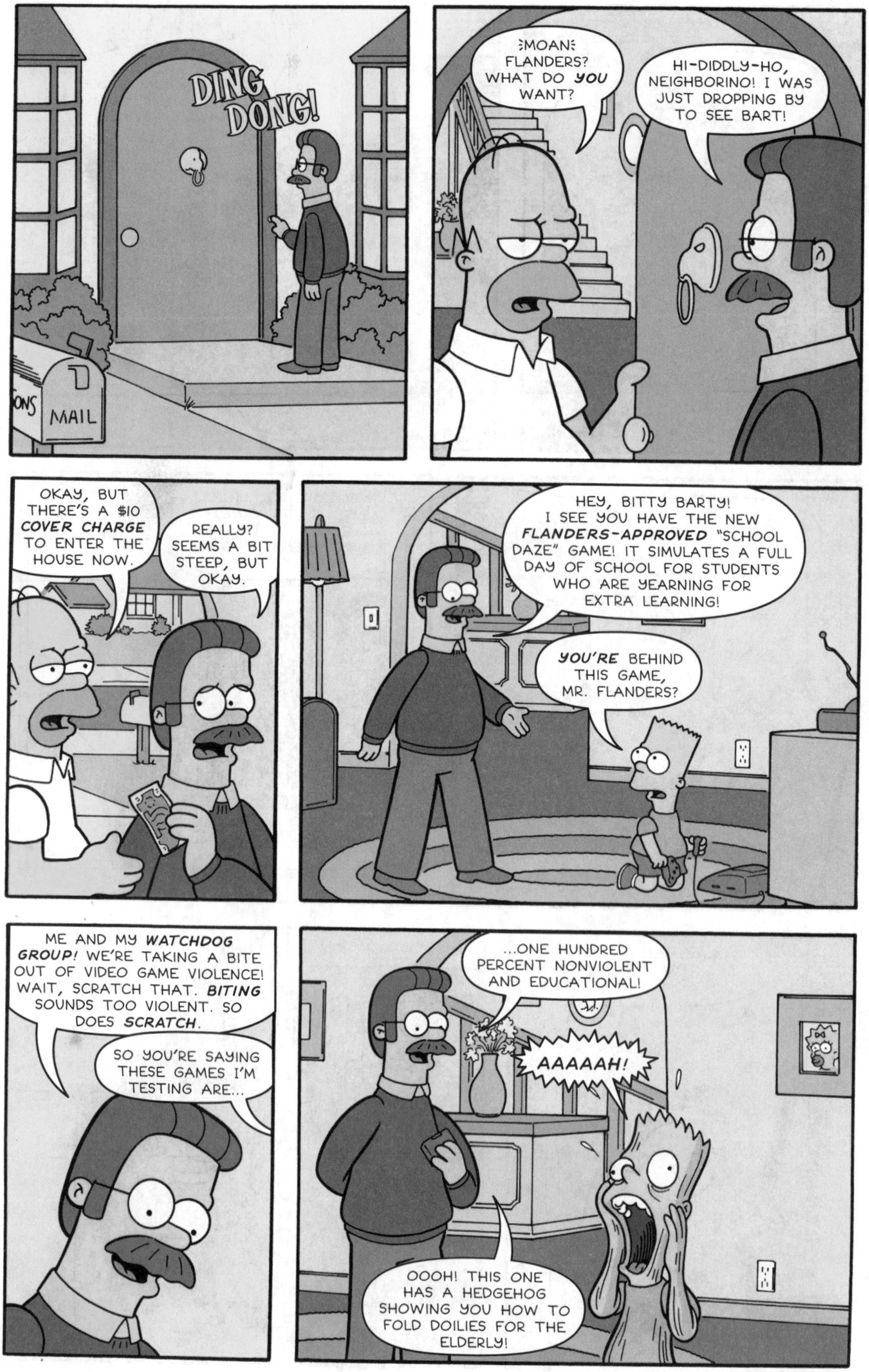
DING DONG!
:MOAN: FLANDERS? WHAT DO *YOU* WANT?
HI-DIDDLY-HO, NEIGHBORINO! I WAS JUST DROPPING BY TO SEE BART!
OKAY, BUT THERE'S A $10 *COVER CHARGE* TO ENTER THE HOUSE NOW.
REALLY? SEEMS A BIT STEEP, BUT OKAY.
HEY, BITTY BARTY! I SEE YOU HAVE THE NEW *FLANDERS-APPROVED* "SCHOOL DAZE" GAME! IT SIMULATES A FULL DAY OF SCHOOL FOR STUDENTS WHO ARE YEARNING FOR EXTRA LEARNING!
YOU'RE BEHIND THIS GAME, MR. FLANDERS?
ME AND MY *WATCHDOG GROUP!* WE'RE TAKING A BITE OUT OF VIDEO GAME VIOLENCE! WAIT, SCRATCH THAT. *BITING* SOUNDS TOO VIOLENT. SO DOES *SCRATCH*.
SO YOU'RE SAYING THESE GAMES I'M TESTING ARE...
...ONE HUNDRED PERCENT NONVIOLENT AND EDUCATIONAL!
AAAAAH!
OOOH! THIS ONE HAS A HEDGEHOG SHOWING YOU HOW TO FOLD DOILIES FOR THE ELDERLY!

THE NEXT DAY...

SUPERINTENDENT CHALMERS WANTED ME TO YELL SOME BAD NEWS TO YOU!

≈SIGH≈ PROCEED!

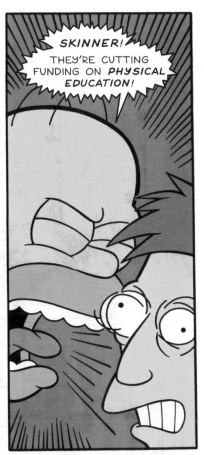

SKINNER! THEY'RE CUTTING FUNDING ON *PHYSICAL EDUCATION!*

WHICH MEANS WHAT?

KEEP CLOSING THE *GYMNASIUM* AND HAVING CLASSES IN YOUR *OFFICE*.

≈SIGH!≈

COME ON, GIRLS! STRETCH THOSE HAMSTRINGS!

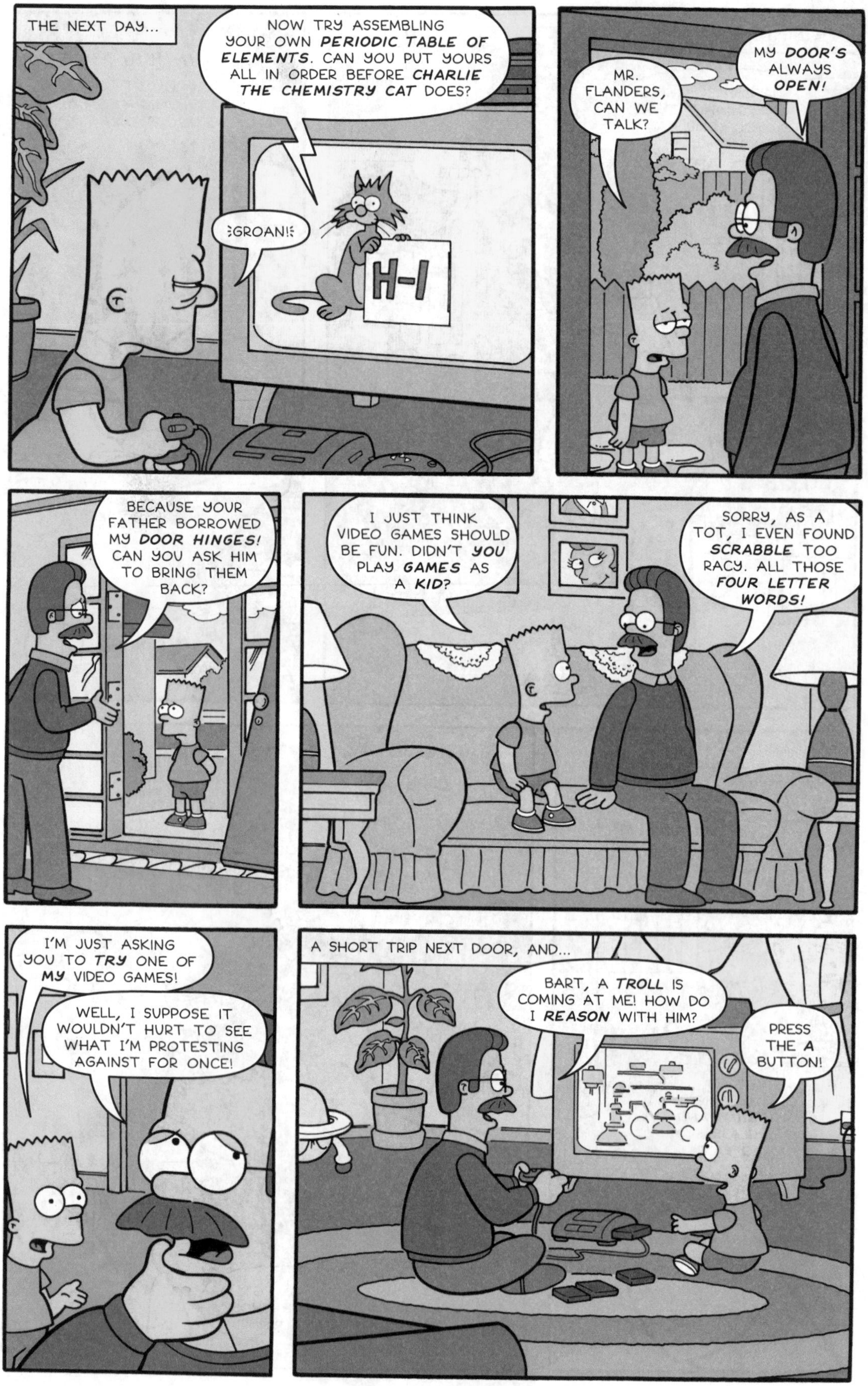

THE NEXT DAY...
NOW TRY ASSEMBLING YOUR OWN PERIODIC TABLE OF ELEMENTS. CAN YOU PUT YOURS ALL IN ORDER BEFORE CHARLIE THE CHEMISTRY CAT DOES?
GROAN!
H-I
MR. FLANDERS, CAN WE TALK?
MY DOOR'S ALWAYS OPEN!
BECAUSE YOUR FATHER BORROWED MY DOOR HINGES! CAN YOU ASK HIM TO BRING THEM BACK?
I JUST THINK VIDEO GAMES SHOULD BE FUN. DIDN'T YOU PLAY GAMES AS A KID?
SORRY, AS A TOT, I EVEN FOUND SCRABBLE TOO RACY. ALL THOSE FOUR LETTER WORDS!
I'M JUST ASKING YOU TO TRY ONE OF MY VIDEO GAMES!
WELL, I SUPPOSE IT WOULDN'T HURT TO SEE WHAT I'M PROTESTING AGAINST FOR ONCE!
A SHORT TRIP NEXT DOOR, AND...
BART, A TROLL IS COMING AT ME! HOW DO I REASON WITH HIM?
PRESS THE A BUTTON!

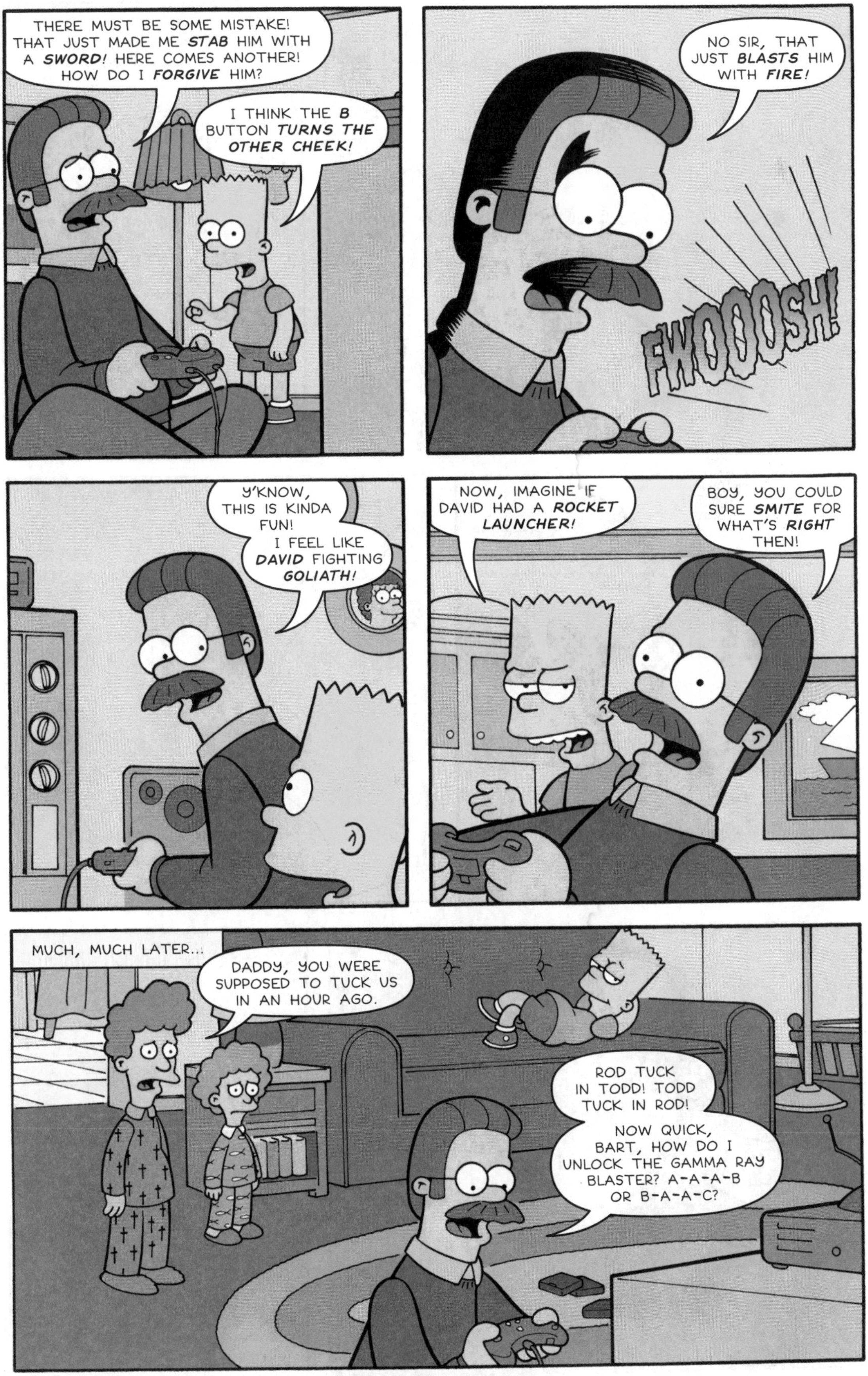

THERE MUST BE SOME MISTAKE! THAT JUST MADE ME STAB HIM WITH A SWORD! HERE COMES ANOTHER! HOW DO I FORGIVE HIM?
I THINK THE B BUTTON TURNS THE OTHER CHEEK!
NO SIR, THAT JUST BLASTS HIM WITH FIRE!
FWOOOSH!
Y'KNOW, THIS IS KINDA FUN!
I FEEL LIKE DAVID FIGHTING GOLIATH!
NOW, IMAGINE IF DAVID HAD A ROCKET LAUNCHER!
BOY, YOU COULD SURE SMITE FOR WHAT'S RIGHT THEN!
MUCH, MUCH LATER...
DADDY, YOU WERE SUPPOSED TO TUCK US IN AN HOUR AGO.
ROD TUCK IN TODD! TODD TUCK IN ROD!
NOW QUICK, BART, HOW DO I UNLOCK THE GAMMA RAY BLASTER? A-A-A-B OR B-A-A-C?

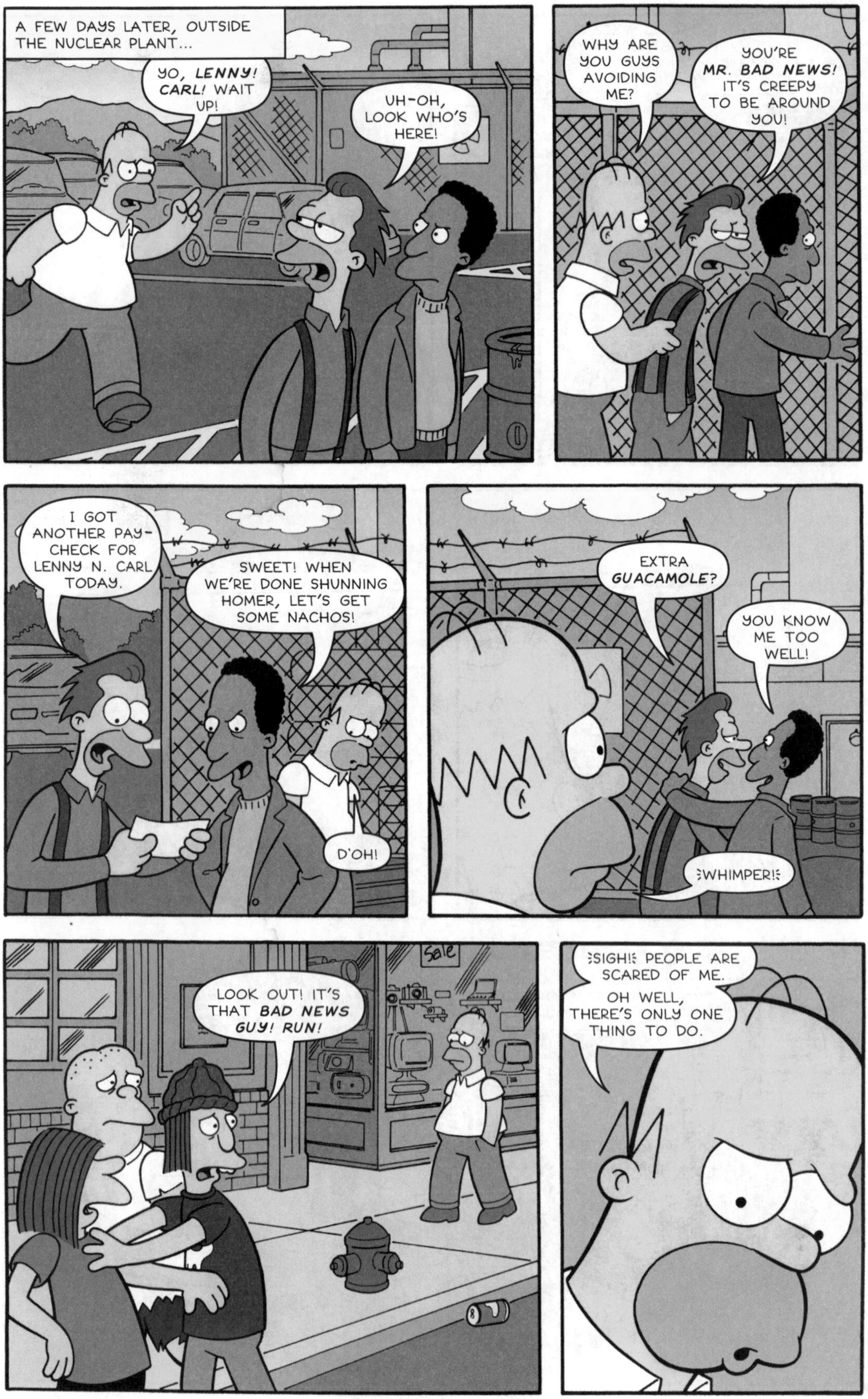
A FEW DAYS LATER, OUTSIDE THE NUCLEAR PLANT...
YO, LENNY! CARL! WAIT UP!
UH-OH, LOOK WHO'S HERE!
WHY ARE YOU GUYS AVOIDING ME?
YOU'RE MR. BAD NEWS! IT'S CREEPY TO BE AROUND YOU!
I GOT ANOTHER PAY-CHECK FOR LENNY N. CARL TODAY.
SWEET! WHEN WE'RE DONE SHUNNING HOMER, LET'S GET SOME NACHOS!
D'OH!
EXTRA GUACAMOLE?
YOU KNOW ME TOO WELL!
WHIMPER!
Sale
LOOK OUT! IT'S THAT BAD NEWS GUY! RUN!
SIGH! PEOPLE ARE SCARED OF ME.
OH WELL, THERE'S ONLY ONE THING TO DO.

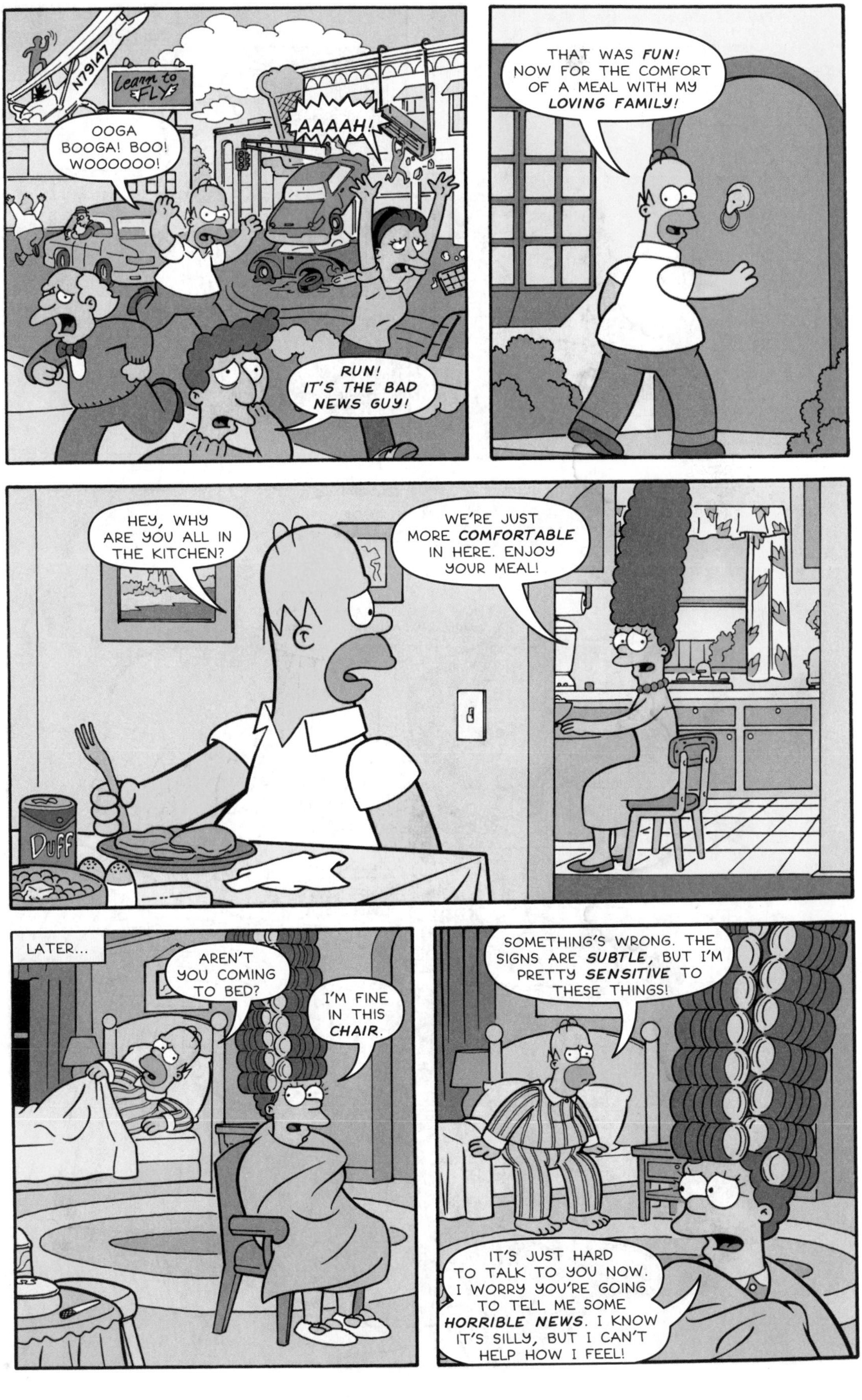
Learn to FLY
N79147
OOGA BOOGA! BOO! WOOOOOO!
AAAAH!
RUN! IT'S THE BAD NEWS GUY!
THAT WAS FUN! NOW FOR THE COMFORT OF A MEAL WITH MY LOVING FAMILY!
HEY, WHY ARE YOU ALL IN THE KITCHEN?
WE'RE JUST MORE COMFORTABLE IN HERE. ENJOY YOUR MEAL!
DUFF
LATER...
AREN'T YOU COMING TO BED?
I'M FINE IN THIS CHAIR.
SOMETHING'S WRONG. THE SIGNS ARE SUBTLE, BUT I'M PRETTY SENSITIVE TO THESE THINGS!
IT'S JUST HARD TO TALK TO YOU NOW. I WORRY YOU'RE GOING TO TELL ME SOME HORRIBLE NEWS. I KNOW IT'S SILLY, BUT I CAN'T HELP HOW I FEEL!

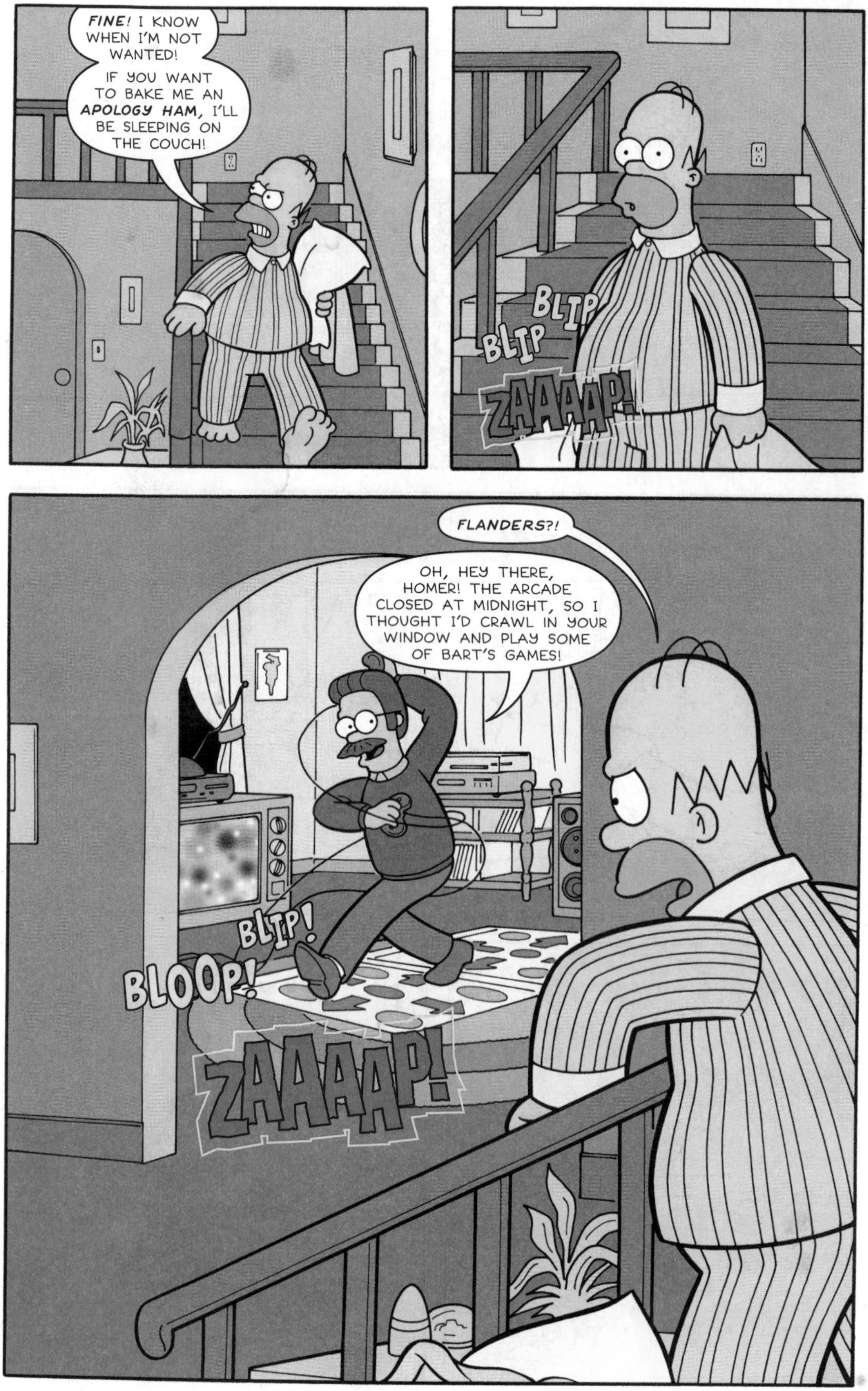
FINE! I KNOW WHEN I'M NOT WANTED!
IF YOU WANT TO BAKE ME AN APOLOGY HAM, I'LL BE SLEEPING ON THE COUCH!
BLIP
BLIP
ZAAAAP!
FLANDERS?!
OH, HEY THERE, HOMER! THE ARCADE CLOSED AT MIDNIGHT, SO I THOUGHT I'D CRAWL IN YOUR WINDOW AND PLAY SOME OF BART'S GAMES!
BLIP!
BLOOP!
ZAAAAP!

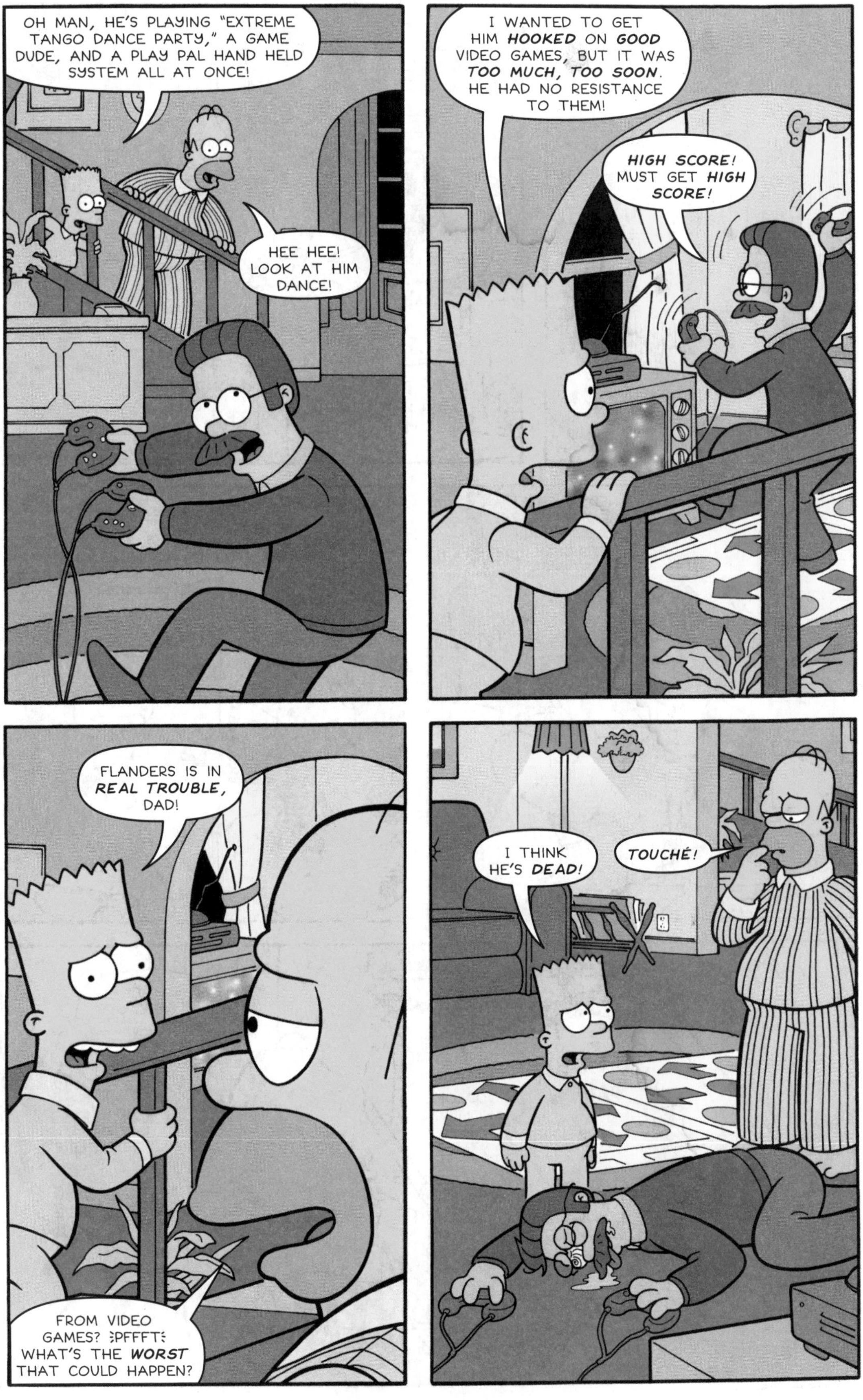
OH MAN, HE'S PLAYING "EXTREME TANGO DANCE PARTY," A GAME DUDE, AND A PLAY PAL HAND HELD SYSTEM ALL AT ONCE!
HEE HEE! LOOK AT HIM DANCE!
I WANTED TO GET HIM **HOOKED** ON **GOOD** VIDEO GAMES, BUT IT WAS ***TOO MUCH, TOO SOON***. HE HAD NO RESISTANCE TO THEM!
HIGH SCORE! MUST GET ***HIGH SCORE!***
FLANDERS IS IN ***REAL TROUBLE,*** DAD!
FROM VIDEO GAMES? ⁝PFFFT⁝ WHAT'S THE ***WORST*** THAT COULD HAPPEN?
I THINK HE'S ***DEAD!***
TOUCHÉ!

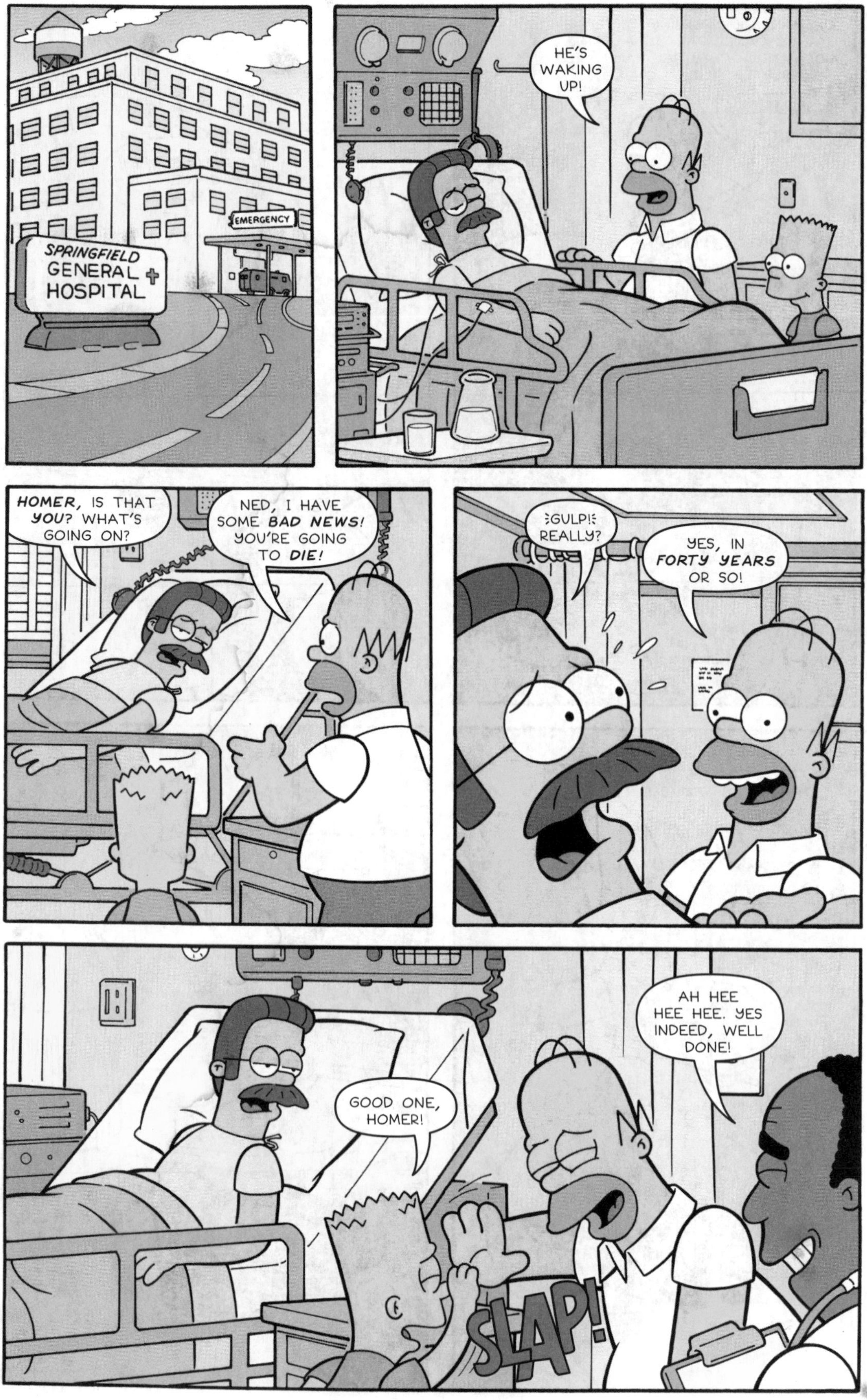
SPRINGFIELD
GENERAL
HOSPITAL
EMERGENCY
HE'S WAKING UP!
HOMER, IS THAT YOU? WHAT'S GOING ON?
NED, I HAVE SOME BAD NEWS! YOU'RE GOING TO DIE!
GULP! REALLY?
YES, IN FORTY YEARS OR SO!
GOOD ONE, HOMER!
AH HEE HEE HEE. YES INDEED, WELL DONE!
SLAP!

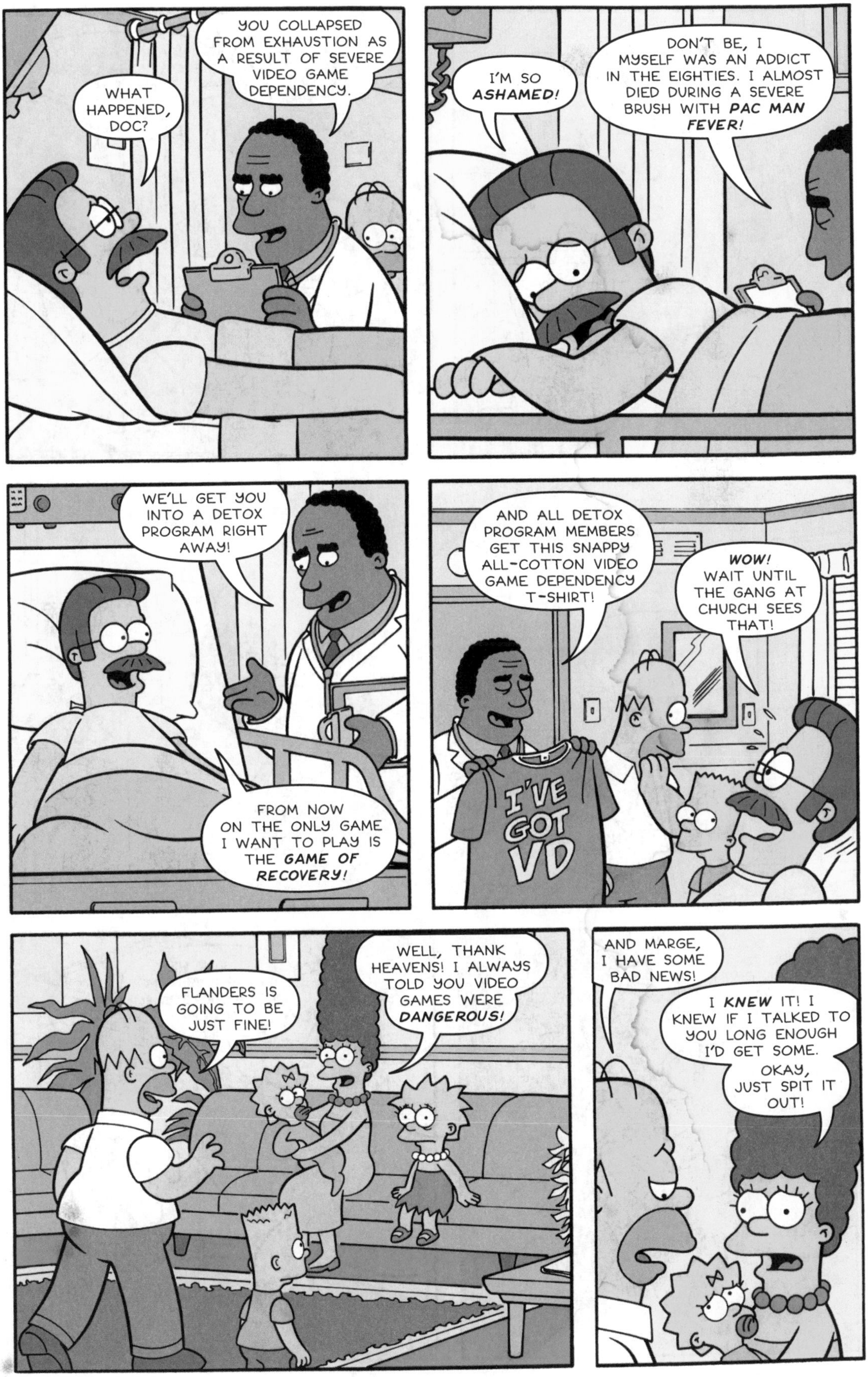

WHAT HAPPENED, DOC?
YOU COLLAPSED FROM EXHAUSTION AS A RESULT OF SEVERE VIDEO GAME DEPENDENCY.
I'M SO ASHAMED!
DON'T BE, I MYSELF WAS AN ADDICT IN THE EIGHTIES. I ALMOST DIED DURING A SEVERE BRUSH WITH PAC MAN FEVER!
WE'LL GET YOU INTO A DETOX PROGRAM RIGHT AWAY!
FROM NOW ON THE ONLY GAME I WANT TO PLAY IS THE GAME OF RECOVERY!
AND ALL DETOX PROGRAM MEMBERS GET THIS SNAPPY ALL-COTTON VIDEO GAME DEPENDENCY T-SHIRT!
I'VE GOT VD
WOW! WAIT UNTIL THE GANG AT CHURCH SEES THAT!
FLANDERS IS GOING TO BE JUST FINE!
WELL, THANK HEAVENS! I ALWAYS TOLD YOU VIDEO GAMES WERE DANGEROUS!
AND MARGE, I HAVE SOME BAD NEWS!
I KNEW IT! I KNEW IF I TALKED TO YOU LONG ENOUGH I'D GET SOME.
OKAY, JUST SPIT IT OUT!

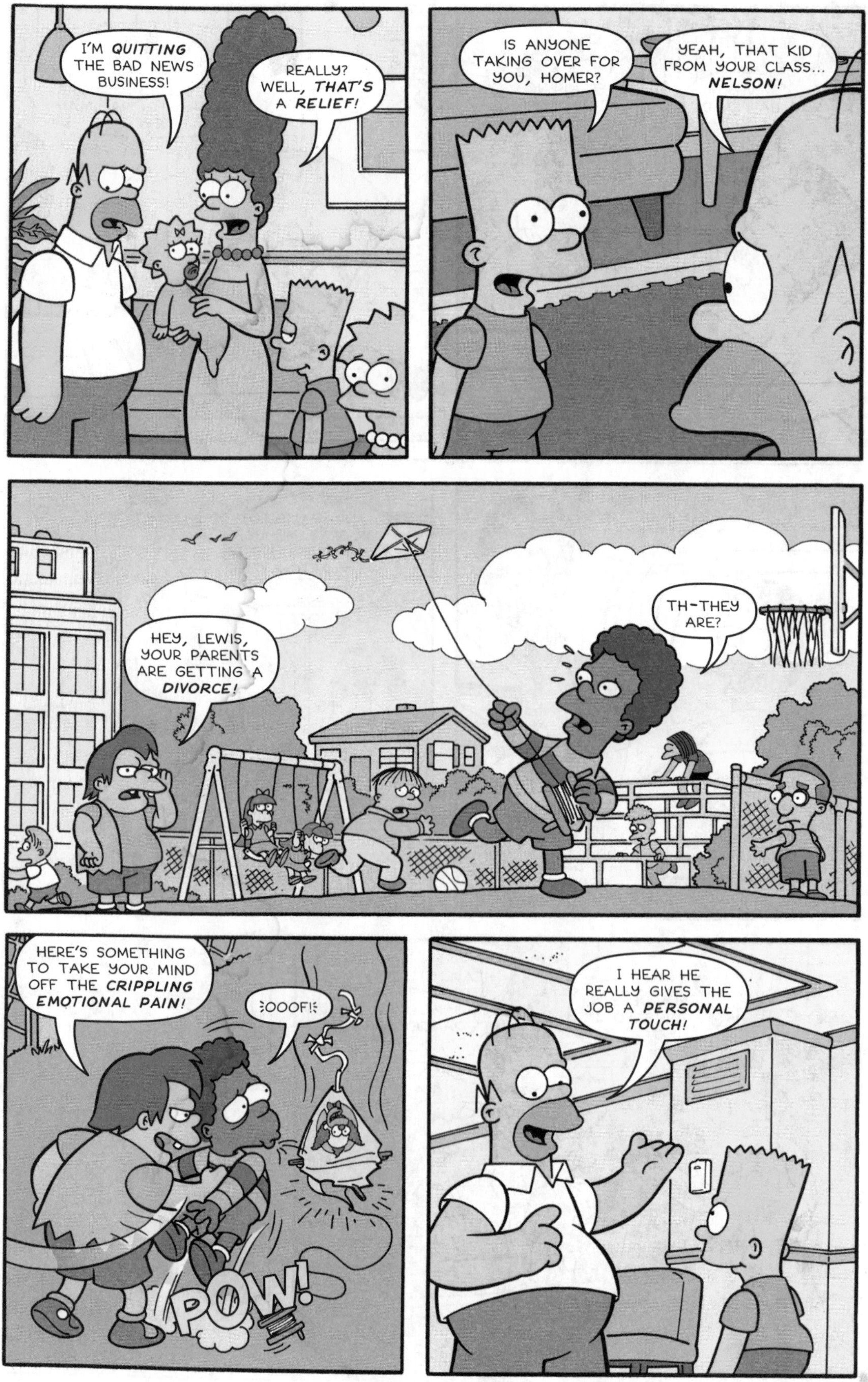

I'M QUITTING THE BAD NEWS BUSINESS!
REALLY? WELL, THAT'S A RELIEF!
IS ANYONE TAKING OVER FOR YOU, HOMER?
YEAH, THAT KID FROM YOUR CLASS... NELSON!
HEY, LEWIS, YOUR PARENTS ARE GETTING A DIVORCE!
TH-THEY ARE?
HERE'S SOMETHING TO TAKE YOUR MIND OFF THE CRIPPLING EMOTIONAL PAIN!
OOOF!
POW!
I HEAR HE REALLY GIVES THE JOB A PERSONAL TOUCH!

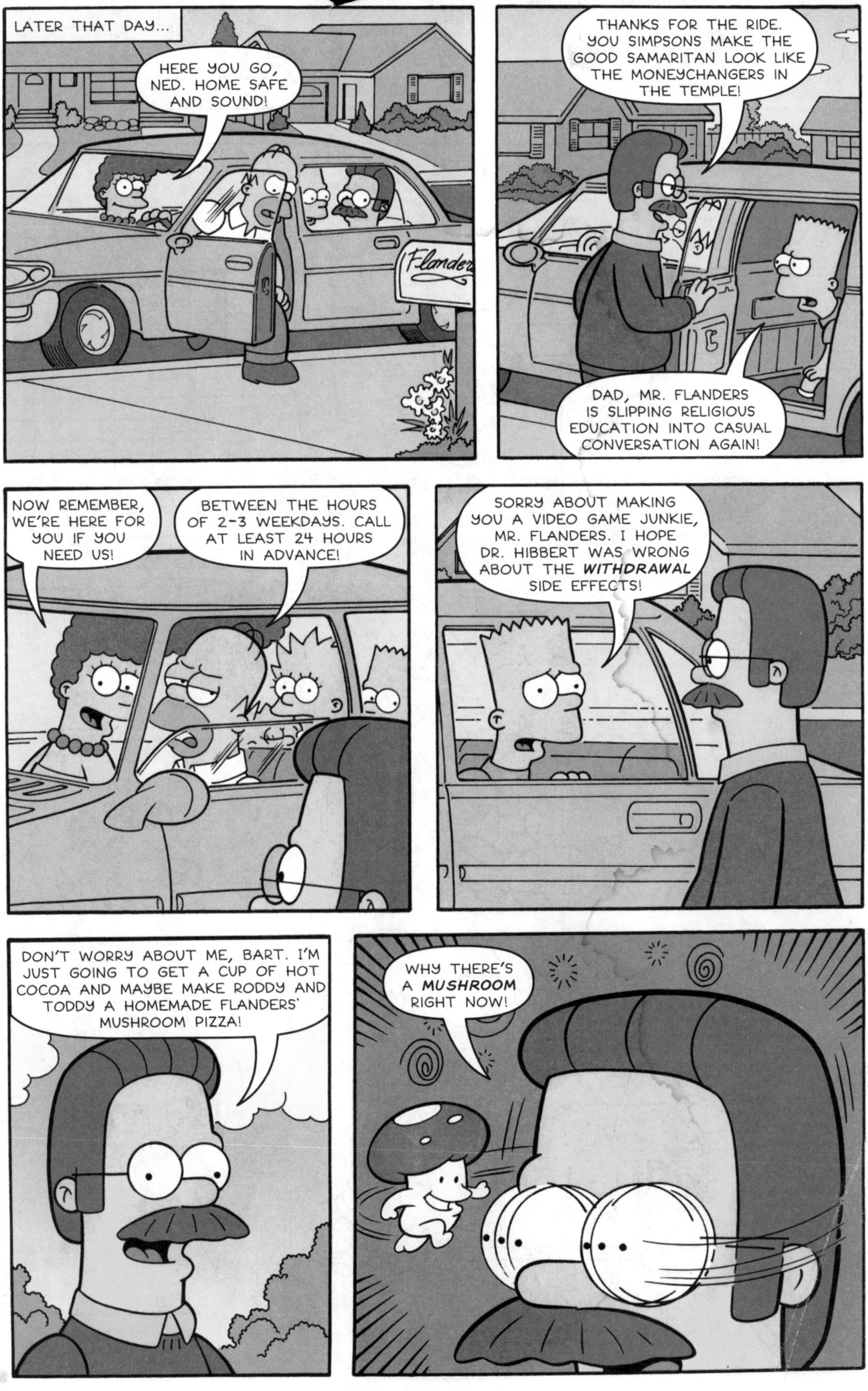
LATER THAT DAY...
HERE YOU GO, NED. HOME SAFE AND SOUND!
Flanders
THANKS FOR THE RIDE. YOU SIMPSONS MAKE THE GOOD SAMARITAN LOOK LIKE THE MONEYCHANGERS IN THE TEMPLE!
DAD, MR. FLANDERS IS SLIPPING RELIGIOUS EDUCATION INTO CASUAL CONVERSATION AGAIN!
NOW REMEMBER, WE'RE HERE FOR YOU IF YOU NEED US!
BETWEEN THE HOURS OF 2-3 WEEKDAYS. CALL AT LEAST 24 HOURS IN ADVANCE!
SORRY ABOUT MAKING YOU A VIDEO GAME JUNKIE, MR. FLANDERS. I HOPE DR. HIBBERT WAS WRONG ABOUT THE **WITHDRAWAL** SIDE EFFECTS!
DON'T WORRY ABOUT ME, BART. I'M JUST GOING TO GET A CUP OF HOT COCOA AND MAYBE MAKE RODDY AND TODDY A HOMEMADE FLANDERS' MUSHROOM PIZZA!
WHY THERE'S A **MUSHROOM** RIGHT NOW!

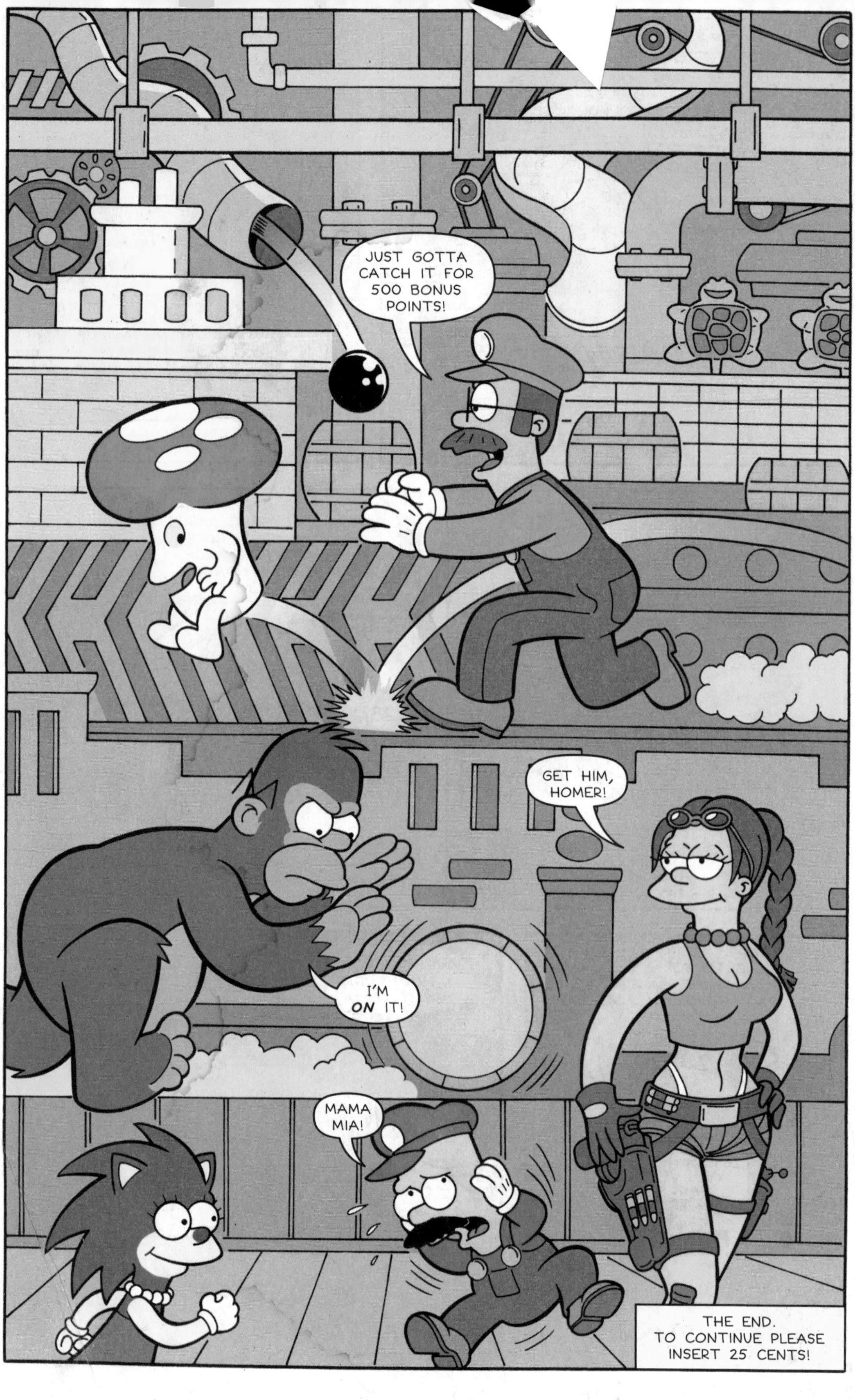

JUST GOTTA CATCH IT FOR 500 BONUS POINTS!
GET HIM, HOMER!
I'M *ON* IT!
MAMA MIA!
THE END. TO CONTINUE PLEASE INSERT 25 CENTS!